The Education of Latino Students in Massachusetts:
Issues, Research, and Policy Implications

The Education of Latino Students in Massachusetts: Issues, Research, and Policy Implications

Edited by

Ralph Rivera *and*
Sonia Nieto

The Mauricio Gastón Institute for Latino
Community Development and Public Policy
The University of Massachusetts Boston

Distributed by the University of Massachusetts Press

Copyright © 1993 by
The Mauricio Gastón Institute for
Latino Community Development and Public Policy
University of Massachusetts Boston
All Rights Reserved
Printed in the United States of America

Distributed by the University of Massachusetts Press
P.O. Box 429, Amherst, MA 01004, USA

ISBN 0-87023-895-7
LC 93-32148

Library of Congress Cataloging-in-Publication Data

The education of Latino students in Massachusetts: issues, research,
      and policy implications / edited by Ralph Rivera and Sonia Nieto
                    p.cm.
      1. Hispanic American students — Education — Massachusetts.
2. Education and state — Massachusetts. I. Rivera, Ralph.
II. Nieto, Sonia.
LC2674.M4E37 1993
371.97'680744—dc20   93-32148
                                                CIP

British Library Cataloguing in Publication data are available.

To
Luna Mari,
Rafael Antonio,
Alicia Marianna,
Marisa April,
and all of the Latino
children in Massachusetts
and their families

Contents

Preface ix
Contributors xi

RALPH RIVERA
Introduction 3

Part I The Context

ANNE WHEELOCK
The Status of Latino Students in Massachusetts Public Schools 11

Part II Educational Issues for the Latino Community

JOSE JAVIER COLÓN-MORERA, NITZA M. HIDALGO,
AIDA A. NEVÁREZ, and ANA M. GARCÍA-BLANCO
Entitlements of Latino Students and Parents: Some Legal Policy
Considerations 35

DIANA LAM
Bilingual Education: Perspectives on Research and Other Issues 58

RALPH RIVERA
Barriers to Latino Parental Involvement in the Boston Public Schools 77

GLENN JACOBS
Latinos and Educational Reform:
The Privatization of the Chelsea Public Schools 88

JAMES JENNINGS
Latino Experiences in Vocational Technical Education:
Implications for Educational Policy and Reform in Massachusetts 106

Part III Research and Policy Implications

ANTONIA DARDER and CAROLE CHRISTOFK UPSHUR
What Do Latino Children Need to Succeed in School?
A Study of Four Boston Public Schools 127

MANUEL FRAU-RAMOS and SONIA NIETO
I was an Outsider: An Exploratory Study of Dropping Out
among Puerto Rican Youths in Holyoke, Massachusetts 147

VIRGINIA VOGEL ZANGER
Academic Costs of Social Marginalization:
An Analysis of the Perceptions of Latino Students at a Boston High School 170

CASTELLANO B. TURNER, AMARO J. LARIA,
ESTER R. SHAPIRO, and MARIA DEL CARMEN PEREZ
Poverty, Resilience, and Academic Achievement among Latino College
Students and High School Dropouts 191

MARTHA MONTERO-SIEBURTH
The Effects of Schooling Processes and Practices on
Potential At-Risk Latino High School Students 217

Part IV Future Directions

SONIA NIETO
Creating Possibilities: Educating Latino Students in Massachusetts 243

Preface

The idea of this book originated primarily from two separate projects of the Mauricio Gastón Institute for Latino Community Development and Public Policy. The first was a conference entitled "On the Policy Agenda in Massachusetts: The Education of Latino Children," sponsored by the Gastón Institute in October of 1990. The purpose of the conference was to create a vehicle for the effective participation of Latinos in education policy development by promoting an exchange of ideas between Latino community activists, parents, teachers, educational researchers, education policymakers, and private sector representatives. The focus of the conference was on four critical educational issues affecting the Latino community in Massachusetts: retention and achievement, entitlements, bilingual education, and school reform. Three of the chapters in this book (Chapters 1, 2 and 3) were originally papers commissioned by the Gastón Institute and presented at this conference.

The second activity that directly contributed to the creation of this book was the Gastón Institute's Latinos, Poverty and Public Policy project carried out during 1991 and 1992. The purpose of this project, which included a research competition, a research seminar, and a policy conference, was to advance the understanding of how poverty and public policy affect the Latino population in Massachusetts and to encouraged research that would be of value both to the Latino community and policymakers. Twelve research studies were sponsored by the project, and Chapters 5, 6, 7, 8 and 10 are products of this initiative.

Our thanks to all those who participated in the creation of this volume. We especially acknowledge the distinguished work of the contributors, the Gastón Advisory Board members, and the research reviewers for their steady guidance of the project, all of the conference participants for their invaluable feedback, and the funders of these projects including the Boston Foundation, The New England, Boston Gas, Shawmut Bank, and the University of Massachusetts. Finally, we want to acknowledge the contribution of all the dedicated Gastón Institute staff members, with special appreciation to Miren Uriarte, former director of the Gastón, Edwin Meléndez, current director of the Gastón and head of the Latinos, Poverty and Public Policy project, Gloria Cardona, the Institute's activities coordinator, and Linda Kluz, production editor for the volume.

Contributors

José Javier Colón-Morera is an assistant professor in the Department of Political Science at the University of Puerto Rico and an associate of the law firm of Colón-Martinez, Colón-Morera. Dr. Colón-Morera holds a J.D. from the University of Puerto Rico School of Law and Ph.D. in political science from Boston University.

Antonia Darder is an assistant professor of education at Claremont Graduate School, Claremont, California, and scholar-in-residence at the Thomas Rivera Center, where she is working on public policy on the education of Latino children. She received a Ph.D. in education from Claremont, and along with teaching credentials, she is a registered nurse and a marriage, family, and child therapist. Her book *Culture and Power in the Classroom: A Critical Foundation for Bicultural Education* was published by Bergin & Garvey in 1991, and she is currently editing another book, *Culture and Differences: Critical Perspectives on the Biculturation Experience in the United States*, to be published by Greenwood Press.

Manuel Frau-Ramos is an adjunct assistant professor in the Cultural Diversity and Curriculum Reform Program at the University of Massachusetts, Amherst. He holds masters degrees in both education and economics and an Ed.D. from the School of Education at the University of Massachusetts. His publications include "Determinantes del Ingreso y la Profesión Seleccionada por Graduados Universitarios: Un Modelo Económico (Chosen Profession and Income Predictors for College Graduates: An Economic Model)," published in *Revista de Administración Pública*, University of Puerto Rico in October 1986, and "Educación y Estratificación Social en Puerto Rico (Education and Social Stratification in Puerto Rico)," also published in *Revista de Administración Pública* in March 1987.

Ana M. García-Blanco received an M.A. from the Harvard Graduate School of Education and is currently a doctoral candidate at Harvard, working on an ethnographic study of a community-based school in Guaynabo, Puerto Rico. Ms.

García-Blanco's other publications include "Race and Racism in American Education" (*Harvard Education Review*, August 1988) and "Constructing a Ship While at Sea" (*Alumni Bulletin, Harvard Graduate School of Education*, November 1988).

NITZA M. HIDALGO is an assistant professor of education at Wheelock College, Boston. She teaches in the areas of multicultural education and urban school reform. Dr. Hidalgo received her Ed.D. from the Harvard University School of Education, and her current research involves an ethnographic investigation of the influence of Puerto Rican families on their children's school achievement. She is the author of the chapter "Multicultural Teacher Introspection," which appeared in *Freedom's Plow*, edited by Perry and Fraser and published by Routledge in 1993, as well as *I Saw Puerto Rico Once: A Review of the Literature on Puerto Rican Families and School Achievement in the United States*, published by the Center on Families, Communities, Schools and Children's Learning in 1992, and "Tensions Spark Debate on Multiculturalism," an article in *New Voices Newsletter* in 1991.

GLENN JACOBS is associate professor of sociology at the University of Massachusetts Boston and the former director of the Latin American Studies Program at the University. He received his doctorate in sociology from Temple University. Dr. Jacobs is currently working on a book entitled *The Great School Caper: The Boston University Takeover of the Chelsea Public Schools and the Rise of the Hispanic Community*. His other books include *Professions for the People: The Politics of Skill*, edited with Joel E. Gerstl (Schenkman, 1976), and *The Participant Observer* (Braziller, 1970). He also writes on social theory and on the sociocultural contexts of Afro-Cuban music.

JAMES JENNINGS is the director of the William Monroe Trotter Institute at the University of Massachusetts Boston and a professor of political science in the College of Public and Community Service at the University. He is received his Ph.D. in American government from Columbia University. Dr. Jennings is the author of *The Politics of Black Empowerment: Transformation of Black Activism in Urban America* (Wayne State University Press, 1992) and coeditor of *Puerto Rican Politics in Urban America* (Greenwood Press, 1984).

DIANA LAM is the superintendent of the Dubuque Public Schools in Dubuque, Iowa. She received her masters in bilingual education from Boston State College and is currently a doctoral candidate at Boston University. Other publications by Ms. Lam include "A Two Year Old is a Linguist," which appeared in the June 1990 issue of *Massachusetts Education Today*, and "Gender and Public Education: From Mirrors to Magnifying Lens," coedited with Meg Campbell and appearing in the National Society for the Study of Education Yearbook, *Gender and Education* (1993).

AMARO J. LARIA has a masters in applied psychology from Boston University. He is currently a Ph.D. candidate in clinical psychology at the University of Massachusetts Boston and is a psychology trainee at the Behavioral Medicine Program, Cambridge Hospital, Cambridge, Massachusetts.

MARTHA MONTERO-SIEBURTH is an associate professor in the Department of Education and Human Services at Simmons College. She received her Ed.D. from Boston University. Dr. Montero-Sieburth's interests are in the direct application of cultural anthropology and qualitative research to the development of instructional materials and curricula, quality teacher education, and research of Latino communities, and she has worked with urban communities including Chelsea and Charlestown for the last 15 years. She is currently preparing two new books for publication: *Immigration, Integration, and Schooling: Restructuring Teachers' Pedagogy and Educational Processes* (Ablex) and *Preparing Educational Qualitative Research in Latin America: The Struggle for a New Paradigm*, with Gary L. Anderson (Garland Press).

AIDA A. NEVÁREZ holds a master in bilingual education from State University of New York and a doctorate in education in reading from Harvard Graduate School of Education. She is currently assistant professor of education at Messiah College in Grantham, Pennsylvania. Dr. Nevárez's editorial experience includes membership on the multicultural review board for McClanahan Co. and Scholastics Inc. and the editorial board of the *Harvard Educational Review.*

SONIA NIETO received a master's degree in Spanish literature from New York University and a doctorate of education in curriculum from the University of Massachusetts Amherst. She is currently an associate professor in the Cultural Diversity and Curriculum Reform Program at the School of Education at the University of Massachusetts Amherst. Dr. Nieto's most recent publication is her book *Affirming Diversity: The Sociopolitical Context of Multicultural Education* (Longman, 1992).

MARIA DEL CARMEN PEREZ has a M.S. in education from the Eliot Pearson Department of Child Study at Tufts University. She is a Ph.D. candidate in clinical psychology at the University of Massachusetts Boston and currently participates in a practicum placement at the Chelsea Memorial Health Center, Chelsea, Massachusetts. Prior to enrolling in the Ph.D. program, Ms. Perez worked as a bilingual psycho-educational specialist for Project C.H.I.L.D., a three-year, preschool, intervention research program at the Martha Eliot Health Center in Jamaica Plain, Massachusetts, a satellite clinic of Children's Hospital.

RALPH RIVERA is an assistant professor at the College of Public and Community Service, University of Massachusetts Boston, and associate director of the Gastón Institute. He received his Ph.D. from the Florence Heller Graduate School for Advanced Studies in Social Welfare, Brandeis University, and his M.S.W. from Boston University School of Social Work. Dr. Rivera's publications include *Latinos in Massachusetts and the 1990 U.S. Census: Growth and Geographic Distribution* (Gastón Institute, UMass Boston, 1991); *Hispanics in Massachusetts: A Demographic Report*, coauthored with Camayd-Freixas and Strom (Commission on Hispanic Affairs, Boston, 1986); and *Latino Parent Involvement in the Boston Public Schools: Preliminary Notes from the Field* (Trotter Institute, UMass Boston, 1988).

ESTER R. SHAPIRO holds a Ph.D. in psychology from the University of Massachusetts Amherst. She is currently the practicum coordinator and an assistant professor in the Clinical Psychology Program at the University of Massachusetts Boston. The Clinical Psychology Program specializes in training for clinical services to underserved populations. Dr. Shapiro's most recent publication is *Grief as a Family Process: A Systemic Developmental Perspective* (Guilford Press, 1993), and she is currently working with Family, Friends and Community on the design of family support services that enhance family development.

CASTELLANO B. TURNER received his doctorate in psychology from the University of Chicago, and he is currently professor and director of clinical psychology in the Department of Psychology at the University of Massachusetts Boston. Dr. Turner's most recent publications include "Through a Glass, Darkly: Psychotherapists' Gender Stereotypes for Women and Men Varying in Age," which appeared in Hess and Markson's (Eds.), *Growing Old in America* (4th ed., Transaction Books, 1990) and "Dimensions of Racial Ideology: A Study of Urban Black Attitudes," which appeared in Kusmer's (Ed.), *Black Communities and Urban Race Relations in American History*.

CAROLE CHRISTOFK UPSHUR received a doctorate of education in clinical psychology and public practice from Harvard University Graduate School of Education. She is an associate professor at the Center for Community Planning at the University of Massachusetts Boston and an associate in pediatrics at the University of Massachusetts Medical School. Dr. Upshur's career has focused on policy issues for children and families, primarily those with disabilities, and traditional risk factors. She has recently coauthored *Development of Infants with*

Disabilities and Their Families (Monographs of the Society for Research in Child Development, Serial No. 230, 57, 1992).

ANNE WHEELOCK is currently an independent education writer and policy consultant in Boston. She worked for 11 years at the Massachusetts Advocacy Center where she prepared a number of major reports on dropout prevention and public school reform, including *Crossing the Tracks: How "Untracking" Can Save America's Schools* (New Press, 1992). Her writing and research interests focus on practices and policies designed to increase equity and excellence in public schools, especially in the middle grades.

VIRGINIA VOGEL ZANGER is the president of the Massachusetts Association for Bilingual Education and a founder of the Massachusetts Coalition for Bilingual Education. She received a doctorate in bilingual education from Boston University, specializing in cross-cultural issues. For the last 20 years, she has participated in the bilingual education community in Massachusetts as a teacher, teacher-trainer, video producer, textbook author, researcher and administrator. Her most recent publication is a revision of her textbook *Face to Face: Communications, Culture, and Collaboration* (Heinle and Heinle, 1992). She is the director of the Hands-On Science Project at the Hurley School in Boston.

The Education of Latino Students in Massachusetts: Issues, Research, and Policy Implications

Ralph Rivera
Introduction

Massachusetts has undergone radical changes in the racial/ethnic composition of its population in the last 20 years. While national demographic projections suggest that the number of Latinos will surpass blacks in the early twenty-first century, the Latino population of Massachusetts, due to its extraordinary growth rate during the last two decades, is already the largest racial/ethnic minority group in the state. The Latino population's high growth rate, combined with its youthfulness, suggests that this group will constitute an increasingly important sector of the state's labor force in the years to come.

The association between educational attainment and economic success has been well established. In recent years, education has become even more important as projections for the 1990s and the twenty-first century indicate that most new jobs will require a work force with high levels of education. Beyond the economic sphere, education is a valuable tool that allows us to deal more effectively and productively with an increasingly complex world. Those members of our population with low levels of education will be limited in their participation in mainstream society and are more likely to be at a disadvantage, both in the world of work and beyond.

If the growing Latino labor force in Massachusetts is well educated and trained, it will contribute positively to the state's economy, and the communities in which Latinos live will experience valuable gains as this labor force seeks full participation in the Commonwealth's social, economic, and political life. On the other hand, if the Latino labor force is poorly educated and trained, the future viability and competitiveness of the Massachusetts economy is threatened, and the Latino population will remain marginalized.

The information available on the educational status of Latino students in the state's public schools indicates that we face a crisis. The Massachusetts public educational system is not responding to the needs of the Latino population, and this population continues to be the most undereducated group in the state. Therefore, it is no surprise that Latinos are the most disadvantaged racial/ethnic minority group in the state, and they consistently hold the highest poverty rate of all Latino state populations in the nation.

The magnitude of the problems faced by Latino children in Massachusetts public schools must be considered within the context of the dramatic growth of Latino students in the state's public education systems. Three urban public school systems are already majority Latino (Lawrence, Holyoke, and Chelsea), while all other cities (and some towns) also have significant proportions of Latino students.

The increasing size of the Latino population poses formidable challenges to state policymakers; however, one of the major obstacles to sound educational policy formulation and program planning that addresses the needs of Latino students is the "information gap." Efforts at educational policy development, planning, and resource mobilization are hampered by the lack of basic information, analysis, and research of the problems and needs of the Latino population in Massachusetts. This book attempts to narrow the information gap on Latino educational issues; it seeks to provide educational policymakers with information and analyses, as well as recommendations for policy formulation.

In Part I, *The Context*, Anne Wheelock's chapter, "The Status of Latino Students in Massachusetts Public Schools" (Chapter 1), provides background information that is critical for understanding the realities faced by Latino students in the Commonwealth's public schools. Wheelock presents a review of the educational status of Latino students and a description of the serious difficulties these students encounter, focusing on enrollment, dropout, grade retention, and school absence patterns. In addition, Wheelock argues that school academic placement practices (i.e., tracking and grouping) have a deleterious effect on Latino students. Wheelock found that Latino students are disproportionately placed below their grade level or in "low-status" courses. She concludes from her analysis that Latino students in Massachusetts "experience nonpromotion, school absence, discrimination by expectation, and unequal access to knowledge as a routine part of their education."

Part II, *Educational Issues for the Latino Community,* addresses five educational issues critical to Latino students and their parents. These issues are educational entitlements, bilingual education, parental participation, school reform, and vocational education. In Chapter 2, "Entitlements of Latino Students and Parents in the Massachusetts Public Educational System: Some Legal and Policy Considerations," Jose Colón-Morera, Nitza Hidalgo, Aida Nevárez, and Ana García-Blanco present an overview of legal mandates that aim to provide equal educational opportunities for Latino students in the Commonwealth. Concentrating on three critical areas — bilingual education, parental involvement, and school reform — the authors review the most important policy debates in each area, discuss the benefits and limits of the entitlements, and note how these can be expanded. They also make recommendation for further research in each area.

In Chapter 3, "Bilingual Education: Perspectives on Research and Other Issues," Diana Lam argues for studies that will contribute to the formulation of public policy that supports and fosters genuine bilingual education programs. She further asserts that in a good bilingual education program, language and culture must be considered assets rather than liabilities to the educational process. Lam also discusses the elements that constitute quality bilingual education, noting the importance of standards for bilingual education and teacher training, an integrated approach to bilingual education programs, and accountability in this vital area of the educational process. She concludes with a discussion of future directions for educational research on bilingual education.

"Barriers to Latino Parental Involvement in the Boston Public Schools" (Chapter 4), by Ralph Rivera, identifies the extraordinary obstacles to effective parental participation that Latino parents encounter in the Boston public school system. Rivera argues that while most Latinos consider parental involvement in the schools important and have indeed developed increasingly effective parent organizations and groups, they face very difficult barriers to individual participation that can be classified as institutional, cultural, socioeconomic, and sociodemographic. He presents three models of programs in Boston schools that have been successful in promoting Latino parent involvement and offers a list of recommendations for schools actively seeking to engage Latino parents.

Chapter 5, "Latinos and Educational Reform: The Privatization of the Chelsea Public Schools" by Glenn Jacobs, provides an insightful account of the Latino community's response to Boston University's takeover of the public school system in the city of Chelsea, Massachusetts. Jacobs presents a detailed description of the forces that led to such an unprecedented arrangement, i.e., the control of a public school system by a private university, notwithstanding the Latino community's opposition. He explains that the silver lining to this takeover lies in the historical mobilization and organization of the Latino community seeking to be active participants in Chelsea's school reform. He points out that this mobilization led to the election of the city's first Latino school committee member.

In Chapter 6, "An Examination of Latino Experiences in Vocational Education: Implications for Educational Policy and Reform in Massachusetts," James Jennings presents perhaps the first analysis of the participation patterns and the status of Latino students in the state's vocational technical education programs in grades 9 through 12. Through interviews with 15 key informants, Jennings also examines the barriers to greater Latino participation in vocational technical education programs, and he identifies areas that require more detailed investigation in the future. Jennings concludes that while there is a serious paucity of information on the experiences of Latino students in vocational education, significant numbers of Latinos are participating in these programs in grades 9 through 12, and, therefore, more attention to this area by educational policymakers is warranted.

The chapters in Part III, *Research and Policy Implications*, report the results of several research studies focusing directly on the experiences of Latino students in Massachusetts. Interestingly, most of the researchers used primarily qualitative research methods in their investigations. Perhaps this is due to an increasing recognition of the limitations of the quantitative approach in elucidating the complexities and intricacies of Latino students' educational experiences. Each of the authors discusses the policy implications of his or her findings.

In Chapter 7, "What Do Latino Children Need to Succeed in School? A Study of Four Boston Public Schools," Antonia Darder and Carole Christofk Upshur report on a qualitative study of the school experiences of fifth-grade Latino children. Through interviews with the students, teachers, principals, and parents, as well as classroom observations, Darder and Upshur sought to identify the educational requisites needed to foster academic attainment for Latino students. The authors analyze nine major educational areas: school leadership, teacher morale, teacher preparation, school environment, curriculum, instructional approaches and teaching strategies, meaningful use of Spanish, teacher expectations, and the future expectations for Latino students. Darder and Upshur conclude with recommendations for educational policies and practices that will strengthen Latino students' academic achievement.

"I was an Outsider: An Exploratory Study of Dropping Out among Puerto Rican Youths in Holyoke" (Chapter 8), by Manuel Frau-Rámos and Sonia Nieto, examines the determinants of dropping out of high school among Latino (mostly Puerto Rican) high school students in Holyoke, Massachusetts. Frau-Rámos and Nieto compared students who completed high school with a group who dropped out along demographic factors such as race/ethnicity, socioeconomic status, and age as well as along school-related experiences such as nonpromotion, participation in the bilingual education program, grades, and academic placement. They also conducted interviews with three Latino students that provide valuable insights into the students' personal experiences with the Holyoke schools. The authors present the implications of their findings for school policy and practice.

Chapter 9, "Academic Costs of Social Marginalization: An Analysis of the Perceptions of Latino Students at a Boston High School," by Virginia Vogel Zanger, examines the social relations within a school from the viewpoint of Latino students. Focusing on academically successful Latino students, Zanger analyzes the relationships that these students have with non-Latino students and with their teachers. She notes that the attitudes and behaviors of non-Latino students and teachers have marginalized the Latino students to such an extent that many of them express a sense of exclusion and isolation, feel that they are in a subordinate position vis-a-vis the non-Latino students, and depict a deep feeling of cultural invisibility. Zanger argues that the social dynamics of the school subvert Latino students' academic achievement, and she discusses the consequences for the students of the lack of language and cultural recognition, the racist attitudes and behaviors, and the lack of trust between them and their teachers. Zanger concludes with a discussion of the implications of her findings for research and practice.

In "Poverty, Resilience, and Academic Achievement among Latino College Students and High School Dropouts: An Exploratory Study," (Chapter 10), Castellano Turner, Amaro Laria, Ester Shapiro, and Maria Perez sought to identify factors that enabled Latino students to overcome their disadvantaged socioeconomic situations and excel academically. The authors developed a psychosocial model to guide the study that encompassed four realms of stress protective factors: individual, family, school, and social. The researchers compared a group of Latino high school graduates who were currently attending college with Latino youths who had dropped out of high school to determine to what extent the protective factors could shed light on the college students' resilience. The proposed psychosocial model is supported by their findings.

In Chapter 11, "The Effects of Schooling Processes and Practices on Potential At-Risk Latino High School Students," Martha Montero-Sieburth examines the impact that a school's codes, norms, and regulations, as well as the attitudes and demeanor of the school personnel, have on Latino students. Montero-Sieburth's qualitative study focuses on eight Latino students, and she utilized participant observation techniques and in-depth interviews to gather detailed information on these students' experiences in school.

Finally, Part IV, *Future Directions*, contains the chapter "Creating Possibilities: Educating Latino Students in Massachusetts" (Chapter 12), by Sonia Nieto, the concluding chapter for this volume. As is emphasized in many of the chapters of this book, as well as in other documentation of the experiences of Latino students in Massachusetts, Nieto argues that change in the state's public educational system must focus on school policies and practices that undermine Latino students' ability to achieve academically rather than concentrating on the characteristics of individual students and their families. She illustrates this argument by briefly reviewing three areas — tracking, curriculum content, and pedagogy — and discussing their negative impact on Latino students. Nieto also discusses how the low expectations that many teachers have for Latino students adversely affects them, and she reviews the literature in this domain. She clamors for the reconceptualization of cultural and linguistic differences so that diversity is celebrated and affirmed. Nieto concludes with a description of a multicultural education model that moves from tolerance to a focus on affirmation, solidarity, and critique.

Like previous migrants and immigrants to Massachusetts, Latinos come here seeking, among other things, economic opportunity for themselves and their families. Like earlier migrants and immigrants they seek peace and a better life for themselves and their children, and they are willing to work hard to achieve this quality of life. The expanded economic opportunities that come with a solid education and training, however, are essential if the rapidly increasing Latino labor force is to contribute to the present and future viability and competitiveness of the Massachusetts economy. The educational success of the Latino population is not only a community concern, but also a matter of self-interest for the Commonwealth as a whole.

Part I
The Context

Anne Wheelock

The Status of Latino Students in Massachusetts Public Schools

In the past decade, national attention has focused on educational policy and school reform. Fueled by perceived failings of the U.S. educational system, failings defined primarily by a decline in standardized test scores, education policy makers in the early 1980s proposed a set of reforms that, for the most part, urged higher standards, longer school days, and tougher graduation require-ments. However, tougher schooling is not necessarily better schooling. By the mid-1980s, a number of constituencies, notably independent advocacy groups, had determined that the impact of the prescribed reforms had not only failed to help the nation's most vulnerable students, primarily in urban districts, but might actually have harmed these students. Included were Latino students who are counted as dropping out of school at the highest rates of any group and who, even when they stayed in school, often find themselves short-changed of a high quality education. Thus, in 1984 the National Commission on Secondary Education of Hispanics called attention to the critical needs of Latino students and urged that these needs be addressed to benefit the broader society. As the Commission pointed out:

> The dropout rates and low school achievement levels of a staggering number of Hispanic high school students have a direct, devastating effect on their communities. The damage inflicted on young Hispanics today threatens society tomorrow.

Other groups since have emphasized the failure of many schools to live up to expectation in relation to Latino students. In a recent report, the National Council of La Raza (no date) noted:

> The American educational system is often described as a pipeline, success-fully transporting individuals from childhood to college or the world of work. National data indicate that Hispanics are slipping through the cracks of the educational pipeline at disproportionate rates — making Hispanics the most undereducated subgroup in the country.

La Raza noted that high numbers of students enrolled below grade level combined with high dropout rates, assignment to nonacademic tracks, and low college-completion rates characterized the overall picture of undereducation. Likewise, the Children's Defense Fund (1990) reports that Latino students perform at reading, math, and science levels lower than their peers, while the National Center for Educational Statistics (1989) has found that Latino dropouts leave school with less schooling and are less likely to return to school than other groups. These reports suggest that while Latino students may be entering the schoolhouse door in record numbers, schools have failed to provide either an equitable or excellent education for them.

Given these data, a general profile of Latino students who leave school before graduation has emerged nationally. For example, a recent study of dropouts conducted by the ASPIRA Association, Inc. (Fernández and Vélez, 1989) in five cities — Milwaukee, Newark, Miami, San Antonio, and Chicago — has defined the "typical Latino dropout" as a student who has repeated at least one grade, is overage for the ninth grade (15.6 years old), has a "D" average, has missed an average of 17 days in a semester, and has no plans to go to college.

This bleak picture, however, should not cloud two important points. First, while Latino dropout rates are consistently the highest for all groups, the profile of the "typical Latino dropout" differs little from that of the "typical non-Latino dropout" as defined by research.[1] Second, as ASPIRA researchers Fernández and Vélez (1989) point out:

> The findings of this study suggest that three of the most important factors in predicting staying in school for Latino high school students are age, grades, and absences, all of which can be affected by school policies and practices.

Indeed, ASPIRA, the Hispanic Policy Development Project, and the Children's Defense Fund have proposed a number of new directions for policy to boost the achievement of Latino children and reinforce their commitment to school. For example, ASPIRA has called for a restructuring of curriculum and a renewed articulation of learning goals and objectives, alternatives to grade retention, and alternative responses to absenteeism that address the school-related causes of nonattendance, including boredom in the classroom and difficulties with teachers (Fernández and Vélez, 1989). Likewise, since 1984 the National Commission on Secondary Schooling for Hispanics (1984) and the Hispanic Policy Development Project (1988) have called for increased collaboration between schools and the community toward a stronger climate of caring, the elimination of tracking to provide equal access to knowledge for all students regardless of their postsecondary plans, and improved school-to-work transitions. More recently the Hispanic Policy Development Project has urged fundamental restructuring of schooling, especially at the middle level, to make schools centers of both learning and caring for Latino youth and their families. Finally, the Children's Defense Fund (1990) has formulated proposals to improve the quality of education received by Latino students, assist parents in helping their children achieve, increase the relevance of school to work, reduce early dropping out, address the needs of Latino youth, and improve postsecondary enrollment.

The wealth of national data and policy proposals is as extensive as the problems are urgent. Both data generated on a national level and proposals for reform suggest potential directions for state-level research and policy making. What is known on a national level provides a springboard for assessing the status of Latino students in Massachusetts.

While federal policies of bilingual education, special education, compensatory education, and early childhood education have enormous impact on Latino students, many of the routines, organizational structures, and practices that characterize the school day are grounded primarily in local and state policy. In fact, because policy at these levels may have the greatest impact on the day-to-day lives of children, analysis of state and local achievement and dropout patterns is key to understanding both the scope of problems facing Latino students and the clues to policy changes needed.

As the Massachusetts Department of Education begins to collect and release more comprehensive educational data for individual school districts and the state as a whole, a rough picture of dropout and achievement patterns for Latino students in Massachusetts emerges (Massachusetts Department of Education, 1989, 1990, 1991).

Enrollment Patterns

According to the U.S. Census Bureau's March 1990 report *U.S. Population Estimates, by Age, Sex, Race, and Hispanic Origin: 1980 to 1988*, the Latino population has grown by 34 percent in eight years. The population of Latinos in Massachusetts schools mirrors this national trend. Furthermore, the number of Latino students in the state's public schools grew from 35,096 in 1980 to 55,275 in 1988, representing a 57 percent change.[2] With 825,409 students enrolled, Latino students now make up nearly 7 percent of the student population of Massachusetts. With these changing demographics, the Hispanic Policy Development Project (1988) has noted:

By the year 2000, in key areas of this nation, the majority population will be Hispanic. In these areas, the future of arts, sciences, and government, the prosperity of business enterprises, and the social health of entire communities will depend mainly on Hispanics: on their participation in community affairs and in the economy, and on their ability to support themselves and their families.

That the future health and well-being of some communities is already dependent on the success of Latino students is no less true for Massachusetts than the nation as a whole.

Of the 20 Massachusetts school districts with the highest number of Latino students, only one — Framingham — is not classified by the Massachusetts Department of Education as an "urbanized center."[3] As table 1 indicates:

In the Lawrence, Holyoke, and Chelsea districts, the Latino enrollment is greater than half the total enrollment.

In the Springfield and Methuen districts, the Latino enrollment is greater than one-quarter of the total enrollment.

Of the remaining 15 districts, all enroll Latino students at a rate higher than the rate of 6.7 for the state overall. Enrollment rates of Latino students in these remaining districts range from 18.7 in Worcester and 19.0 in Boston to 7.1 in Somerville.

Moreover, even within the top 20 districts, Latino students are concentrated in only a handful of communities. For example:

More than half of all Latino students in the state's public schools are enrolled in four districts — Boston, Springfield, Lawrence, and Holyoke — although these districts enroll only 12 percent of all public school students in the state.

Three-fifths of all Latino public school students are enrolled in five districts — the top four and Worcester — although these districts enroll only 15 percent of all public school students in the state.

While the 10 districts with the greatest number of Latino students enroll only one-fifth of all public school students, they enroll nearly three-quarters (73.7 percent) of all Latino students.

Massachusetts enrollment data on Latino students have particular policy implications related to excellence and equity. To the extent that most Latino students are in urban districts, they also cope with the troubling conditions that characterize many of these districts, conditions that include deteriorating buildings, a politicized bureaucracy, an aging teaching force, a fragile tax base, and a low percentage of households with children in public schools. Moreover, despite their high numbers, Latino children — and their parents — may have limited or no political representation in forums where decisions concerning public schools are made, particularly on city councils or school committees.

Families whose first language is not English may also find it difficult to promote their children's interests at the school level. Indeed, Massachusetts enrollment data suggest that many Latino children may find themselves with only a tenuous link between their home and school language. For example, according to data shown in table 2:

> Statewide, four out of five Latino students come from families whose first language is not English.

> In all 10 of the highest-Latino-enrollment districts, more than half of all Latino students come from families whose first language is not English, with nine out of 10 students in Lawrence in this category.

> Statewide, slightly more than one-third of Latino students whose first language is not English are considered limited- English-proficient (LEP), that is, they cannot perform regular classroom work in English.

Table 2 describes these findings based on the population of Latino students whose first language is Spanish as well as students whose English proficiency is still too limited to allow them to succeed in all-English classrooms.

Latino students may also be victims of traditional educational policies and practices that offer a poor "fit" with students' real needs — a curriculum and instructional focus geared toward standardized tests, a reliance on special education or pull-out approaches as a means to address academic and behavioral problems in separate settings, rigid tracking and ability grouping, developmentally inappropriate middle grades schools, punitive and ineffective attendance and retention policies, and inadequate mechanisms to communicate with parents. And again, given a lack of political representation, Latino parents may have no vehicle to raise concerns about such practices or mobilize resources to provide alternatives.

Finally, in urban districts with high rates of Latino enrollments, Latino students may find themselves in the vanguard of integration efforts. In such circumstances, Latino students are likely to be particularly vulnerable to inequitable and racist school exclusion practices, particularly when desegregation requires that they attend schools that are largely white.

Dropout Patterns

In 1989, the state released its first report on dropouts, which revealed patterns that largely parallel national patterns. The *Massachusetts Dropout Report: 1987-88* (Massachusetts Department of Education, 1989) noted "large differences" among subgroups in the student population, with Latino students having the highest annual dropout rates for both 1987-88 and 1986-87, the first year data were collected. Some of the findings of this report are presented in table 3. Specifically, the data shows:

> 1,631 Latino students dropped out of Massachusetts schools in 1986-87, while an additional 1,727 dropped out in 1987-88.

> Annual dropout rates for Latino students of 15.2 percent in 1986-87 and 14.4 percent in 1987-88 were more than three times the rates for white students for both years and just under three times the rate for all students.

> Latino dropout rates were substantially greater than the annual rate of 8.9 percent for all urban districts.

> Although the annual dropout rate for Latino students dropped slightly from the first to second year, the proportion of Latino students represented in the dropout population was greater the second year than the first — 11.4 percent in 1986-87 and 12.4 percent in 1987-88.

> The projected four-year rate is highest for Latino students, equal to the national average for this group, and nearly three times the projected rate for white students.

Massachusetts Department of Education data (1989) by race for each district portrays the drama of the dropout phenomenon for Latino students in the 20 districts that enroll the vast majority of Latinos:

> In the 20 districts with high Latino enrollments, 1986-87 annual dropout rates for all students ranged from 3.9 percent in Framingham to 17.1 percent in Chelsea compared to rates for Latino students ranging from 4 percent in Brockton to 25 percent in Methuen.

> In every one of these 20 cities except Brockton, the dropout rate for Latino high school students is higher than the rate for all students. Even in cities where larger Latino enrollments might be expected to reduce the differ-

ences, the gap is considerable. For example, compared to the annual rate for all students within a district, the rate for Latinos is:

Approximately two times greater in Springfield, Haverhill, Salem, Waltham, and Somerville;

Approximately two and one-half times greater in Southbridge;

Approximately three times greater in Cambridge and Framingham.

These figures represent only two years of baseline data on dropouts. It will be several years before the data revealed here are considered entrenched patterns. However, we have little reason to be optimistic. National Center for Educational Statistics data (1989) already shows that despite declines in national dropout rates for other subgroups, rates for Latinos have remained high and have not declined over time. In addition, Boston public schools data collected over six years indicate that the gap between Latino dropout rates and those for other groups in the district with the largest number of Latino students in the state has not narrowed significantly over time and remains near 50 percent (Massachusetts Advocacy Center, May 18, 1990).

Why do Latino students drop out of Massachusetts schools at such high rates? No large, systematic study exclusive to this state has taken on that question, but some data is suggestive. In the 1988 report *Too Late to Patch: Reconsidering Second-Chance Opportunities for Hispanic and Other Dropouts* (Miller, Nicolau, Orr, Valdivieso, and Walker, 1988), the authors, writing for the Hispanic Policy Development Project, reviewed data from the National Center for Educational Statistics High School and Beyond Study and a related Ford Foundation study and outlined factors with special relevance to Latino students dropouts.

The report cited poor quality schools, discrimination by school professionals against Latinos, and teachers' low expectations for Latino students' achievement as fundamental to the dropout phenomena. The report also noted that among all students, Latino students were more apt to be overage for their grade (a factor that has emerged in numerous reports as a major correlate of dropping out) and more likely to drop out because of family-related reasons, including being married or pregnant or needing to work. Finally, data from the study indicated that students from non-English speaking backgrounds were three times as likely as other Latinos to drop out of school, and researchers found that while poverty contributes significantly to dropping out, Latino youth still drop out more frequently than other students, even when rates are controlled for family income, suggesting that language-minority status is a more significant factor than it is for students of other subgroups.

Clearly, while some of the factors associated with Latino students dropping out are not related to school policies, many are. As ASPIRA (Fernández and Vélez, 1989) has pointed out, it is school-related variables such as nonpromotions that put students below their appropriate grade, absences, and discrimination by expectation that must be the focus of educational policies affecting Latino achievement and retention.

Grade Retention Patterns

With the implementation of increasingly rigid grade promotion and graduation requirements in the 1980s, a number of states embarked on a course of "toughening up" their schools through approaches designed to ensure that students who were deemed "unready" for their next grade would be required to repeat their grade, ostensibly to have more time to master the knowledge and skills necessary for further success. As a result, Shepard and Smith (1990) have recently determined that approximately 2.4 million students across the country — some 6 percent — are not promoted every year. Moreover, based on analysis of data from 13 states and the District of Columbia, Shepard and Smith estimate that half of all students in the United States arrive in ninth grade having failed at least one grade.

To a certain extent, Massachusetts, by avoiding rigid mandates in its Educa-tion Reform Act of 1985, Chapter 188, has also avoided extremely high nonpromotion rates statewide. Indeed, compared to the retention rate estimated for the country as a whole, the Commonwealth's 3.5 percent rate of students recommended for retention seems almost inconsequential (Massachusetts De-partment of Education, 1990). However, the lack of mandates for "tougher" standards on the state level has not prevented certain local districts from imposing what Shepard and Smith have called "fierce" nonpromotion rates on vulnerable students. The state's relatively low rate masks rates for urban districts, and especially for Latino students in those districts, that signal severe consequences for these students in terms of both achievement and attachment to school.

In fact, according to the first report on nonpromotion released by the Massachusetts Department of Education (1990), high grade retention rates for Latino students raise questions regarding the quality and appropriateness of education being offered many Latino students in the state. According to the report:

4,058 Latino students were recommended for grade retention in June 1989.

With 8.3 percent of all Latino students recommended for grade retention in 1989, Latinos were more than twice as likely as all students statewide and three times as likely as white students to be held back in grade.

While Latino students made up 6.1 percent of the Massachusetts public school enrollment in October 1988, they made up 14.4 percent of all Massachusetts students recommended for grade repetition in June 1989.

A statewide summary of the number of students recommended for retention in June 1989 by race is presented in table 4.

"High retention rates are a signal that large numbers of students are not learning and achieving at acceptable levels within many of our schools," the Massachusetts Department of Education report states. And according to data collected in Massachusetts, a large number of schools with high nonpromotion rates are located in the urban districts with the highest Latino enrollments. For example, the data indicate that in seven of the state's 10 highest-Latino-enrollment districts — Springfield, Lawrence, Holyoke, Worcester, Chelsea, Brockton and Lynn — Latino students experience the highest retention rates for any group. And while the 36,693 Latinos enrolled in the top 10 districts make up approximately one out of every five students (21.3 percent) enrolled in these 10 districts combined, the 12,179 Latino students recommended for retention in these districts represented more than one out of every four (26.9 percent) retained students.

Perhaps many policy makers, educators, and even parents would argue that nonpromotion is a way of providing remediation for students whose work does not reflect grade-level expectations. Indeed, "common sense" suggests that grade retention is a well-intentioned effort to provide students who are "behind" with more time and attention which will allow them to experience success later. If this were true, Latino students would be among the beneficiaries of such practices and would experience improved achievement. Sadly, this is not the case.

In fact, as Shepard and Smith (1990) note, grade retention undermines students' attitude toward school, their behavior, their self-esteem, and their persistence in school until graduation. But most relevant to the status of Latino students is what Shepard and Smith call "the most critical finding — that retention worsens rather than improves the level of student achievement in years following the repeat year." As they observe, contrary to expectations, retained students rarely catch up with their peers or even improve their performance in relation to students in their new grade. Indeed, had these students moved ahead with their peers, particularly in the early grades, their chances of improvement would have been significantly better than had they repeated their grade.

Moreover, Shepard and Smith point out that nonpromotion is cumulative and that any annual rate eventually compounds to create much higher rates of students who are overage for grade by legal school-leaving age, creating a pool of students who are highly vulnerable to dropping out. Because of this dynamic, the younger students are when they are held back in grade the first time, the more quickly they suffer the problems associated with being overage for their grade. And when they experience repeat nonpromotions, as many do, they are likely to reach school-leaving age in earlier and earlier grades.

This dynamic has particular application for Latino students in Massachusetts. According to Massachusetts Department of Education data (1990), Latino students experience the greatest chances of being recommended for retention in the earliest grades. Indeed, the 8.6 percent rate of retention for Latino children through third grade is two and one-half times the retention rate for white children at that grade level. Furthermore, while available data does not yet allow for a precise analysis, the 1989 retention rates for Latino students suggest that approximately one out of nine Latino students (11.4 percent) in the Commonwealth may enter the sixth grade already one year below age-appropriate grade, compared to one out of 20 (4.9 percent) students overall, making Latino students more than two times as vulnerable as all Massachusetts students to dropping out, assessed on that criterion alone. By the time Latino students enter ninth grade, nearly one out of every five Latino students may be overage for grade by one year, compared to one out of every 13 students overall and one out of every 17 white students, making Latino students nearly three times more vulnerable than students overall to dropping out.

While the Massachusetts Department of Education report on grade retention (1990) notes that across-the-board rates vary from grade to grade, aggregated grade-level rates mask differences among groups of students and districts. It is these differential rates of students recommended for retention that dramatize the achievement gaps between Latino and white students. These gaps vary from district to district, and given that the gaps begin in the earliest grades and are never closed, the net effect is the entrenchment of achievement differences over time, with Latino students being increasingly disadvantaged by their continuing exposure to failure.

Moreover, nonpromotion in different grades may have different consequences in terms of students' subsequent school experiences. For example, nonpromotion in the early grades may trigger placement in "special" remedial programs, many of which rely on a slower paced pull-out approach. These programs can sometimes be helpful, but frequently any gains recorded are only short-lived, and reviews of such programs by such researchers as Gartner and Lipsky (1987) suggest that once students are classified into such programs, they may never return full time to the mainstream. In seventh grade, nonpromotion can serve as a sorting mechanism to determine which students will be enrolled in which courses. Indeed, Useem (1990) has described the critical nature of seventh grade in particular to school-based course placement decisions and students' access to high-level curriculum. Finally, in ninth and tenth grade, nonpromotion may be the final straw for discouraged learners whose next step is to withdraw from school. For example, according to researcher Byrne (1988), 62 percent of all students retained in Boston's ninth grade ultimately drop out of school, a rate double that of students who receive ninth-grade promotions.

A review of retentions at particular grades, then, suggests more subtle sorting patterns at work in a given system, patterns which then may also differ by race or ethnicity. The patterns of nonpromotion for Latino students in Massachusetts are particularly disturbing because grade retention is almost entirely a function of policy. Even given different levels of school performance, individual schools and school districts can respond to varying achievement levels in different ways. Since nonpromotion is only one possible school intervention, and since it is arguably among the most discriminatory and least effective of the alternatives available, its persistent use as a means of addressing the educational needs of Latino students clearly falls short and should be eliminated.

School Absence Patterns

As extensive studies — especially by the National Commission on Secondary Education for Hispanic Students (1984), the Hispanic Policy Development Project (1988), and ASPIRA (Fernández and Vélez, 1989) — have noted, school absence is a powerful correlate of dropping out, particularly among Latino students; and this topic deserves a place of its own in a focus on issues related to achievement and retention of Latino students.

School absence must also be understood within the framework of school practices, district attendance policies, and social needs. For example, Weitzman's five-year Boston City Hospital-based study (1985) of students in six Boston middle schools found few health or family differences between students with excessive absences and those with regular attendance patterns. However, this study did find that students with high absence patterns were more likely to be overage for their grade and placed in special education. "Problem absence" was also highly correlated with the specific school attended.

Typically, poor attendance patterns begin to show up in the middle grades, with truancy considered an important predictor of dropping out. In Massachusetts, state-level data indicate that Latino students are especially vulnerable to attendance problems and truancy. For example, a draft Massachusetts Department of Education report (1991) reveals that in 1987-88, almost 2,000 Latino students in Massachusetts were defined as truant, that is they were absent from school at least once for an unapproved reason. The report also indicated that the truancy rate for Latino students is highest for all groups of students enrolled in Massachusetts public schools, and Latino students were overrepresented in the state's truant population, comprising 8.1 percent of all students defined as truant one or more times in 1987-88, compared to their 5.9 percent statewide enrollment rate.[4]

Massachusetts truancy data by race or ethnicity for 1987-88 are shown in table 5. These data suggest that just as Latino students experience nonpromotion at the highest rates in the earliest grades, Latino students also reveal truancy problems earlier in their schooling. Specifically, according to the Massachusetts Department of Education (1991): At the elementary level — through fifth grade — Latino students are three times more likely to have at least one unexcused absence than their white peers; at the middle level, Latino students are more than twice as likely to be truant from school at least once than their white peers; and at the high school level, when truancy rates are highest for all groups, Latino students still experience truancy rates that are 60 percent higher than those of their white counterparts.

District- and school-level data will be critical to a deeper understanding of attendance and absence patterns for Latinos students. Moreover, a review of school policies and practices needs to accompany such an analysis. While some evidence exists that students' social, economic, or family demands may have a negative effect on attendance, evidence also suggests that school- and district-based practices also discourage attendance. Interviews with Boston students, both by the Massachusetts Advocacy Center (1986) and by Kahn for the *Boston Phoenix* (1990), consistently have revealed that schools at all levels may turn tardy students away at the door, thus undermining attendance that day or on subsequent days when students find themselves late to school. Moreover, *The Way Out: Student Exclusion Practices in Boston Middle Schools* (Massachusetts Advocacy Center, 1986) found that a districtwide policy of linking grade failure and nonpromotion to failure to attend school 85 percent of each marking period contributed substantially to attendance that declined from marking quarter to quarter through the school year, as students, knowing they would fail subsequent to their missing a certain number of days, found little point in continuing to attend. These findings suggest that further policy research concerning the attendance patterns of Latino students must focus at both the district- and school-level.

Discrimination by Expectation: Tracking and Grouping

As noted in the Hispanic Policy Development Project report *Too Late To Patch* (Miller, Nicolau, Orr, Valdivieso, and Walker, 1988), teachers' "self-fulfilling prophecies" fueled by low expectations for the performance of Latino youth constitute a significant school-related barrier to achievement and engagement among Latino students. Schools' placement practices, both in "special" programs and in the academic mainstream, often institutionalize these low expectations. As a result, Latino students are more likely to find themselves placed below their grade level or in low-status courses outside a grade-appropriate academic curriculum. Since students can learn only what they are taught, the placement of Latino students in settings below their grade level inevitably depresses their academic achievement and commitment to school.

In Massachusetts, a 1986 Department of Education study documented the extent to which different students have different experiences in Massachusetts schools. The report, *The High School Experience in Massachusetts*, found that African-American and Latino students take fewer academic courses than white students, specifically in science, math, and foreign languages. Moreover, although they take more English courses, these are typically in business English or remedial reading. Overall, according to the report, minority students are less likely to be enrolled in specific courses that are designed to lead to more advanced work in subsequent years. The report provided the following examples:

> White students average three times more college preparatory courses than minority students;

> While 14 percent of all white students take Algebra I in the eighth grade, only 3 percent of all minority students — both Latino and African-American — do so;

> Only 2 percent of all minority students are enrolled in both Algebra I and a foreign language in eighth grade, markedly decreasing the likelihood they will be involved in the top track in all courses.

While these findings apply statewide, detailed data available for Boston suggest similar patterns. In a recent report, *Locked In/Locked Out: Tracking and Placement Practices in Boston Public Schools*, the Massachusetts Advocacy Center (1990) analyzed Boston course enrollment data and found serious patterns of institutionalized low expectations for the district's Latino students. Overall, Boston's school placement patterns indicate that Latino students are, on one hand, least likely to be placed in settings that offer access to valued knowledge and expanded opportunity (for example, in Algebra I in ninth grade) and, on the other hand, most likely to be placed in settings characterized by attention to "basics" and low expectations (for example, in Basic Math I in ninth grade).

Moreover, absolute numbers of students enrolled in "high status" settings in Boston tell a dramatic story of exclusion from opportunity and access to knowledge. For example, the Massachusetts Advocacy Center reports (1990):

In 1988-89, only 59 out of 2,390 Latino students in all Boston high schools (2.4 percent) were enrolled in higher level math courses (beyond trigonometry) including 20 in advanced math or advanced math-honors, 15 in elementary analysis, 23 in advanced placement math, and 1 in calculus. The 2.4 percent rate of placement for Hispanic students in these courses is less then half the rate of 5.5 percent for all students.

In 1987-88, only 124 (5.3 percent) of Latino students in grades 4, 5, and 6 were enrolled in advanced work classes compared to 177 (19.0 percent) Asian students, 268 (10.9 percent) white students, and 481 (8.3 percent) African-American students.

By seventh grade, only 8 percent of all Latino students are enrolled in Boston's selective examination schools compared to 18 percent of all Boston seventh graders.

Students requiring bilingual programs have virtually no access to Boston's examination schools or magnet high schools. Even the Snowden School for International Studies, which features second-language courses for English-speaking students, has no Spanish bilingual program.

Finally, at every grade level in Boston, Latino students are far more likely to be enrolled in "remedial" settings like special education than in "advanced" settings (Massachusetts Advocacy Center, 1990). Furthermore, once in these remedial settings, Latino students in Boston are further segregated from their peers by special disability (Camayd-Freixas and Horst, 1987).

According to the Massachusetts Advocacy Center's report (1990), the low expectations that accompany these placement practices have not escaped the notice of students. Thus several Latino students commented, "They don't expect enough from us, and if they don't expect enough we can't give enough," and "Nobody wanted to push me because they thought I would fall over the edge. We have to be challenged." Such comments suggest that students in low-track settings may be prepared to work much harder than their schools have recognized.

As a policy matter, findings of discriminatory and disproportionate placement practices that exclude Latino students from high opportunity settings raise serious doubts that Latino students have equal access to knowledge in the public schools of Boston. If such patterns are replicated in other districts, as the Massachusetts Department of Education's 1986 study suggests, the undereducation of thousands of Latino students is virtually guaranteed in Massachusetts public schools.

Conclusions

Data from across the state as well as from particular school districts with large numbers of Latino students portray a disturbing picture. In Massachusetts, the Latino student population is growing rapidly, so much so that a number of urban communities in the state will depend on the Latino students currently enrolled in their schools for their future health. However, the present status of these very students suggests that neither the state nor these communities are taking seriously the future welfare of either the students or the society of which they are a part.

While some data, particularly on school attendance, are incomplete, they are nonetheless compelling. Both statewide and in specific districts, Latino students are not getting the education they need and deserve. Already vulnerable because of their "dominated" status in the larger society, Latino children experience nonpromotion, school absence, discrimination by expectation, and unequal access to knowledge as a routine part of their education. These experiences are likely to contribute substantially to their dropout rate, the highest for any group in the state.

Given this picture, the need to develop state and local policies to address educational inequities affecting Latino children is urgent. This requires exploring the purposes of educational policy and engaging in broad discussion about the expectations for the achievement of Latino students.

On one hand, the needs of thousands of Latino students statewide are immediate. Overage for their grade, truant from school, and placed below their grade level in such a way that depressed achievement is inevitable, Latino students need immediate support. On the other hand, a strategy that relies completely on developing services for vulnerable students risks conveying the message that students carry deficits that must be fixed by personal, social, or academic support. And while such a strategy may improve the academic performance of some students, it will fail to address the inequitable and ineffective district-based and school-level practices, policies, routines, structures, and relationships that depress achievement and contribute to early school leaving among Latino students.

Thus, while further analysis could refine the profile of the Latino students who are most "at risk" in Massachusetts schools, the sheer numbers of students who can be defined as vulnerable argues for a closer examination of the relationship between these Latino students and their schools. Writing about the contribution that schools themselves make to the dropout problem, researchers Wehlage and Rutter (1986) recommend reviewing schools' own policies and practices for the causes of disengagement "not only in the characteristics of the dropout, but also in relation to those institutional characteristics that affect the marginal student in a negative manner." As Wehlage and Rutter argue,

"Presumably the school is obligated to create an environment in which these [marginal] youth can experience some kind of success, find institutional partici- pation rewarding, and develop aspirations for additional schooling that can lead to satisfying employment." It is clearly necessary to describe the school-related factors that make those outcomes more likely for Latino youth.

A focus on services need not necessarily exclude a focus on institutional change. Indeed, a two-pronged strategy that offers support for specific students and also creates schools that live up to the obligations defined by Wehlage and Rutter is entirely consistent with a commitment to educational policy that promotes both equity and excellence. The challenge, then, is to identify supportive interventions that can benefit individual Latino students as well as school-level practices, policies, and relationships that will be responsive to Latino students and their communities.

Notes

1. This is not to say that no differences exist. As the ASPIRA study notes, differences exist within the Latino population when data is broken down into such national categories as Mexican-American, Puerto Rican, Cuban-American, or Central American. As this report will point out, the profile of the "typical Latino dropout" may emerge earlier in the schooling process than for other groups. Moreover, reviewers of the data base generated by the national High School and Beyond study noted that grades appear to be more important in dropping out for whites and Latinos than for African Americans (Ekstrom, Goertz, Pollack, and Rock, 1986). However, it should be noted that because this data base only includes students surveyed from tenth grade, this study has limited application to understanding many Latino dropouts who leave school prior to that grade.

2. In some communities, the growth in Latino students enrolled in public schools was dramatically greater for the same period. For example, Latino enrollment grew by 131 percent in Lawrence, 122 percent in Lynn, and 77 percent in Worcester (Beane, Pineda, Rivera, and Rivera, 1990).

3. For purposes of comparing districts, the Massachusetts Department of Education has clustered districts according to the kind of community (KOC) they represent. Such grouping is thought to allow for more appropriate comparisons of districts of similar demographics.

4. Enrollment figures may vary due to the failure of some schools in some districts to report data to the Massachusetts Department of Education.

References

Beane, G., Pineda, C., Rivera, L., and Rivera, R. (1990, May). *A Profile of Latinos in Massachusetts: Demographic, Education, and Economic Status.* Boston, MA:

University of Massachusetts, Mauricio Gastón Institute for Latino Community Development and Public Policy.

Byrne, G. (1988, June). High School Dropouts in Boston. Paper submitted to the Department of Urban Studies, Massachusetts Institute of Technology, Boston, MA.

Camayd-Freixas, Y., and Horst, L. (1987, August). *The Special Education Program: An R and D Accountability Study.* Boston, MA: Boston Public Schools.

Children's Defense Fund. (1990, January/March). *Latino Youths at a Crossroads.* Washington, DC: CDF Adolescent Pregnancy Prevention Clearinghouse.

Ekstrom, R., Goertz, M., Pollack, J., and Rock, D. (1986). Who Drops Out of High School and Why? Findings from a National Study. *Teachers College Record,* Spring.

Fernández, R. R., and Vélez, W. (1989, October). *Who Stays? Who Leaves? Findings from the ASPIRA Five Cities High School Dropout Study.* Working Paper #89-1. Washington, DC: ASPIRA Institute for Policy Research.

Gartner, A., and Lipsky, D. K. (1987, November). Beyond Special Education: Toward a Quality System for All Students. *Harvard Educational Review, 57,* 4.

Hispanic Policy Development Project. (1988). *Closing the Gap for U.S. Hispanic Youth: Public Private Strategies.* Report from the 1988 Aspen Institute Conference on Hispanic Americans and the Business Community. Washington, DC: Author.

Kahn, R. (1990, January 19). Better Late than Never: Boston's Bogus School Policy. *Boston Phoenix.*

Massachusetts Advocacy Center. (1986). *The Way Out: Student Exclusion Practices in Boston Middle Schools.* Boston, MA: Author.

Massachusetts Advocacy Center. (1990, May 18). Non-Promotion and Dropout Data: 1986-87, 1987-89. Memorandum. Boston, MA: Author.

Massachusetts Advocacy Center. (1990). *Locked In/Locked Out: Tracking and Placement Practices in Boston Public Schools.* Boston: Author.

Massachusetts Department of Education. (1986, April). *The High School Experience in Massachusetts.* Quincy, MA: Massachusetts Department of Education, Bureau of Research and Assessment.

Massachusetts Department of Education. (1989, June). *Massachusetts Dropout Report: 1987-88.* Quincy, MA: Massachusetts Department of Education, Office of Planning, Research, and Evaluation.

Massachusetts Department of Education. (1990, April). *Structuring Schools for Student Success: A Focus on Grade Retention.* Quincy, MA: Massachusetts Department of Education, Division of School Programs; Bureau of Student Development and Health; Office of Planning, Research, and Evaluation.

Massachusetts Department of Education. (1991). *Massachusetts Attendance and Truancy Report.* Draft. Boston, MA: Author.

Miller, S. M., Nicolau, S., Orr, M. T., Valdivieso, R., and Walker, G. (1988). *Too Late to Patch: Reconsidering Second-Chance Opportunities for Hispanic and Other Dropouts.* Washington, DC: Hispanic Policy Development Project.

National Center for Education Statistics. (1989, September). *Dropout Rates in the United States, 1988.* Analysis Report. No. NCES 89-609. Washington, DC: U.S. Department of Education, Office of Educational Research and Improvement.

National Commission on Secondary Education for Hispanics. (1984). *Make Something*

Happen: Hispanics and Urban High School Reform. Washington, DC: Hispanic Policy Development Project.

National Council of La Raza. (no date). *Reversing the Trend of Hispanic Undereducation.* Washington, DC: Author.

Shepard, L. A., and Smith, M. L. (1990). Synthesis of Research on Grade Retention. *Educational Leadership,* 84-88.

U.S. Bureau of the Census. (1990, March). *United States Population Estimates, by Age, Sex, Race, and Hispanic Origin: 1980-1988,* Washington, DC: U.S. Bureau of Census.

Useem, E. (1990, April). *Getting on the Fast Track in Mathematics: School Organizational Influence on Math Track Assignment.* Paper presented at the American Educational Research Association Conference, Boston, MA.

Wehlage, G. G., and Rutter, R. A. (1986, Spring). Dropping Out: How Much Do Schools Contribute to the Problem? *Teachers College Record, 87,* 3.

Weitzman, M., M.D., et al. (1985, July). Demographic and Educational Characteristics of Inner City Middle School Problem Absence Students. *American Journal of Orthopsychiatry, 55,* 3.

Table 1

Massachusetts Enrollment of Latino Students in 20 Public School Districts,
October 1988

City*	Total Enrollment	Latino Enrollment	Latino Enrollment Rate (%)	Cumulative Enrollment as % of Total	
				Total	Latino
				825,409	55,275
Boston	59,184	11,267	19.0	7.2	20.4
Springfld.	23,355	7,146	30.6	10.0	33.3
Lawrence	10,379	6,655	64.1	11.3	45.4
Holyoke	7,222	4,002	55.4	12.1	52.6
Worcester	20,766	3,888	18.7	14.6	59.6
Lowell	13,505	2,033	15.1	16.3	63.3
Chelsea	3,468	1,746	50.3	16.7	66.5
Brockton	14,929	1,474	9.9	18.5	69.1
Lynn	11,337	1,312	11.6	19.9	71.5
New Bdfrd.	14,418	1,213	8.4	21.6	73.7
Cambridge	7,551	928	12.3	22.5	75.4
Fitchburg	4,914	902	18.4	23.1	77.0
Frmnghm.	7,549	862	11.4	24.1	78.6
Haverhill	6,549	595	9.1	24.9	79.6
Salem	3,966	541	13.6	25.3	80.6
Waltham	5,375	541	10.1	26.0	81.6
Sthbrdge.	2,617	480	18.3	26.3	82.5
Smervlle.	6,370	453	7.1	27.1	83.3
Methuen	1,445	393	27.2	27.2	84.0
Chicopee	2,368	377	15.9	27.5	84.7

*Cities are ranked in descending order according to the number of Latino students in the
district.
SOURCE: Beane, G., Pineda, C., Rivera, L., and Rivera R. (1990, May). *A Profile of
Latinos in Massachusetts: Demographic, Education, and Economic Status.* Boston, MA:
University of Massachusetts, Mauricio Gastón Institute for Latino Community Develop-
ment and Public Policy.

Table 2

Massachusetts Latino Students Whose First Language Is Not English (FLINE) and Who Are Classified as Limited-English-Proficient (LEP), for the 10 Highest-Latino-Enrollment Districts, October 1988

City	FLINE*	LEP	Enrollment	% FLINE*	% LEP
Boston	9,118	5,980	11,267	80.9	53.1
Springfield	4,929	1,944	7,146	69.0	27.2
Lawrence	5,935	2,996	6,655	89.2	45.0
Holyoke	3,522	2,267	4,002	88.0	56.6
Worcester	2,617	1,128	3,888	67.3	29.0
Lowell	1,637	679	2,033	80.5	33.4
Chelsea	1,486	604	1,746	85.1	34.6
Brockton	759	310	1,474	51.5	21.0
Lynn	1,028	420	1,312	78.3	32.0
New Bedford	875	386	1,213	72.1	31.8
Statewide	44,448	20,135	55,275	80.4	36.4

*Includes LEP students who are counted as a subset of students whose first language is not English.
SOURCE: Beane, G., Pineda, C., Rivera,L., and Rivera R. (1990, May). A Profile of Latinos in Massachusetts: Demographic, Education, and Economic Status. Boston, MA: University of Massachusetts, Mauricio Gaston Institute for Latino Community Development and Public Policy.

Table 3

Massachusetts Dropout Data, by Race/Ethnicity, Grades 9 to 12,* 1986-87 and 1987-88

	1986-1987			1987-1988			
Race/ Ethnicity	9-12 Enroll- ment	Number Drop- outs	Annual Rate (%)	9-12 Enroll- ment	Number Drop- outs	Annual Rate (%)	Projected 4-Year Rate
African- American	17,153	1,826	10.6	17,078	1,808	10.6	36.0
Asian	5,190	331	6.3	6,152	298	4.8	18.0
Latino	10,671	1,631	15.2	12,017	1,727	14.4	45.0
Native American	387	36	9.3	458	54	11.8	40.0
White	234,779	10,530	4.4	222,841	10,096	4.5	17.0
Urban	107,052	9,569	8.9	103,712	9,274	8.9	31.0
Statewide	268,180	14,354	5.3	258,564	13,983	5.4	20.0

*Because data on dropouts has been collected statewide only since 1986-87, annual rates are more accurate than projected cohort rates. However, the Massachusetts Department of Education has estimated four-year dropout rates for all students by district.
SOURCE: Massachusetts Department of Education. (1989, June). *Massachusetts Dropout Report: 1987-88.* Quincy, MA: Massachusetts Department of Education, Office of Planning, Research, and Evaluation.

Table 4

Massachusetts Students Recommended for Grade Retention, by Race/Ethnicity, June 1989

Race/Ethnicity	Number Enrolled	Number Retained	Rate (%)
African-American	57,314	4,862	8.5
Asian	21,543	838	3.9
Latino	49,172	4,058	8.3
White	679,178	18,410	2.7
Urban	18,477	18,537	5.6
Statewide	808,289	28,233	3.5

SOURCES: Massachusetts Advocacy Center. (1990, May 18). *Non-Promotion and Dropout Data (1986 - 87, 1987 - 89)*. Memorandum. Boston, MA: Author; Massachusetts Department of Education. (1990, April). *Structuring Schools for Student Success: A Focus on Grade Retention*. Quincy, MA: Massachusetts Department of Education, Bureau of Student Development and Health, Office of Planning, Research, and Evaluation.

Part II
Educational Issues for the Latino Community

Jose Javier Colón-Morera, Nitza M. Hidalgo, Aida A. Nevárez, Ana M. García-Blanco

Entitlements of Latino Students and Parents: Some Legal Policy Considerations

The purpose of this chapter is threefold: to analyze and review some of the important issues on the subject of entitlements that are supposed to guarantee equal educational opportunity rights for Latino students currently enrolled in the Massachusetts public educational system; to review some of the policy debates on these issues; and to recommend areas for future research and policy analysis. The primary focus is to reveal specific areas where these entitlements can be expanded, where the limits lie, and where there is need for further advocacy, research, and litigation. Emphasis is placed on how locally organized Latino parental and student initiatives can play a crucial role in this endeavor.

The reflections shared in this chapter are the result of an active and direct contact with a substantial number of Latino parent organizations including Bilingual Education Parent Advisory Councils, Parents United for the Education of Others (PUEDO), Latino and other parent groups who aim to reduce dropouts among Latino students, and groups confronting the lack of bilingual, special education services. These reflections are augmented by a critical review of the literature in each of the areas and the work and experiences of the authors in the public schools.

The long-term efforts to improve the education of Latino students depend on the sustained activation of Latino parents in a comprehensive effort to reform the educational environment in which the learning process occurs. It is essential to concentrate the present debate on how to provide equal educational opportunities to Latino students on the following issues:

The limited access Latino parents have in the school decision-making processes, in curriculum planning and development, and in disciplinary actions;

The assessment and placement practices (tracking) that stigmatize Latino students; and

Teaching practices and curriculum that are not culturally relevant to the

Latino population, are not addressing specific cultural needs, or are not incorporating Latino cultural strengths.

This chapter analyzes various areas in which legal mandates or entitlements are intended to benefit Latino students enrolled in the Massachusetts public educational system. Some of these mandates are described and the benefits and limitations of these mandates for the Latino population are explored. Recommendations for further research and for possible legal or advocacy efforts are provided. Coverage in the chapter is limited to two main areas: bilingual education and parental involvement. All three areas are essential elements of a comprehensive school-reform process that will reverse the current cycle of failure, frustration, and eventual school withdrawal of Latino students.

Context

The educational status of Latinos in the United States demands immediate attention by educators and policy makers. Ten and one-half percent of all children attending public schools in the United States in 1988 were Latino. For every ten Latino students who graduated from high school, six other Latinos dropped out of school. Comparatively, the rates for black students are ten high school graduates to three student dropouts; for white students the rates are ten graduates to two dropouts (Children's Defense Fund, 1990, p. 8). Dropping out of school occurs at an earlier age for Latinos — by their sophomore year. Latino students (ages 12 to 15) are also more likely to be two or more grades behind in school, 2.5 times more likely than white students (Children's Defense Fund, 1990, p. 9).

Recent U.S. Department of Education figures indicate that only 33 percent of children ages 5 through 14, who are limited-English-proficient, receive bilingual education, English-as-a-Second-Language (ESL), or some other kind of special language services in school (National Council of La Raza, 1990). Latino students are also tracked[1] into lower grade-level classes to a greater degree than all other students.

In high school, Latinos are placed more often in basic courses instead of at-grade courses. In Boston, for example, 40.9 percent of Latino ninth graders were placed in Basic Math 1 or 2 (ASPIRA, 1987, p. 4). This insidious local practice has national ramifications: 75 percent of all Latino high school seniors "have been placed in curricular programs that make a college education improbable" (National Council of La Raza, 1990). The lack of appropriate language services, high dropout rates, and persistent tracking characterize the poor education received nationally by Latinos.

The national picture is replicated at the local level. In Boston public schools, the districtwide dropout rate for all students for 1988 was 37.2 percent, but for Latinos the dropout rates are much higher: 1985: 49.9 percent; 1986: 49.1 percent; 1987: 53.8 percent; 1988: 48.5 percent (Wheelock, 1990). For the year 1988 almost one half of all Latino students left school without graduating. In 1988-89, Latino students also suffered the highest nonpromotion rates in the city within six different grade levels. In the 1987-88 school year, 28.6 percent of all ninth grade Latino children were held back (Massachusetts Advocacy Center, 1989).

According to Daniel French of the Massachusetts State Department of Education, a direct correlation between nonpromotion and dropping out exists. Statewide, students who are not promoted one grade have a 40 percent chance of leaving school. For the students who are retained two or more years, there is a 90 percent chance they will drop out of school (French, 1989, p. 34). The high rates of nonpromotion for Latino youth may be one reason why 54 percent of the Latino students who entered the ninth grade in 1983 in the Boston public schools left school before graduation. One survey found that the most critical educational needs identified by Massachusetts Latino leaders was the reduction of the escalating dropout rate among Latino youth and the promotion of higher daily attendance rates for Latino students (ASPIRA, 1987, p. 35).

Nationwide, over 70 percent of Latino youth attend predominantly minority schools. While attending an all-minority school is not in and of itself problematic, the situation is complicated when most of those schools are located in poor socioeconomic class neighborhoods within large urban centers with low tax bases. In the Northeast, the Latino population is concentrated in these urban communities. Thus most Latino children in the Northeast attend urban schools where there are too few books and educational materials and deteriorating physical plants (Kozol, 1991).

Looking at the condition of education for Latino students nationally and in the Massachusetts public schools makes the need for reform evident. School reform that addresses the needs of Latino students must include the use of bilingual education, parent participation, and school restructuring. This three-pronged approach is necessary in order to make lasting and in-depth reforms in the quality of education for Latino students, to involve parents and communities in the decision-making process of schools to a greater extent, and to develop comprehensive efforts to retain Latino students in school, including programs that combine myriad services: individual tutorials, counseling, referrals to outside agencies, and part-time job placements. The following sections of this chapter discuss bilingual education and parental involvement.

Bilingual Education

LEGAL ENTITLEMENTS OF BILINGUAL EDUCATION

This nation's courts and legislatures provided the essential guarantee to quality educational practices for students of limited-English-proficiency by developing the legal standards to evaluate school districts that serve this particular student population. In doing this, they have responded to the cry of parents and students for quality education; until the action by the courts this cry was not heard by school districts. Under the Fourteenth Amendment to the Constitution, "No state shall....deny to any person within its jurisdiction the equal protection of law." While this clause has been the foundation for the litigation of most bilingual education cases, the courts have held consistently that "denial of bilingual education is not in violation of the equal protection clause" (Fernández, 1989). Therefore, the principal legal basis for the courts mandating bilingual education has come from legislative acts such as Title VI of the Civil Rights Act of 1964 (42 UUSC sec. 2000 (d) (1976)), the Equal Educational Opportunity Act (EEOA) of 1974 (20 sec. 1703 (f) (1982)), and desegregation efforts, i.e., *Kayes v. School District No. 1*, 670 F. Supp. 1513 (1987).

In particular, *Lau v. Nichols* (414 US 563 (1974)) is considered a landmark case in the education of limited-English-proficient (LEP) students because it was the first time that the proscription of discrimination in federal assistance programs by Title VI of the Civil Rights Act of 1964, as applied to education equality for linguistic-minority children, was enforced. That is, this case exposed the educational practices of a particular school district as discriminatory against students who do not speak English as a first language, and it questioned the equal educational opportunities available to LEP students in federally assisted programs. In the *Lau* case, it was undisputed that there were almost 2,800 Chinese children attending the San Francisco Unified School System that did not speak, understand, read, or write the English language. The Supreme Court decided that under Title VI of the Civil Rights Act, "there is no equality of treatment merely by providing students with the same facilities, textbooks, teachers and curriculum; students who do not understand English are effectively foreclosed from any meaningful education" (Rom, 1985, p. 17).

Furthermore, the Supreme Court held that the Department of Health, Education and Welfare (HEW) had the authority to require that school districts receiving federal funds "must take affirmative steps to rectify the language deficiency in order to open its instructional program to [LEP] students" (Rom, 1985, p. 17). Following that decision, in 1975, HEW issued guidelines for minimum compliance with the requirements of the *Lau* decision. These guidelines are commonly known as the Lau Guidelines or Lau Remedies and are summarized below.

1. School districts, if found in noncompliance with Title VI, need to submit remedial plans and detail procedures for identifying the students' primary home language, classifying each student into one of five "Lau Categories" regarding language dominance, and assessing the student's linguistic proficiency and academic achievement level in order to "prescribe an educational program utilizing the most effective teaching style to satisfy the diagnosed educational needs" (Rom, 1985, p. 18).

2. The course offering should not be culturally biased. The contributions of minority peoples should be expressed in the curriculum.

3. Teachers and instructional staff are required to be "linguistically/ culturally familiar with the background of the students to be affected."

4. The student/teacher ratio has to be equal or less than the ratio found in the district.

5. It is not educationally necessary nor legally permissible to create racially/ethnically identifiable schools or classes to implement these programs.

6. Parents of children whose primary language is not English are to be informed of all school programs and activities to the same extent that other parents are informed of these programs. When necessary, appropriate translations are to be provided.

7. Specific descriptions are to be given to parents regarding the Transitional Bilingual Education Act or other program assistance the school district offers.

8. School districts have to submit periodic reports to the Office of Civil Rights of the Department of Health, Education and Welfare (OCR/HEW) concerning the implementation and the effectiveness of their remediation plans in eliminating language barriers (Rom, 1985, p. 18).

Before 1981 the courts used the Lau Guidelines as the legal standards to evaluate the soundness of particular bilingual programs. In many cases school districts were restricted in their ability to choose educational models to serve linguistically diverse students since the courts frequently imposed remedies providing for specific ones, such as the transitional bilingual model. However, this has changed since "one of the first acts of the Reagan Administration in January 1981 was to revoke the Lau Guidelines" (Rom, 1985, p. 21). In more recent cases, *Castaneda v. Pickard* (648 f. 2d 989 (1981)) for example, the courts have used a three-part test to evaluate a program under sec. 1703 (f) of the EEOA instead of the Lau Guidelines. The test requires answering the following questions:

> Is the program based on educational theory recognized as sound or at least as a legitimate experimental strategy by some of the experts in the field?

> Is the program reasonably calculated to implement that theory?

> Has the program, after being used for a sufficient time to afford it a legitimate trial, produced satisfactory results? (Rom, 1985, p. 22).

The generality of these questions reflects the reluctance of the courts, in recent years, to impose specific educational remedies. After 1981 there has been a willingness to give more flexibility to particular school districts in choosing educational programs that fit their needs. But as Rom (1985) warns, "these recent decisions are putting school districts on notice; while they are being given the responsibility and authority they long for, they will be held accountable for producing results..." (Rom, 1985, p. 23).[2]

In 1971, Massachusetts enacted the first state law mandating any form of bilingual education. The Transitional Bilingual Education Act (TBE) was enacted more than two years before the United States Supreme Court decision in *Lau v. Nichols.* Among the legal entitlements provided by TBE are the following:

> 1. Instruction in the dominant language while teaching in English for school districts with 20 or more children of a particular non-English language group "incapable of performing ordinary class work in English."

> 2. Instruction for students on their own background and history.

> 3. Exit students from program after three years or when "he achieves a level of English language skills that will enable him to perform success-fully in classes in which instruction is given in English, whichever comes first" (Mass. General Law, 1990).

> 4. Creation of a Parent Advisory Committee to increase parent participation in the school.

> 5. Creation of a committee composed of representatives from the school

administration, the TBE Committee, and the Parent Advisory Committee to evaluate the program on an annual basis (Mass. General Law, 1990).[3]

6. Evaluation of students' oral comprehension, speaking, reading, and writing skills in English in order to enter and exit from a program.

7. Maximum student-teacher ratio should be 15 to 1; in cases where it is 20 to 1 a teacher's aide should be assigned.

Advocates of bilingual education in Massachusetts identified three issues that are currently the focus of their efforts in guaranteeing the continuation and improvement of the programs developed under the TBE act. First, since 1989 advocates have had to battle efforts to reappeal or change the TBE act. So far, these attempts have not been successful. The continuing attempts to change the law have focused on: providing local school districts with the power to choose which option of program, bilingual or English-as-a-Second-Language (ESL), is best for their schools; placing a three-year cap to the amount of time a student can stay in a bilingual program; eliminating the courses on history and culture on the student's native country given as part of the curriculum in bilingual programs; and removing the student-teacher ratio limit in the law so that bilingual classes can be larger and, therefore, bilingual personnel in the schools can be decreased.

Second, advocates have identified the need to closely monitor the implementation of the state bilingual law in the various school districts. Investigations done by advocacy groups, such as the Multicultural Education, Training and Advocacy Inc. (META), have uncovered multiple cases where the law is being violated in Massachusetts. In many instances the implementation of the law has been poorly monitored or followup to the recommendations on how to improve programs and abide by the law presented to school districts by the monitors has not occurred. Recently, the state's Education Department agreed to improved their monitoring process by: developing a document that can be used by all monitors, thus providing consistency in the criteria used to evaluate programs; using a schedule for monitoring to guarantee that all school districts will be assessed; and developing a procedure to guarantee the enforcement of the suggestions from monitors. This new procedure specifies that the Division of Bilingual Education must inform the Commissioner of Education of any districts that are not complying with the law, and if after 30 days the districts do not reform their practices the Commissioner can then present the case to the Massachusetts State Board of Education.

Third, advocates of bilingual education have focused on the fact that more than 60 percent of all teachers in Massachusetts who work in English-as-a-Second-Language (ESL) classes have not been appropriately trained in this field

(Rice, 1991). The State Education Department has been made aware of the problem and proposes that the current efforts to reform the educational system in Massachusetts provide for the adequate training of ESL teachers.

CURRENT DEBATES IN BILINGUAL EDUCATION

Bilingual education has aroused heated debates since its enactment in 1968. These debates cover issues of educational effectiveness, political power, and social status. In his book *Bilingual Education: History, Politics, Theory, and Practice* (1989), James Crawford suggests that the complex issues and the passionate discussions about bilingual education have four main explanations:

1. The goals of the bilingual education law were never clear. The question is whether bilingual education "was intended to ease the transition to English or to encourage the maintenance of minority languages" (Crawford, 1989, p. 13).

2. The increasing number of immigrants in recent years has been interpreted as a threat to the cultural, societal, and political unity of this country because of the erroneous, yet common, belief that newcomers do not know and are not willing to learn English.

3. The implementation of bilingual programs has caused schools to change administration and education patterns that historically were used to serve a white, majority, middle-class, student population. According to Crawford the changes are unwelcome because of the apparent extra work for school staff and because of a lack of direct benefits to the majority school population.

4. Bilingual education theory and empirical research has challenged notions strongly held by people in the United States about language and language learning. The studies on second-language learning and the advocacy for a multilingual society that are embedded in bilingual education have exposed the common myths and the ignorance of Americans, even within educational circles, on linguistic issues.

In Massachusetts, the most recent debates about bilingual education have been spurred by the actions of the English-only movement and the introduction of bills that advocate the elimination of bilingual education. Crawford's explanation of the origins of the English-only ideology in the United States is helpful in order to understand the growth of this restrictive movement in

Massachusetts and the rationale used to attack bilingual education and immigrant rights in general:

> The English Only movement, an outgrowth of the immigration-restrictionist lobby, has skillfully manipulated language as a symbol of national unity and ethnic divisiveness. Early in this century, those who sought to exclude other races and cultures invoked claims of Anglo-Saxon superiority. But in the 1980s, explicit racial loyalties are no longer acceptable in our political discourse. Language loyalties, on the other hand, remain largely devoid of association with social injustice. While race is immutable, immigrants can and often do exchange their mother tongue for another. And so, for those who resent the presence of Hispanics and Asians, language politics has become a convenient surrogate for racial politics (Crawford, 1989, p. 14).

The leaders of the English-only movement attack bilingual education as a "barrier to students' full participation in American life" (Crawford 1989, p. 54).

From the beginning of the 1980s there have been continued legislative threats against bilingual education. Some of the arguments against bilingual education stem from a misguided interpretation of research and its use by policy makers, educators, and politicians. Bilingualism, it is argued, is a detriment to children's development and prevents non-English speaking children from achieving their academic potential. Some critics interpret the research to mean that there is insufficient evidence about bilingual education to conclude that it is superior to other methods. The high dropout rate of Latinos and their low academic achievement in Massachusetts are believed to be signs that bilingual education is not working. Other arguments concern the manner in which bilingual education programs are implemented in schools. It is believed that bilingual education programs often foster separatism in schools and that teachers in bilingual programs often do not speak English well enough. These teachers, the argument goes, by teaching exclusively in the native language, do not promote the learning of English.

What does research tell us about bilingualism, academic achievement of Latinos and effectiveness of bilingual education programs? Crawford (1989) and Secada (1990) argue that research that uses empirical data to confirm or reject theories about why limited-English-proficiency (LEP) students succeed or fail in school, research that uses factors like age, minority social status, and native-language proficiency in analyzing the process of acquiring English, and research on how linguistic development interacts with cognitive development has shown positive results. This research, known as basic research, has provided data on the benefits of bilingualism and the conditions where it can be best promoted. Crawford (1989) cites the work of Hakuta (1986) as showing some of the findings of basic research that contradict misconceptions about bilingualism. Hakuta (1986) found evidence in basic research that support the following hypotheses:

> 1. Early childhood is not the optimum age to acquire a second language; older children and adults are "more often efficient language learners." Thus the "sense of urgency in introducing English to non-English-speaking children and concern about postponing children's exit from bilingual program" are misplaced.

> 2. Language is not a unified skill, but a complex configuration of abilities....Language used for conversational purposes is quite different from language used for school learning, and the former develops earlier than the latter.

> 3. Because many skills are transferable to a second language, "time spent learning in the native language...is not time lost in developing English" or other subjects. To the contrary, a child with a strong foundation in the first language will perform better in English over the long term.

> 4. Reading should be taught in the native language, particularly for children who, on other grounds, run the risk of reading failure. Reading skills acquired in the native language will transfer readily and quickly to English and will result in higher ultimate reading achievement in English.

> 5. There is no cognitive cost in the development of bilingualism in children. Very possibly, bilingualism enhances children's thinking skills.

Similarly, since the 1960s, studies by Peal and Lambert (1962) and Hakuta (1984, 1985, 1986) have shown positive consequences of bilingualism for linguistic and cognitive development. The findings of these studies contradict earlier research by a majority of educational psychologists who regarded bilingualism as a cognitive liability for young children. These earlier studies have been criticized for poor design and possible anti-immigrant biases that were prevalent at the time.[4]

Additional criticism of bilingual education blames the use of bilingual education for the high dropout rate. Secada (1990) writes:

> Bilingual education is a small program. As Bennett's own data demonstrate, more Hispanic were served through Title I and Chapter I. Moreover, even larger numbers of Hispanic students attend woefully inadequate

schools without any additional services. To place the blame for these events at the door of bilingual education, while arguing that the goal of the program is to develop English language skills, stretches credibility.

Crawford believes that although sufficient research exists to disprove the criticism hurled at bilingual education, it has been ignored by policy makers and politicians who prefer to "keep the debate within the bounds of evaluation research (this research attempts to establish the effectiveness of bilingual models in comparison to other educational models), where the case for bilingual education is weaker, where findings are more qualified, and where discussion is more useful to politicians than to educators" (Crawford, 1989).

IMPLEMENTATION OF BILINGUAL EDUCATION

Many practitioners would argue that although bilingual education philosophy is based on sound theory and research, its implementation lacks effectiveness in many cases. These practitioners see a need to identify problems of implementation, so that effective solutions can be incorporated and programs can truly achieve the goals of the philosophy. One such problem is the separatism that sometimes is created when administrators and teachers do not promote the interaction between students in bilingual programs and students in mainstream classes. Although separatism does exist in some schools with bilingual programs, it is incorrect to assume that this separatism is promoted by the bilingual education philosophy. Charles Glenn (1990) provides two possible reasons for separation in schools:

> Programs controlled by educators who do not understand or sympathize with the goals of bilingual education tend to become a form of remedial instruction. Such programs have few educational expectations other than to develop English-language skills to a point that will permit survival in a "mainstream" class but not development of the pupil's full potential.

> Programs directed by strong advocates of bilingual education place a much more positive emphasis upon the home language of the children. However, many programs keep linguistic minority children separate from other children far too long (1990, p. 28).

Therefore, there is a need to identify and provide solutions for cases where administrators and teachers, because of a lack of understanding, do not promote integration between students and teachers in bilingual and mainstream classes. In this regard Glenn (1990) states "studies of language acquisition stress the importance of using language with peers in activities designed to promote cooperation and reduce anxiety. Real proficiency in the use of English may never be acquired without deliberate efforts to promote integration and the interaction it encourages" (p. 28).

Glenn recommends more efficient integration of bilingual programs into the life of the school. Further, since the basic erroneous premise posits bilingual education as a remedial program that "overcome[s] a deficiency in limited English proficient children..., [educators mistakenly believe the children's] real education will begin when they are mainstreamed" (Glenn, 1990, p. 28).

CURRENT TRENDS IN BILINGUAL EDUCATION

In recent years Massachusetts has begun to implement programs that follow a different model than the widely used Transitional Bilingual Education (TBE). The model emphasizes the integration of students, teachers, and curriculum to learn each others' languages and work academically in both languages. This model is known in Massachusetts as the two-way program.

The implementation of such a model is seen by some as representing the true spirit of bilingual education — "bilingual education for all members of society, rather than for minorities alone" (Fishman, 1976). Ovando and Collier (1985) state that "it is the only model that places both groups at the same starting point and thus sensitizes English speakers to the complex process of learning a second language and becoming more aware of other systems of thought" (p. 41). Glenn (1990) states that, "The best setting for educating linguistic minority pupils — and one of the best for educating any pupil — is a school in which two languages are used without apology and where becoming proficient in both is considered a significant intellectual and cultural achievement" (p. 30).

In Massachusetts the Rafael Hernandez School in Dorchester has been a two-way bilingual school since the 1970s. In Chelsea, the Shurtleff Elementary School has followed an integrated bilingual model in which both languages are used for instruction, but only linguistic-minority students are expected to become proficient in both. The goal in this school is to integrate the bilingual and regular curriculum, teachers, and students. Other elementary schools like the Blackstone and the Hurley in Boston are planning to start pilot programs using integration and two-way models.

FURTHER RESEARCH IN BILINGUAL EDUCATION

Because of the increasing numbers of students who are not proficient in English in the U.S. school systems there is a need for continuing the research on how best to educate these students and how to improve the educational programs that already serve them. For example, studies that could identify the general support levels for bilingual education in communities (i.e., level of understanding of bilingual education, prejudices against minority groups and immigrants) and the factors that influence the support levels, and then suggest ways of improving support for bilingual education are necessary to design policy for the future of bilingual education in Massachusetts. These types of studies have been done already nationwide.[5] In this state studies are needed regarding the attitudes of the Anglo majority towards bilingual education.

Studies that document the quality of implementation of programs in Massachusetts are necessary in order to identify factors that contribute to effective bilingual education practices and suggest ways to improve less effective programs. The use of a case study methodology has proven effective for this purpose (Crawford, 1989; Morrison, 1990; Holm and Holm, 1990).

Teacher training in bilingual education is another area that needs to be seriously investigated. How is Massachusetts training its future teachers to work with the increasing numbers of language-minority and immigrant students, both in bilingual and in regular programs? What training programs exist that can provide continued support to teachers already working in schools with an increasingly diverse student population (i.e., students from different countries, students from different social classes, students who have different levels of literacy)? What is the quality of such training programs? What exists elsewhere that may be a model to improve programs in Massachusetts? Are the standards designed by the state Department of Education realistic in producing enough teachers who can effectively work in bilingual education programs?

Parent Participation

Many educators believe that Latino parents are not interested in their children's education, are hard to reach, or do not value education. But Latino parents do value education. The Latino value of interdependency and the responsibility Latinos feel about helping others has aided Latino families and communities in the struggle towards improvements in education. Within Latino communities across the nation, there exist long-standing grassroots organizations that promote educational achievement and work to improve the educational achievement of Latino students.[6] If Latino parents are welcomed in the schools, if Latino parents have access to information about their children's rights and how the school system functions, if educators are informed about Latino socialization patterns, and if Latino parents hold influential positions within school management, then schools can be made responsive to Latino student needs.

But educators create barriers between their schools and the communities they serve. Educators are not trained to embrace parental participation in school. Too often educators do not live in the communities they serve, nor are they sympathetic to those communities. Latino parental involvement requires educators to undergo a paradigm shift to redefine parental involvement in nonracist, cultur-ally-consonant ways that are inclusive and empowering of the members of the communities the schools serve. According to Sonia Nieto, educators should expand their definition of parental involvement to include the following: motivating a child to do well in school, talking to the child about everyday things, providing an environment of high expectations, and sacrificing their lives to help their children (Nieto, 1992). Parents and their children are not consumers of education, but owners of the educational institutions; as such, the schools should reflect their needs and concerns.

The barriers to parent participation in school can be traced to attitudes that both educators and parents hold that obstruct access. From the educators' viewpoint, teachers and administrators can get defensive when a parent com-plains about the school. Because of the quasi-professional status of teaching, educators can feel there are no rewards for outreach to parents. On the other hand, parents may have had negative experiences during their own schooling years and can feel alienated from the institution of school. Parents may believe that complaining about a school issue will have ramifications for their children, that the teachers will make the child pay for the parents concerns. (Grant, 1981).

Further barriers to parent participation stem from school practices that are insensitive to cultural differences. Sending important notices to Spanish-speaking parents in English insures the information will be missed. Holding parent meetings only in English or not having transportation and childcare arrangements will result in low Latino-parent turnout. Closing the school building to the community in the evenings does not allow people to view the school as a site for community activities.

LEGAL ENTITLEMENTS FOR PARENTAL PARTICIPATION

To assure minimal levels of parental involvement in schools, two possible legal strategies could be pursued: the bilingual parent advisory councils created by the Massachusetts bilingual law and the mechanisms for parental involvement required by Chapter 1 regulations.[7] Both structures would help Latino parents to gain initial access to schools in order to influence policy decisions essential to the academic success of language-minority children.

The Massachusetts Transitional Bilingual Education Act (TBE) provides for the creation of parent advisory councils (PACs) to spur parental involvement in schools. It also requires the use of native-speaking teacher aides in classrooms, native-speaking community coordinators to act as liaisons between the school and the parents, native-speaking guidance or pupil-adjustment counselors, and the creation of a committee composed of representatives from the school administration, the transitional bilingual education program, and the parent advisory committee to evaluate the program on an annual basis (Mass. General Laws).

Chapter 1, formerly Title I of the Elementary and Secondary Education Act, requires state educational agencies to develop specific mechanisms for parent participation in schools. Some of these requirements are:

1. Develop written policies after consultation with parents to ensure that parents are involved in the planning, design, and implementation of programs.

2. Explain to parents annually the programs and activities funded by Chapter 1.

3. Make available reports on children's progress, parent-teacher conferences, and conferences with other related personnel.

4. Provide opportunities for regular meetings of parents.

5. Develop programs, activities, and procedures that provide training for parents, use parents as volunteers, provide timely information, solicit parent suggestions, provide reports of parents' recommendations, and create parents' advisory councils.

POLICY DEBATES ON PARENTAL PARTICIPATION

There is an urgent need for Latino parent and community involvement in schools. Parents and teachers share common concerns. Latino parents and their children's teachers are interested in Latino children's spiralling educational achievement, the increasing numbers of teenage pregnancies, and the disproportionate dropout rates. Teachers would benefit from learning more about their students' home experiences since students learn both in the classroom and at home. Latino parents would benefit from gaining knowledge about how schools function. Carl Grant (1981) recommends a number of strategies for teachers to encourage more parent participation in the classroom:

At the start of the school year, contact all parents by phone or in person, listen to them, and solicit their views about what they would like for their children.

Look into home visits. Is it acceptable in the school community?

Hold parent/teacher meetings during the first month of school. Ask for concrete assistance. Ask for topics for curriculum.

Have parents share how they have seen their children learn best.

Maintain a comfortable, inviting, working classroom climate.

Introduce parents working in or visiting your class to other staff and to security personnel.

These strategies, with some modifications, can be used to elicit Latino parent involvement in classrooms. The teacher who wishes to reach out to Latino parents can contact a parent liaison to make introductions, have a person on hand to serve as a translator when a Latino parent visits, supply childcare at school during parent visits, make arrangements for transportation for parents, and be willing to meet during after-school hours to accommodate working parents.

Another set of strategies that incorporates the participation of parents on a schoolwide basis is found in the work of James Comer (1988). The Comer model "promotes [children's] development and learning by building supportive bonds that draw together children, parents and the school" (p. 42). Comer believes children who are successful in school are children who have received from their parents the "social skills and confidence that enable them to take advantage of educational opportunities" (p. 42). Comer believes some children need to be educated in the mainstream social skills because their parents have not had an opportunity to learn them. This process requires trust and confidence between teachers, students, and parents. Once children have learned these skills, teachers will raise their expectations of the students.

In order to foster positive interactions between parents and school staff, Comer's program created a governance and management team composed of parents, teachers, principal, mental health specialists, and nonprofessional support staff. His intervention also includes a parent program (described below) and a mental health team composed of the school psychologist, a social worker, and a special education teacher. The mental health team meets regularly to discuss individual cases and to foresee and prevent problems.

The Comer model has numerous components addressing different areas of the school culture. The parent program focuses on involving parents in the school decision-making process, increasing outreach to parents, promoting parent attendance at social and academic school events, enhancing the inclusion of parents in the school community, and hiring parents to work in classrooms. The following are some of the components of the parent program:

School-based councils: Parents work on the governance team, share control of the school, collaborate on policy decisions.

Parent service workers: The school provides training for parents who conduct home visits and make referrals to social service agencies.

Parents' program: Engages parents in academic and social projects, such as pot luck dinners, book fairs, fashion shows, cultural nights (Comer, 1988, p. 47).

Parent fundraising: Invites parents to contribute skills they possess for fundraising activities. Some parents can sew costumes or band uniforms, some can build a ramp for the school auditorium.

Parent center: Creates a meeting place for parents to congregate to discuss school and community issues.

Parent classroom aides: Employs parents to assist in classrooms through-out the school. They can read to children in both Spanish and English, create curriculum materials with teachers, assist during field trips, and provide cultural linkages between the school and the home.

These programs exhibit six different levels of parental involvement ranging from involvement solely at home to decision-making involvement in school: (1) Parents can work at home with children, teaching them social skills and primary school skills. (2) Parents can work with children on their homework assignments, enhancing the academic skills children learn in school. (3) Parents can attend school functions, teacher conferences and parenting workshops arranged at school. (4) Parents can volunteer in school, providing either classroom assistance or fundraising help. (5) Parents can serve on advisory panels, targeting special concerns, for example, curriculum changes. (6) Parents can serve on school-based management teams, making wide-ranging decisions.

These levels of parental involvement are often viewed as hierarchical with the minimal level being helping children at home and the most profound level being some form of school-based management participation. It is unreasonable to expect all parents to strive for what is perceived to be the best form of parent involvement. An inclusive definition of parent involvement holds the parental activities in the home to be of equal value to participation on decision-making school bodies.

Researchers using a social contextual approach to investigate family literacy practices have found the social-cultural context of children's lives to be essential components of the children's learning (Auerbach, 1989). The social contextual approach examines the contributions of the differing teaching and learning activities in the home to children's school success.

For example, Dinah Volk (1992) looked at the parent/child interactions in three Puerto Rican homes with kindergarten-aged children. She found both formal and informal learning activities taking place. Two mothers initiated learning activities that were teacher-like; the mothers directed the learning with cues and questions that resembled teacher/student activities. The third mother did not take on teacher-like activities with her children, but she nonetheless engaged in culturally specific activities (for example, holding conversations with her children about daily events in the home) that may influence children's school success. Volk's research finds that all of these parents had information and skills that helped their children's school achievement.

Concha Delgado Gaitan (1990) incorporates the culturally relevant skills and resources Latino parents offer and expands the meaning of parental involvement in another direction. She believes "parents need to understand not only how to help their children with specific tasks in the early years, but also to understand how the school system functions so they can continue to help their children as they move through the grades" (1990, p. 59).

While educators expand the meaning of parental involvement to be more inclusive of the resources and activities found within Latino homes, we understand the necessity of providing Latino parents with capacity-building information in order for them to be effective advocates of their children's education.

The underlying philosophy of all parent participation strategies should be based on the partnership model. The partnership model of parental involvement revolves around mutual respect and shared power (Children's Defense Fund, 1990, p. 8). Parents are seen as partners in the educational enterprise, both at home and at school. Their presence in the school and their activities with children in the home are valued for the experience, knowledge, and perspective they add to the learning community. In order for the partnership model to be successful, parents need knowledge of how schools operate to educate children.

The child is seen within the context of her/his community. Instead of blaming parents and the community for school failure, the community and families within it are viewed as resources to the work of the school. Every dimension of the school is touched and changed by the work of parents. The mission and goals of the school reflect a community presence. The teachers' and administrators' beliefs about families have to change to correlate to the new information they have from working closely with parents. The curriculum is enriched by the connection to the students' lives. The school forms linkages with the community and community-based agencies, making the school a functional member of the community.

FURTHER RESEARCH ON PARENTAL PARTICIPATION

How can we restructure our schools to support Latino parents? Research on the beliefs and attitudes of teachers and administrators toward diversity is needed. Oftentimes Latino parents do not feel welcomed at their children's school. More concrete information on how these parents come to feel this way is needed in order to know what changes are needed from teachers and administrators. The flow of information between the school and the home is vital to a child's success. How are messages sent to the home? Are messages translated in Spanish for non-English speaking parents? The work of Comer needs to be piloted with Latino parents in predominantly Latino communities since his programs are geared to African-American parent involvement.

Children come to school with many cultural riches. Studies should be conducted to investigate whether the strengths of the home are translated into classroom competence and whether good teachers use the strengths children come in with to build new learning. Research into the unique cultural ways Latino parents motivate and help their children at home should be conducted. Studies on the effects of parental involvement in schools on student achievement, specifically with Latino parents and children, are necessary.

Surveys of the Latino community concerning beliefs, concerns, and experiences within the public school system could be used to mobilize the community toward school reform. Studies on the collected knowledge Latino parents have gained from working in schools could help create Latino parent leadership training modules. Future research should be directed towards helping educators undergo the paradigm shift needed to open access to Latino parental involvement.

Conclusions

This chapter describes the need for reform in the education of Latino children, but critique without recommendations for change is a fruitless venture. The chapter presents a definition and philosophical framework by which to understand Latino parental involvement in schools — one that expands the common definition to include what parents do at home and their involvement in the different dimensions of school organization. Improving Latino parent involvement in the education of their children requires educators to make themselves and the schools accessible to parents and provide training to parents on how to be effective advocates for their children. The Latino parent advocate could utilize the mechanisms for parental involvement provided by Massachusetts Transitional Education Act and Chapter 1 regulations.

A number of strategies for how teachers can encourage more parental participation within individual classrooms and incorporate the participation of parents on a schoolwide level are provided, but this process has to be facilitated by the school principal who welcomes parents to the school and by a committee-generated school mission that guides the work of the school.

The urgency of the future work towards the improvement of education for Latino students is illustrated in this quote from Edna Suarez Columba, a child specialist:

> Our children begin receiving drops of water on them, like drops hitting a rock, from the time they leave their homes. By the time our children get to the middle school, each child, like the rock, is cut in half.

Addressing these educational problems would not require new outpourings of federal monies or new legislation. Many of the problems facing Latino students in Massachusetts are within the existing authority of the Department of Education as addressed under Chapter 1, under the Civil Rights Act monitored by the Office of Civil Rights, and under various federal acts regarding special education. To continue to fail to address these problems will, in the long run, cost a great deal, beginning with the lost of opportunity and hope for the future of Latino children and the community.

Notes

1. Research suggests that tracking is detrimental to students, both academically and emotionally. For example, tracking can confine students to curriculum and instruction that is continuous drill and practice rather than creative thinking and problem solving (QEM Project, 1990). Also, this instructional practice can generate student problems by lowering student self-esteem and teacher expectations (Rosenbaum, 1971 in Oakes, 1986). In addition, students, once tracked into the lower level groups, find it very difficult to move out into the higher level groups or more heterogenous groups (Oakes, 1986).

2. See also *Gomez v. Illinois* 811 f 2d 1030 (1987). In this case the U.S. Court of Appeals for the Seventh Circuit held that the Eleventh Amendment did not foreclose action brought on behalf of students with limited-English-proficiency who alleged that state officials failed to discharge duties imposed by federal law by failing to promulgate uniform and consistent guidelines for the identification, placement, and training of limited-English-proficient children. Also, this court held that under the Equal Educational Opportunities Act an action to enforce rights under the Act could be maintained against the state and local agencies that were ordinarily immune from the Eleventh Amendment. Indeed, the procedures required for determining whether educational agencies were adequately assisting students with limited-English-proficiency under Equal Educational Act did not apply only to local school districts but also to state educational agencies.

3. Successful litigation in the cities of Lynn and Lowell in Massachusetts produced

two court enforceable consent decrees providing a wide variety of legal entitlements for the limited-English-proficient children of these school districts. Successful litigation in the cities of Lynn and Lowell in Massachusetts produced two court enforceable consent decrees, providing a wide variety of legal entitlements for the limited-English-proficient children of these school districts. The Multicultural Education, Training, and Advocacy, Inc., (META) monitors the implementation of the decrees for the court each year.

4. For a further discussion of these findings, see California State Office of Bilingual Bicultural Education. (1981). *Schooling and Language Minority Students: A Theoretical Framework*. Los Angeles: California State University; Cummins, J. (1986). Empowering Minority Students: A Framework for Intervention. *Harvard Educational Review* 56(1); Hakuta, K., and Gould, L. (1987, March). Synthesis of Research on Bilingual Education. *Educational Leadership, 44;* Staff. (1986, November). When Children Speak Little English: How Effective is Bilingual Education? *Harvard Educational Letter* 2(6); McLaughlin, B. (1978). *Second Language Acquisition in Childhood*. Hillsdale, NJ: Lawrence Erlbaum; Zamora, G. (1987). Understanding Bilingual Education. *Background Series*. Boston: National Coalition of Advocates for Students.

5. See for example: Cole, S. (1983). Attitudes toward Bilingual Education among Hispanics and a Nationwide Sample. Manuscript, Center for the Social Sciences, Columbia University; Hakuta, K. (1986). Bilingual Education in the Public Eye: A Case Study of New Haven, Connecticut. *Journal for the National Association of Bilingual Education, 9;* California Opinion Index. (1987). *Immigration*. Report. California: Field Institute; Citrin, J. (1988, July). *American Identity and the Politics of Ethnicity: Public Opinion in a Changing Society*. Paper presented at the annual meeting of the International Society of Political Psychology, Secaucus, NJ; Huddy, L., and Sears, D. (1990, March). Qualified Public Support for Bilingual Education: Some Policy Implications. In C. Cazden and C. Snow (Eds.), *The Annals of the American Academy of Political and Social Science. English Plus: Issues in Bilingual Education*. England: Sage Publication.

6. Examples of these grassroots organizations on the national level are ASPIRA and the National Council of La Raza; on the local level they include El Barrio Popular Education Program in New York and La Alianza Hispana in Boston.

7. Chapter 1 regulations refer to the federal programs designed to provide instructional support services to children who are identified as being educationally disadvantaged; these programs are also known as compensatory education.

References

ASPIRA Association, Inc. (1987). *Northeast Hispanic Needs: A Guide for Action*. Washington, DC: Author.

Auerbach, E. (1989). Toward a Social-Contextual Approach in Family Literacy. *Harvard Educational Review, 59*(2), 165-181.

French, D. (1989, March 12). On Tracking. *The Boston Sunday Globe*.

Children's Defense Fund. (1990). *Latino Youths at a Crossroads*. Washington, DC: Children's Defense Fund's Adolescent Pregnancy Prevention Clearinghouse.

Comer, J. (1988, November). Educating Poor Minority Children. *Scientific American, 259*(5).

Crawford, J. (1989). *Bilingual Education: History, Politics Theory, and Practice.* Trenton, NJ: Crane Publishers.

Fernandez, A. (1989). The Right to Receive Bilingual Education. *West's Education Law Reporter, 53*(4), 1067.

Fishman, J. (1976). *Bilingual Education: An International Sociological Perspective.* Rowley, MA: Newbury House.

Glenn, C. (1990, May). How to Integrate Bilingual Education without Tracking. *School Administrator, 28.*

Grant, C. (1981). The Community and Multiethnic Education. In J. Banks, (Ed.), *Education in the 80's: Multiethnic Education.* Washington DC: National Education Association of the United States.

Hakuta, K. (1984). *The Causal Relationship Between the Development of Bilingualism, Cognitive Flexibility, and Social-Cognitive Skills in Hispanic School Children.* Report for the National Institute of Education (NIE-G-81-0123). Washington, DC: Government Printing Office.

Hakuta, K. (1985, July). *Cognitive Development in Bilingual Children.* Paper presented at a meeting of the National Clearinghouse for Bilingual Education and the Georgetown University Bilingual Education Service Center, Rosslyn, VA.

Hakuta, K. (1986). *Mirror of Language: The Debate on Bilingualism.* New York: Basic Books.

Holm, A., and Holm, W. (1990, March). Rock Point, A Navajo Way to Go to School: A Valediction. In C. Cazden and C. Snow (Eds.), *The Annals of the American Academy of Political and Social Science.* English Plus: Issues in Bilingual Education. England: Sage Publication.

Kozol, J. (1991). *Savage Inequalities.* New York: Crown Publishers, Inc.

Massachusetts Advocacy Center. (1989, March 8). *Non-Promotion and Dropout Data: 1986-87, 1987-88.* Memorandum. Boston, MA: Author.

Massachusetts General Laws Chapter 71a, section 2, (1990): 4.

Morrison, S. (1990, March). A Spanish-English Dual-Language Program in New York City. In C. Cazden and C. Snow (Eds.), *The Annals of the American Academy of Political and Social Science. English Plus: Issues in Bilingual Education.* England: Sage Publication.

National Council of La Raza. (1990). *Multiple Choice: Hispanics and Education.* Newsletter. Washington, DC: Author.

Nieto, S. (1992). *Affirming Diversity: The Sociopolitical Context of Multicultural Education.* New York: Longman Publishers.

Oakes, J. (1986). Tracking, Inequality, and the Rhetoric of Reform: Why Schools Don't Change. *The Journal of Education,* Boston University, Boston, MA.

Ovando, C. and Collier, V. (1985). *Bilingual and ESL Classrooms Teaching in Multicultural Contexts.* New York: McGraw-Hill.

Peal, E., Lambert, W. (1962). The Relation of Bilingualism to Intelligence. *Psychological Monographs, 76*(546).

QEM Project. (1990). *Education that Works: An Action Plan for the Education of Minorities.* Cambridge, MA: MIT Press.

Rice, R. (1991, Fall). Personal conversation with Roger Rice, director, Massachusetts Education, Training, and Advocacy, Inc.

Rom, A. (1985, September/October). The Evaluation of Legal Requirements for the Education of Students of Limited English Proficiency. *Boston Bar Journal, 29* (4), 17.

Secada, W. (1990). Research, Politics, and Bilingual Education. In C. Cazden and C. Snow (Eds.), *The Annals of the American Academy of Political and Social Science. English Plus: Issues in Bilingual Education.* England: Sage Publications.

Volk, D. (1992, April). *A Case Study of Parental Involvement in the Homes of Three Puerto Rican Kindergartners.* Paper presented at the 1992 annual meeting of the American Educational Research Association, San Francisco.

Wheelock, A. (1990, April 26). Testimony before the President's Commission on Hispanic Education, Boston, MA.

Diana Lam
Bilingual Education: Perspectives on Research and Other Issues

Although my family was of modest means, we had a truly bilingual education in grades one through twelve in Peru. We learned to think, write, read, and speak in both Spanish and English from native speakers of Spanish and English. My 54 classmates, who were a heterogeneous group in terms of ability, were all expected to learn in Spanish and English. There was no choice or decision to be made on our part. Teachers had the expectation that all of us could learn to think and express ourselves in speech and writing in two languages. We did. More critically, we who were all native Spanish speakers, learned English to some purpose beyond rudimentary oral communication. When we read Shakespeare in high school, we read the original. At the same time, we studied Peruvian history and literature in Spanish. We studied science in Spanish and mathematics in English, crisscrossing concepts and vocabulary in two languages to make a tight weave. We did not travel back and forth across a bridge. Our entire school experience took place on the bridge. We camped out and made a home there, internalizing two languages so we would own them for the rest of our lives — the true meaning of language acquisition. The bridge was sturdy enough to support our aspirations to build a structure of our own design that would span and celebrate the roots of two cultures and two languages. In this most fundamental sense, we felt entitled, from first grade, to possess a second language — not to replace our own but to enrich our lives, our minds, and opportunities. That sense of entitlement is entirely a question of school culture, expectations, and the messages, including nonverbal ones, sent out by adults working with children. For us, school was a place to learn in two languages, and in the course of learning in two languages, we learned a great deal about two languages. In fact, I learned a third language in high school, as did most of my classmates.

What a different bridge we have built for most Hispanic children in Massachusetts. The reasons why the current bridge is predicated on a temporary experience are obvious: lack of money and increasing hostility from certain well-organized factions within the English-dominant community. The bridge is shaky rather than strong.

Nevertheless, we have a unique opportunity in public education to redefine bilingual education. This unique opportunity is a result of the growing movement toward parental choice in selecting public schools on the one hand, and the stunning world events of the last 30 years that have succeeded in bringing international issues into the lives of ordinary Americans. Shaped themselves by an increasingly global village viewpoint, there is a growing sentiment among English monolingual parents of school-age children (African-American and Anglo) of the value of second-language instruction. This is a new and potentially powerful ally in an expanded coalition for genuine two-way language instruction.

Hispanic parents, as evidenced by the popularity and waiting lists at the handful of two-way language schools and programs in Massachusetts, remain eager to encourage their children to "camp out on the bridge" rather than be forced to one side or the other.

Up to now, advocates of bilingual education have had to struggle hard to win and maintain any native language instruction in the curriculum and to defend their programs from attacks from English-only and other groups, and so there has been a tendency to protect the status quo with its widely differing programs and quality. Bilingual education, as a field of professional study, is relatively new, and research in the field has followed an existing political agenda rather than shaping a future one. The study of how children learn, including how children learn a first and second language, is at once totally political and totally nonpolitical. It is political in that political winds determine whether society values the study of how children learn, particularly of how limited-English-proficient Hispanic children learn. For example, is money allocated for such research? It is nonpolitical in that the necessary research, once funded, is insulated from those political crosswinds. How? Either because it is a longitudinal study and transcends the political winds of the moment, or because it is basic research that crosses disciplines to develop theory that stands up in practice to the scrutiny of different political sectors.

In this chapter, I argue for new directions in research in order to shape a public policy that promotes truly bilingual education and delineate the aspects of quality programming that should be embedded in future research studies. I argue further that language and culture should be seen as assets rather than handicaps in the educational process, and I address the importance of an integral approach to bilingual education and of ending the isolation of bilingual students. I review the issue of accountability of teachers, administrators, and students as addressed by entry and exit criteria and raise the issue of standards for bilingual education and teacher training.

The discussion is directed toward bilingual education in Massachusetts and draws primarily on the Massachusetts experience. Yet the debate on bilingual education is a national debate, and as such this and all discussion must go beyond the confines of a single state's experience.

Much of the current research that purports to discredit bilingual education has been based on the wrong questions — questions shaped by a political rather than an educational public policy agenda. Many educators in bilingual education have long believed that Hispanic children were smart and capable and should retain and even expand their native language proficiency in addition to learning English. However, these practitioners, with their widely differing programs and populations, consistently use research studies that ask the wrong question. When evaluating programs, instead of asking "How quickly can limited-English-proficient children learn English," the question should be "How do students learn a second language," and "What other factors combined with instruction in first language must we consider in program design?" Before turning to the major questions for future research in bilingual education, let us review how such a limited question came to dominate center stage in the political and public arena.

Background

Research is the shadow of public policy, and public policy is shaped by history and aspiration. The United States first acknowledged that government had a responsibility to play a role in meeting the particular educational needs of students with limited- or no-English-proficiency when President Lyndon Johnson signed the Bilingual Education Act (Title VII) into law in 1968. Politically, these students could be ignored no longer. Yet embedded in the 1968 federal statute was a view that students needed to be stuffed like sausages with a filling of English; limited-English-proficient students were empty casings, deprived, in need of remediation and compensatory education. The law did not require the use of any native language instruction in meeting these students' needs, nor any expansion or revision of the standard curriculum. According to a 1977-1978 study by the American Institute for Research, 49.6 percent of bilingual teachers interviewed lacked proficiency in their students' native language (Crawford, 1989).

Massachusetts passed the first state law promoting bilingual education in November 1971, the Transitional Bilingual Education Law, Chapter 71A, which permitted the use of native language instruction and delineated certification requirements for bilingual teachers (Crawford, 1989). That law, as well as the landmark *Lau* v. *Nichols* case decided by the U.S. Supreme Court in 1974, became the foundation, with Title VII, for building a bridge between the dominant English-language culture and a tremendously diverse Hispanic culture spanning two continents with roots to a third. Yet again, despite research evidence to the contrary, that second-language acquisition takes five to seven years (Cummins, 1986; Hakuta, 1986; Collier and Thomas, 1989), the law called for a transitional program. Students were not to camp on the bridge; after three years they were to sink or swim in the regular education classroom.

Still today, bilingual education is viewed primarily as a remedial or compensatory program — philosophically a catch-up operation — by school administrators and school committees. Even the labels with their implied sorting and ranking — regular education, bilingual education, vocational education, special education — serve to separate and fragment the delivery of services. Heaven help the student who crosses boundaries and is bilingual, special needs, and a vocational student! That child will most certainly be relegated to the basement of a school building, the least well-lit place where special needs, vocational, and bilingual classes are traditionally housed — effectively segregated and out of the way.

Administrative decisions have compounded these separations in larger systems, where often the principal does not view bilingual or special needs programs as within administrative responsibility: "They report to downtown." Bilingual children and staff exist as best they can, misunderstood, tolerated but rarely embraced by the school community of which they are members.

The view of bilingual education as a transitional program to English instruction was never universally accepted, however. Santiago Polanco-Abreu, Puerto Rico's congressional delegate, argued during the 1967 deliberations on the Bilingual Education Act:

I wish to stress that I realize the importance of learning English by Puerto Ricans and other minority groups living in the States. But I do not feel that our educational abilities are so limited and our educational vision so shortsighted that we must teach one language at the expense of another, that we must sacrifice the academic potential of thousands of youngsters in order to promote the learning of English, that we must jettison and reject ways of life that are not our own.

Polanco-Abreu called for the establishment of programs that (a) would utilize two languages, English and the non-English mother tongue, in the teaching of the various school subjects, (b) would concentrate on teaching both English and the non-English mother tongue, and (c) would endeavor to preserve and enrich the culture and heritage of the non-English speaking student.

Nor was the view of the importance of one language only — English — for instruction based in historical fact. According to von Maltitz (1975):

The concept of teaching in two languages (or in a language other than English) is not a completely new idea in the history of education in the United States. Some bilingual public schools existed here before the Civil War and flourished in various places thereafter. In localities with heavy concentrations of German-speaking families, such as Cincinnati, Cleveland and Milwaukee, there were schools in which at least part of the curriculum was taught in German; in an earlier era, French was used in public schools in Louisiana and Spanish in New Mexico (p. 7).

But because bilingual education, or teaching in any language but English in public schools, did not conform to the melting-pot philosophy of twentieth-century United States society, it fell into disfavor and in many states was declared illegal. The resurgence of interest in bilingual teaching, which came about in the decade of the 1960s, was fostered by two factors: the growing determination of various ethnic minorities to maintain their ancestral languages and lifestyles and the schools' inability to educate many of the children from these ethnic groups when using a language that the pupils had not yet mastered as the only medium of instruction.

A drowning person will grab anything that floats, and Hispanic children in 1971 were drowning in their attempt to reach shore in an educational system indifferent, and more often hostile, to their needs (Massachusetts Task Force of Children Out of School, 1971). The bridge of bilingual education, even with its weaknesses, offered thousands of Hispanic children for the first time access to public education in their native language. Despite claims to the contrary, the majority of these children fared better than their counterparts who did not have equivalent supports (Hakuta, 1986).

The Association for Supervision and Curriculum Development (ASCD) argued in a 1987 report that "Rather than emphasize research that might give insights to teachers on effective classroom practices and on how they might help limited-English-proficient students, [policy makers have] expended ... much energy on research of questionable quality and validity that asks, 'Has it worked?'" The simplistic question "Has it worked?" ignores the complexity of bilingual programs and "serves to fuel a divisive debate."

What makes bilingual education work? Underlying good bilingual education, as under all good education, are fundamental assumptions about language and culture.

Language and Culture as Assets

"We have room for but one language in this country and that is the English language, for we intend to see that the crucible turns our people out as Americans, of American nationality, and not as dwellers in a polyglot boarding house," argued President Theodore Roosevelt 75 years ago. The debate of whether one must be English dominant to be a "true American" continues today.

Curiously, the same English-only proponents who insist one must be able to read the U.S. Constitution in English to understand it forget the link between the ideas of today's democratic society, with its protection of the rights of the few from the trespass of the many, to early Greece and Rome — where English was a foreign tongue. These same English-only proponents fail to acknowledge the native American contribution to the Constitution, an acknowledgment made by Benjamin Franklin and other colonists who sought living examples of self-governing unions as they contemplated their break from England. "What made colonists American as opposed to English was their experience with the Indians," according to Lyons (1987) who cites numerous instances of the influence of the Iroquois Confederacy in the development of the Constitution. The United States itself is predicated on ideas, not the English language manifestation of those ideas, however beautiful and powerful the words in the English language may be. As a country, we have never been defined by only one tongue. The words Massachusetts, Los Angeles, Baton Rouge, the Dakotas, and many more remind us of the rich tongues of Spain, of France, and of native American tribes.

Hispanic students often experience school as the "others," the "outsiders." Very few schools embrace and acknowledge that Hispanic children bring a rich cultural legacy with the potential to enrich the entire school community.

What is culture? The history and literature of a people, their life patterns from birth to death and from generation to generation; it is a people's governance, music, art, science, dance, games, humor, customs, beliefs, and rituals. Most dazzling, many dimensions of other cultures are accessible to the motivated, patient learner; I know this as a long-term observer of and participant in contemporary American culture.

Culture is vastly more than a people's native foods and dress. Yet this is often the depth of exposure that bilingual children may have in their curriculum to their ancestors' rich contributions to world culture. Mainstreamed to the regular classroom, former bilingual students may no longer have these native celebrations.

Von Maltitz (1975) notes:

> Some of the differences between one ethnic group and another, of course, go much deeper than superficial variations in manners and habits. Underlying some of them are attitudes toward life and death, love and family relationships, concepts of time — not in the meaning of hours and minutes but in the larger sense. There are also different views concerning the way humans should conduct their lives, motivated by a competitive, acquisitive spirit or guided by an acceptance of what fate brings. The attitude toward land — humans' use of the earth — also varies (p. 2).

Teachers and school administrators need to understand all of these varied aspects of the cultural backgrounds of the pupils whose education is entrusted to them. A study of the cultural roots of the various segments of the American nation is an important part of the bilingual-bicultural movement in public education.

How Do Language and Culture Play a Role?

If the teacher (bilingual and regular education) role shifts to explorer and learner with students, together they can make an in-depth inquiry into the students' cultures. Just as Europeans cherish distinctly different traditions (who would argue French culture is identical to Welsh or Hungarian cultures?), Hispanics celebrate a rich diversity of culture, dating from ancient times.

Why should the inquiry be in-depth? "As teachers, I think one major role is to undo rapid assumptions of understanding, to slow down closure, in the interest of breadth and depth, which attach our knowledge to the world in which we are called upon to use it," Duckworth writes in *The Having of Wonderful Ideas and Other Essays on Teaching and Learning* (1987, p. 78). Duckworth makes an eloquent, persuasive case for encouraging children to learn how to generate and then explore for answers to their own meaningful questions. Every child has meaningful questions about his or her culture and ancestry if we educators will only create classroom environments for such questions.

A student who spends time exploring an aspect of culture that holds his fascination is far beyond the experience of a parade of multiethnic banquets. How did the Mayans invent the idea of zero? How has geography shaped the history of Ecuador? What are the favorite fables of children from Chile? What role does music play in the daily life of Puerto Ricans? The questions are endless. Asking the students to generate the questions affirms their abilities as generators of valid questions; asking the students to research these substantive questions validates their own culture as worthy of serious inquiry and scholarship.

Ideas translate, but the rhythms and syncopations, the warmth and familiarity of colloquial expressions cannot. Each language plays its music on a different instrument. The notes may be the same, but the timbre of a piano has a resonance the harpsichord can never match. Children deserve the riches of literature in its original Spanish and English.

What Is Quality Bilingual Education?

"Good bilingual education is good education which happens to be in two languages," argues Brisk (1990). Good education has a seamless quality. All the pieces fit because there is an underlying shared purpose and theoretical framework for whole learning. Teachers make choices — select a book, plan a lesson, engage students in discourse — based on educational thought, not externally generated political or bureaucratic reasons. Students make choices — ask a question, explore an idea, work through a problem cooperatively — because they understand that they are validated as individuals. They also know that their best thinking and expression are expected, whether in language, music, art, or physically. The expression of both ideas and feelings are at home in good education.

Teachers, administrators, and parents develop and share a vision for their school that draws on the uniqueness of that community of individuals. Because teachers have articulated a shared vision of how children learn, including how they learn in two languages, high expectations for children's achievement and teaching approaches are consistent throughout the program. Teachers and administrators are conversant with the latest research and curriculum developments within and beyond bilingual education and apply findings to their own classroom.

If that sounds like a fairy tale impossibility in urban schools, it is because of the external demands that buffet and direct the deployment of teachers, administrators, and resources for bilingual education, resulting in a short-changed, fragmented program directed by and accountable to administrators who are most often off-site. Bilingual education, in far too many schools, is effectively a segregated program for both staff and students.

A quality program cannot exist within a school without the full support and involvement of the on-site educational leader: the principal. A quality program cannot make the transition to becoming quality education without the active participation of the entire staff of the school; to provide a child with an exemplary year or two experience is only a piece of the patchwork. Administrators and teachers — bilingual, special education, and regular education — have a responsibility to look to the entire design and examine the educational experience the school system is providing the child from entrance at age four or five to graduation from high school. Each piece is every educator's responsibility.

Duckworth (1987) describes good education in this way:

> What is the intellectual equivalent of building in breadth and depth? I think it is a matter of making connections: breadth could be thought of as the widely different spheres of experiences that can be related to one another; depth can be thought of as the many different kinds of connections that can be made among different facets of our experience (p. 7).

Questions and ideas are central to this process. When Duckworth (1987) notes that good education cannot be rushed, we may remind ourselves of the fallacy of externally prescribing a timetable for children to master a second language:

> Exploring ideas can only be to the good, even if it takes time. Wrong ideas,

moreover, can only be productive. Any corrected, wrong idea provides far more depth than if you never had a wrong idea to begin with. You master it much more thoroughly if you have considered the alternatives, tried to work it out in areas where it didn't work, and figured out why it was that it didn't work — all of which takes time (pp. 71-72).

While they are addressing issues of early childhood education in particular, the following three components by Hall and Wortis (1990), of Literacy/Curriculum Connections, can be applied as a benchmark to good education for every age, including adults: developmentally appropriate practice, multicultural education, and a whole-language theory. They emphasize "a firm belief in the efficacy of the acquisition learning model and the communal cooperative learning environment that supports it," and they define their terms in the following ways:

Developmentally appropriate practice emphasizes learning as an interactive process. Teachers observe and record each child's special interests and the developmental process. The curriculum is then planned to be appropriate for the age span of the children within the group and is implemented with attention to the different needs, interests, and developmental levels of the individual children. Teachers prepare the environment for children to learn through active exploration and interaction with adults, other children, and materials. Through an integrated curriculum, all areas of a child's development are addressed: physical, emotional, social, and cognitive.

Multicultural education is inclusive rather than exclusive. It encompasses many dimensions of human difference, including culture, race, socioeconomic status, exceptional need, gender, and sexual orientation. It affirms and validates each child's culture and background. It provides for the growth of positive self-esteem among all children and guarantees that each child will feel successful. By providing all children equal opportunity to learn, multicultural education gives each child a chance to reach her/his full potential. The ultimate goal of multicultural education is to develop children's abilities to function competently within multiple cultures.

Whole language is a theory about language, literacy, and learning in general. The key premise is that babies the world over acquire a language through actually using it in meaningful contexts. The major assumption is that this model of acquisition through real use, not through practice exercises, is the best model for learning to read and write. In the classroom reading and writing are done for real purposes. Language is considered a tool for making sense of something else. Subjects under study have prominence and provide the contexts for much of the reading and writing.

Clearly, high quality teachers and home-school collaboration are essential to all effective schools. What additional criteria should be considered in developing effective two-way bilingual programs? Lindholm (1990), of the Center for Language Education at the University of California, Los Angeles, suggests:

> Programs must provide long-term treatment (four to six years), optimal input in two languages, focus on academic subjects, integration of language arts with curriculum, separation of languages for instruction, additive bilingual environment, balance of language groups, sufficient use of minority language, opportunities for speech production, administrative support and an empowerment objective of instruction (p. 96-101).

Quality education encompasses a view of children as active and engaged learners, a view diametrically opposed to the philosophical underpinning of transitional bilingual education, which is "quick, compensatory and remedial education." Those engaged in good education refuse to reduce their goals or methods to those prescribed from the outside, including federal or state government. Good education makes its own way, based on the needs of students.

What Does It Take to Get There?

TEACHER TRAINING

"I think the teacher's job is to raise questions about even ... a simple right answer — to push it to its limits, to see where it holds up and where it does not hold up," Duckworth says (1987, p. 78).

The changes in state certification of teachers in Massachusetts hold many hopeful signs, including the elimination of education as a field of undergraduate study and replacing it with a liberal arts major which in most cases includes a foreign language requirement. However, there remains a gaping hole that may not be filled by graduate requirements of individual schools of education. Regular education teachers in Massachusetts are not required to complete any courses for certification or continuing education that address the needs of limited-English-proficient students.

If we are to promote the notion of all teachers taking responsibility for the education of all students, then regular education teachers must be required to take courses in second-language acquisition, and there must be incentives for all teachers to develop their own second-language capability beyond simple foreign language requirements. There is ample lip service in education today for the value of intercultural training for teachers, yet such courses remain optional electives for entering the teaching profession. Students who seek out these courses already are motivated enough to realize that as educators they have an expanded responsibility to assist children in affirming and celebrating their cultures. What about the education students who are not yet motivated? What incentive is there for them to alter their ethnocentric view of teaching and learning?

Given secondary and higher education's poor track record of teaching English-dominant students to achieve oral and written fluency in a second language, we cannot expect a quick turnaround in an outdated system of foreign language instruction that produces such poor results, including among future teachers. Realistically, while graduate schools of education may have a foreign language prerequisite, students will require further study to approach fluency as bilingual teachers.

Nevertheless, every Massachusetts teacher should be required to complete a course, with a field experience, in intercultural training and second-language acquisition. English speakers who have struggled through high school and college Spanish — and still are not fluent — should have new insight into why mastering a second language has its own developmental timetable for children. Furthermore one child's timetable is often quite distinct from the next.

Similarly, the widely held practice in bilingual education of requiring all teachers to teach in both languages regardless of native- and second-language abilities should be challenged. In the move to school-based decision making, the entire teaching staff of a school should work together to design a truly bilingual education program that uses teachers' strengths. For example, the language instruction of my own education played to teachers' strengths. While all teachers could speak both Spanish and English, I learned English composition from a native English speaker and Spanish composition from a native Spanish speaker.

Barth (1990) notes that "in good schools, good thinking pervades the curriculum and decision making." Good thinking is holistic. By putting bilingual teachers, special education teachers, and regular education teachers in effect on three separate certification tracks, we have instituted separate standards and promoted fragmented thinking. To what extent does teacher preparation, including language ability in English and Spanish and knowledge of current learning theory and content areas, impact students' achievement when enrolled in two-way bilingual programs? To what extent does it impact in transitional bilingual programs? Monolingual and bilingual teachers (as well as special education teachers, for there are a significant number of limited-English-proficient students enrolled, even over-enrolled, in special education) are not adversaries but allies in this scenario, working together to educate all the children in their care.

Bilingual education has been shortchanged in two ways: Many bilingual teachers teach initially under waiver — an acknowledgment that either they are not yet fluent in two languages and/or they have not yet completed their professional training required for certification. Regular education teachers also have suffered from inappropriate sorting and tracking within the profession. Many are ignorant of the most rudimentary elements of bilingual education as a field. Separate professional development, if any at all, has been characteristic of bilingual, regular education, and special education teachers with different administrators responsible for professional development design and programs. In the future, ongoing professional development must be at the core of a school system's values and action agenda. Examples include offering teachers a range of professional development, from one week mini-sabbaticals to model classrooms as pioneered in the Chelsea public schools during the 1989-90 school year, to inservice, after-school, and summer workshops and courses.

The mini-sabbatical model holds particular promise as an accelerated, intensive professional growth opportunity. Hosting teachers have a chance to reflect on their successful practices while visiting teachers can observe a model practitioner and work side-by-side in a real classroom setting. The 42 early childhood Chelsea teachers who volunteered for the first round of mini-sabbaticals attested to the value of the experience for lifting morale as well (Chelsea Public Schools, 1990).

DEVELOPING AN INTEGRATED APPROACH

Traditionally, bilingual classes have been isolated from standard curriculum classes. Paralleling the move toward clustering in middle and high schools, we have a separate "bilingual cluster." That is, despite the mandate by Massachusetts General Law for integration of bilingual students in nonacademic subject areas, integration happens only sporadically in Massachusetts.

Staking out extreme positions — everything must be taught in the native language versus rapid total immersion in English — ill serves students' needs. Bridge building connects both sides and, in the process, creates new structures.

Brisk (1990) has outlined principles for the academic and social integration of bilingual students, noting that "Education that isn't integrated can't be good education." These principles include clustering bilingual and monolingual classes for the delivery of a full curriculum to students:

Bilingual students should receive at least one block in which all the teaching is in the native language ... and should be in one class in which they will need to use English. Teachers should teach what they like and do best in the language that they do best. Integration should not be done just with students who are in the top English group. Monolingual personnel need to be trained to work with bilingual students. They need to understand that having bilingual students in their classes does not mean that they have to lower expectations or water down material (p. 24).

ACCOUNTABILITY

After 20 years of bilingual education, we know precious little about the ability of students to acquire two languages, because so few truly bilingual programs exist and because the federal government, with its increasingly restrictive vision of bilingual education, has failed to fund research and evaluation of these most promising programs. While standardized tests have their own tyranny and obvious limitations, Edmonds (1981), in his research on what makes schools effective, points out the value of such tests as a benchmark for measuring individual school's progress (as opposed to individual student's progress) over time. Clearly, they contribute a very flawed and limited benchmark, but they are something. The fact that we in Massachusetts have not yet created any testing instrument for children enrolled in bilingual education programs means we cannot judge how schools or programs are improving bilingual instruction over time.

The stepchild of public education in so many ways, testing and evaluation is the great uncharted water of bilingual education. Bilingual educators need immediate assistance in this area from educational researchers.

Gardner (1983), for instance, is developing alternative assessments to uncover the many facets, from musical to kinesthetic, of any one child's intelligence. He defines linguistic intelligence as one of the major facets of intelligence and calls special attention to the development of the core operations of language that all of us possess in significant degrees. These he defines as: a sensitivity to the meaning of words — appreciation of the subtle shades of difference, for instance, between spilling ink "intentionally," "deliberately," or "on purpose;" a sensitivity to the order among words — the capacity to follow rules of grammar and on carefully selected occasions to violate them; a sensitivity at a somewhat more sensory level to the sounds, rhythms, inflections, and meters of words — that ability which can make poetry even in a foreign tongue beautiful to hear; and a sensitivity to the different functions of language — its potential to excite, convince, stimulate, convey information, or simply to please.

Future Directions for Research

"I was looking at the stars last night," a student tells her teacher. "What are they? Why do they shine? Do they burn out in the day?"

"Those are hard questions," the teacher replies. "You are not ready. You wouldn't understand. I have never taken astronomy myself. You must study and pass elementary, junior, and high school science and mathematics before you can answer those questions. You should be reading at night, not looking at the stars, if you want to succeed in school."

A different answer, the invitation to explore the curriculum together, seems obvious to us. What if the student was Spanish-speaking and asked a monolingual English teacher the same questions in Spanish or hesitant English? Many such students would not even risk asking the questions. But the questions, and the imagination behind the questions, would still be there. How can public policy and research help this student get the quality teaching in two languages that she richly deserves? How can this student further develop and refine her linguistic intelligence in two languages? How can we provide incentives to teachers and administrators to create schools and programs where students can flourish in two languages? What real consequences should there be for schools that fail to educate our children?

There are schools in Massachusetts, such as the Rafael Hernández in Boston and programs such as Project Amigos in Cambridge, that provide a rich learning environment that supports the development of truly bilingual linguistic intelligences. There are other examples nationally, such as the Oyster School in Washington, DC. These efforts share the characteristics of a culture that promotes the continued development into adulthood of linguistic intelligence; of alternative assessment and teaching strategies that include a strong emphasis on providing children with ample "practice time" to use the languages in meaningful ways; and of a willingness on the part of educators to expose themselves to public, parent, and research scrutiny.

Researchers in the field of bilingual education and beyond have a unique role to play in advancing public policy. They can pose the unasked questions and collaborate closely with practitioners to uncover answers. By inviting the public, particularly parents, teachers, and students, to assist in generating questions, researchers are more likely to maintain the connection between their initial purpose and the ultimate outcome. By remembering the stargazer, and her striking linguistic intelligence, researchers will be emboldened to ask thorny and difficult questions for the sake of all children.

Margaret Geller, astronomer and a recipient of the MacArthur "genius" fellowship for her work mapping the universe, notes "You try to be as correct as you can, but to make advances in science you have to have a certain willingness to be wrong. The hardest thing in science is to ask the question." In research on bilingual education I would call for a boldness in asking questions in fresh ways. We must cast a wide net of questions beyond the scope of individual schools or programs.

We all speak glowingly about parent involvement, for example. What specific kinds of parent involvement and training have a positive impact on children learning in two languages? What kind of school governance has a positive impact on children learning in two languages? We often find that successful programs have been created by teachers and parents working together, often at odds with the school administration or in spite of them. Does the fact that a school or program has created itself — in effect, become a chartered effort with a distinct purpose — affect student achievement and learning in two languages? What role does parent choice play in having a positive impact on truly bilingual education?

Successful public education bilingual programs and schools are obvious through the most telling barometer of all: waiting lists. Parents vie to enroll their children. What factors inhibit and often prevent such successful bilingual programs from being replicated, despite their popularity? These questions all demand research. We cannot afford to diminish ourselves by diminishing the scope of our research questions.

We must be willing to ask politically sensitive questions. Is there a way to address issues of equity for bilingual and special needs students in a within-city-limits-school-choice plan that includes mechanisms for the chartering and decommissioning of schools? Would a chartering mechanism:

> Allow successful programs to become full-fledged autonomous schools, perhaps sharing a site with other chartered schools?

> Provide an incentive to teachers and parents to replicate popular and successful two-way bilingual schools?

> Reward rather than punish excellent two-way bilingual schools by giving them greater autonomy and control of their own resources?

Would a school decommissioning mechanism affect schools that currently refuse to provide truly bilingual education, despite the desire of their parents and needs of their students?

The currency of schools is time and resources, with the greatest resource being the human beings (students, families, staff) affiliated with the institution. An agenda for bilingual education in the next century entails questioning and chronicling every aspect of how time and resources are valued and used within a program, a school, and a school system. Wherever children are not valued, bilingual education is not going to be valued either. As bilingual, regular education, and special needs teachers crisscross lines and develop a team approach to teaching, researchers must also step across the boundaries of disciplines to develop new research designs that have an overriding goal of supporting the education of every student. Researchers must also, as we have noted, design the instruments that can measure the effectiveness of bilingual programs and the needs of students in such programs. What is possible and what works? What testing and evaluation tools assess school strengths and weaknesses? What tools assess individual students' progress and proficiency? What are we testing to find out? How do a student's wrong answers illuminate our understanding of what a child knows? Is there a pattern to the wrong answers?

Another major issue researchers must vigorously address is how humans learn a second language, and its corollary, what role do age and development play in learning a second language? This question begs an earlier one: How do children learn a first language? Pinker, Director of the Center for Cognitive Science at Massachusetts Institute of Technology, has called language "the jewel in the crown of cognition — it is what everyone wants to explain" (DeCuevas, 1990, p. 63).

Brown (1973), in his seminal work on language development in children, says the way children learn a first language is "approximately invariant across children learning the same language and, at a higher level of abstraction, across children learning any language" (p. 403). According to DeCuevas (1990):

> Brown's pioneering work became the model for countless studies of child language that followed and gave rise to the flourishing field known as developmental psycholinguistics. By now so much has been written on language learning in children that no one could ever read it all, but in spite of all the work, no one has yet been able to explain fully how children learn their first language, although the pattern of development is well established for children learning English and a number of other languages as well (p. 62).

Let us invite researchers to work with teachers, students, and parents as allies in finding the answer to how people learn a second language. What can we learn from students and teachers who reflect on this question over time? Lampert (1986) models the role of researcher-as-teacher/teacher-as-researcher; she teaches an elementary mathematics class every morning while also holding a teaching appointment at Michigan State University. Lampert asks her elementary students to write their thoughts on what they learned that week in mathematics. What did they understand? What are they working to understand? Is there a comparable rich field of longitudinal data from students of all ages reflecting on learning a second language? What about longitudinal reflections by teachers on teaching in two languages?

What other factors combined with instruction in the first language must we consider in program design? Researchers must examine systematically the identified facets of good education in the context of instruction in two languages.

Researchers should be directed to study the impact of in-depth cultural learning on Hispanic achievement. What difference does reading from an original Spanish literature text make? What barriers do teachers and administrators face in developing a culturally relevant curriculum in Spanish and English? How can school-family ties be strengthened when enlisting family resources for the serious study of the child's native culture?

Curriculum is a major area for future research and development. Why do we still have such a shortage of quality literature in Spanish by Hispanic authors for children in kindergarten through grade 12. Reading a Spanish translation of a children's classic is preferable to reading a Spanish translation of a balkanized basal reader; but why must teachers be faced with such a poverty of choices? Read *Alice in Wonderland* in the original English, and *Platero y Yo* in the original Spanish. Education means empowering our youngsters to meet great authors "face to face;" bilingual education means giving them the advantage of meeting the writers, poets, playwright, and storytellers in their native tongues.

English and American children's literature has flowered in the past 100 years. There is not yet a comparable body of children's literature from Latin America, but there is a treasure house of legends, fables, and myths to disseminate more widely. The poetry of Latin America suitable for children could alone fill volumes. What rich volumes they would be and how preferable to a basal translation from English of a poem of little literary value in its original tongue. How can researchers and teachers work together on the collection, publication, and promotion of an expanding body of children's literature in Spanish?

Curriculum resources in Spanish, whether science, social studies, literature, music, or mathematics, lag behind and when available, are often more expensive. We must find incentives and create opportunities, such as summer institutes, for teachers and educational researchers to work together in the development of state-of-the-art trade books, interdisciplinary kits, curriculum units, and quality interdisciplinary children's magazines for classroom use. These Spanish-language magazines would be the equivalent of *Cobblestone*, which focuses on U.S. history, *Faces,* which focuses on anthropology, or *Calliope*, which focuses on world history, all for students in grades four through nine. Our curriculum in public education is neither multicultural nor gender-balanced. It is up to us to join forces as researchers and educators to create the curriculum resources in Spanish that our children deserve.

Dworkin (1987) notes that "Despite the plethora of research devoted to the effects of teachers and schools upon student achievement, there appears to be almost no work which addresses the impact of teacher work commitment upon students." In a heavily tracked system, Hispanics are disproportionately relegated to the remedial and basic regular education courses once they are "mainstreamed" out of bilingual education. These courses remain low-status within schools and may even be assigned the least talented rather than most talented teachers. What difference does it make to Hispanic student achievement if it is the lesser skilled or burned-out teacher who is assigned to teach our children?

Similarly, what impact does administrators' work commitment and attitude have on Hispanic student achievement? In my tenure as superintendent and the first Hispanic administrator in Chelsea, a school system 52 percent Hispanic, I was touched by the private expressions of support from students, staff, and community in telling me what a difference my presence made. "You can speak to us in Spanish," one mother said gratefully. "You show us our children can go far."

There has been a certain hesitancy on the part of educational researchers outside bilingual education to join with us in studying how we can all serve all children better. I extend an enthusiastic invitation to all educational researchers — whether studying cooperative learning, whole language, critical and creative thinking, school restructuring, parent involvement, school climate, early childhood education, middle schools, tracking, retention or curriculum development, within or across any discipline — to work with bilingual practitioners. We need each other.

The day must come when a state bilingual conference is flooded with educators and researchers who traditionally have not attended and choose no longer to abdicate responsibility for the education of bilingual children to one particular group. The researchers and teachers of the future will present their shared findings on "good education that happens to take place in two languages."

References

Association for Supervisors of Curriculum Development, Panel on Bilingual Education. (1987). *Building an Indivisible Nation: Bilingual Education in Context.* Alexandria, VA: Author.

Barth, R. (1990, August). Interview with Diana Lam. Cambridge, MA.

Brisk, M. (1990, May). Presentation to the Boston Public Schools, Thompson Island, Boston, MA.

Brown, R. (1973). *A First Language/The Early Stages.* Cambridge, MA: Harvard University Press.

Collier, V. and Thomas, W. (1989). How Quickly Can Immigrants Become Proficient in School English? *Journal of Educational Issues of Language Minority Students, 5.* Boise State University. Boise, IO.

Chelsea Public Schools. (1990, June 21). *Creating a School System that Thrives on Change and Diversity.* Chelsea, MA: Author.

Crawford, J. (1989). *Bilingual Education: History, Politics, Theory and Practice.* Trenton, NJ: Crane Publishing Company.

Cummins, J. (1986). Empowering Minority Students: A Framework for Intervention. *Harvard Educational Review, 56*(1), 18-36.

DeCuevas, J. (1990). No, she holded them loosely. *Harvard Magazine, 93*, 1.

Duckworth, E. (1987). *The Having of Wonderful Ideas and Other Essays on Teaching and Learning.* Columbia University, NY: Teachers College Press.

Dworkin, A. G. (1987). *Teacher Burnout in the Public School: Structural Causes and Consequences for Children.* Albany, NY: State University of New York.

Edmonds, R. (1981, November). *The Characteristics of Effective Schools: Research and Implementation.* Unpublished paper. This material also appears in: Northwest Regional Educational Laboratory. (1990). *Effective School Practices: A Research Synthesis 1990 Update.* Portland OR: Author. Pp. 15-23.

Gardner, H. (1983). *Frames of Mind: The Theories of Multiple Intelligences.* New York, NY: Basic Books.

Hakuta, K. (1986). *Mirror of Language: The Debate on Bilingualism.* New York, NY: Basic Books.

Hall, L., and Wortis, S. (1990). Infusing Multiculturalism in a Whole Language Classroom. *The Whole Language Teachers Association Newsletter, 5*, 2.

Lampert, M. (1986). Knowing, Doing and Teaching Multiplication. *Cognition and Instruction, 3*, 305-342.

Lindholm, K. (1990). Bilingual Immersion Educational Criteria for Program Development. In A. M. Padilla, H. H. Fairchild, C. M. Valadez (Eds.), *Bilingual Education Issues and Strategies*, pp. 91-105. Newbury Park, CA: Sage Publications.

Lyons, O. (1987, June 28). Iroquois Constitution: A Forerunner to Colonists Democratic Principals. *New York Times.*

Massachusetts Task Force on Children Out of School. (1971). *The Way We Go to School: The Exclusion of Children in Boston.* Boston, MA: Beacon Press.

Von Maltitz, F. W. (1975). *Living and Learning in Two Languages: Bilingual-Bicultural Education in the United States.* New York, NY: McGraw-Hill.

Ralph Rivera
Barriers to Latino Parental Involvement in the Boston Public Schools

Introduction

There is an increasing interest in parental involvement in the Boston public schools. Before the obstacles to parental involvement are discussed, it is important to understand the many roles that parents can play in their children's education. According to Henderson, Marburger, and Ooms (1986), parental roles can be classified into five basic categories:

1. *Partners*: Parents performing basic obligations for their child's education and social development. These obligations include getting the child ready for school every day, purchasing supplies, filling out forms, and reviewing report cards.

2. *Collaborators and problem solvers*: Parents reinforcing the school's efforts and helping to solve problems. This role can include encouraging academic achievement, reading to a young child, taking trips to the museum, and showing concern when the child falls behind in school.

3. *Audience*: Parents attending and appreciating the school's and their child's special programs, performances, and productions.

4. *Supporters*: Parents providing volunteer assistance to teachers in the classroom, becoming active in parent organizations, and helping with fund raising.

5. *Advisors and/or codecision makers*: Parents providing input on school policy and programs through membership in ad hoc or permanent governance bodies.

Unfortunately, most of the attention paid to parental involvement in Boston has focused on the activities of formal, organized parental groups (i.e., a limited part of the "supporters" role). Scant attention has been given to the unique circumstances of Latino parents and how these circumstances may limit their ability to engage in any parental roles.

This chapter focuses on the major obstacles to Latino parental involvement in the Boston public schools. Model programs that look beyond the "supporter" role in seeking to engage Latinos in their children's education are presented. In closing, recommendations on how to promote Latino parental involvement are offered.

The author has relied on the reservoir of knowledge and experience of 16 key Latino informants representing parents, teachers, principals, school administrators, parental organizers, guidance counselors, and others as sources of primary information for this chapter. These individuals were asked to: (a) identify what they considered to be the major obstacles to Latino parental participation in the Boston public schools; (b) identify programs that they considered effective in promoting Latino parental involvement; and (c) provide general recommendations for the promotion of Latino parental participation.

An effective partnership between home and school can improve the educational performance and experience for Latino children. It is hoped, therefore, that this information will be used to guide the development of culturally appropriate, innovative parental involvement programs for Latino parents throughout the Boston public school system.

Importance of Parental Involvement

It has been well documented that parental involvement has a positive impact on a child's academic achievement. The following statements (cited in Crespo and Louque, 1985) are summarized from Henderson's *Parent Participation-Student Achievement: The Evidence Grows* (1981):

> Families provide the child's most important learning environment. Parental involvement in almost any form can improve student achievement.

> When parents show a strong interest in their children's schooling, they promote the development of attitudes that are key to achievement. These attitudes are more a product of how a family interacts than of its social class or income.

> When parents play significant roles as paraprofessionals, decision makers, tutors, volunteers, observers, or learners themselves, student achievement seems to directly reflect the level of parental involvement.

> The degree of parental and community interest in quality education is a

critical factor affecting the impact of the high school environment on the achievement and educational aspirations of students.

High-achieving students are more likely to have active, interested, and involved parents than low-achieving students. Children whose parents are most involved make the greatest gains.

The form of parental involvement does not seem to be critical.

It is critical that parental involvement be well-planned, comprehensive, and long-lasting. One-time public relations campaigns seem to have little effect.

Research on Latinos reinforces the value of parental involvement. For example, a 1984 Michigan State Department of Education study on Latino dropout rates found that parents were critical to their child's academic survival (Crespo and Louque, 1985). The study found a strong relationship between parental involvement and graduation rates.

There is also evidence that the schools and programs most successful in improving the educational attainment of linguistic-minority children in general, and Latinos specifically, make strong efforts to involve parents and collaborate with families at all levels (Make Something Happen, 1984; Parent Involvement, 1986; Success in Bilingual, 1987).

Not only has the value of promoting Latino parental involvement been established, but the need to do this is becoming increasingly evident. A survey of 250 Latino leaders in the Northeast conducted by ASPIRA Institute for Policy Research found that the need to promote parental involvement among Latinos was the third most pressing priority identified under the education and training needs category. It was preceded in importance only by the need to increase Latino school attendance and reduce dropout rates and by the need to increase Latino representation in administrative and policy-making positions at all levels of the educational system (Northeast Hispanic Needs, 1987).

Factors Associated with Low Parental Involvement

It is widely acknowledged that Latino parents have relatively limited participation in the Boston public school system. The individuals interviewed for this chapter shed some light on the many factors that contribute to the low level of Latino parental involvement in the school system. These factors can be classified into four major categories: institutional, cultural, socioeconomic, and sociodemographic.

INSTITUTIONAL BARRIERS

Many of the obstacles to effective parental involvement faced by Latino parents are the same barriers encountered by all parents with children in the Boston public schools. These obstacles can be considered institutional.

Former superintendent Laval S. Wilson's *Boston Educational Plan: Parent and Community Support Report* (1987) accurately acknowledges that "the school system has failed to effectively reach out and build networks and linkages to the community and our parents," and that "parent involvement historically has not been a priority in the Boston Public Schools." The report identifies three major reasons for the low level of parental participation in Boston's schools. It refers to the inconsistent views held by Boston public school teachers and administrators regarding the role of parents; the lack of a commitment by the Boston public schools to promote parental involvement; and the poor communication between the school system and parents that limits parents' abilities to effectively contribute to their children's education.

The lack of a consistent, clear view of parents' role in the school system that prevails today, coupled with the lack of commitment of the Boston public schools to support parental participation, inevitably means that the strong promotion and encouragement required to engage Latino parents does not materialize.

Communications in their native language as well as the presence of bilingual school personnel are essential if Latino parents are expected to understand how they can contribute to their children's education. Currently, information given to parents is in English, and there are few Spanish-speaking staff in school administration offices. As was stated in the *Parent and Community Support Report*:

> With few exceptions, notes about holidays, half-days, testing schedules, parent meetings, and school policies are sent home in English only. The lack of multilingual staff in schools and district offices who can communicate with non- or limited-English-speaking parents results in the parents becoming frustrated, alienated and consequently uninvolved. (pp. 6-7)

An important exception to this trend appears in schools that have Latino principals and/or assistant principals. These administrators' bilingual abilities make these schools more accessible and open to Latino parents, and these schools seem to make an extra effort to ensure that information sent home to Latino parents is translated into Spanish.

Many Latino parents (as well as many non-Latino parents) feel that the Boston public school system is confusing and difficult to understand. Attempts by the Boston public schools to address this problem have not been successful. For example, the Student Assignment Information Booklet, designed to make parents aware of the school assignment process and published in many different languages, is considered by many parents to be too lengthy and difficult to understand. Moreover, these booklets have been found to contain inaccurate information. If Latino parents (or any parent for that matter) are to involve themselves in the school system in a significant way, efforts to address parental understanding of the school system must be made.

CULTURAL RELEVANCE

While the public education system of the United States assumes a partnership between school and home and while many North American parents have historically been involved in their children's education, this is an alien concept for most Latinos. Even though Latino parents place a very high value on education, in their countries of origin the separation between the roles of parents and the roles of schools is relatively clear. Most Latinos parents are used to seeing themselves as responsible for getting their children to school and consider it appropriate to leave their children's educational matters to the teachers and administrators. In their native countries, many would rely on the authority of the teachers and school administrators to decide what is in the best interest of their children.

As Latinos learn about the new and different school environment they face in this country, they have shown the capability to assume different parental roles required both to improve the quality of education their children receive and to help their children achieve in school. A clear example of this is the work of the Latino Parents Association and the Master Parent Advisory Council, two organizations that have made the Boston public schools more responsive to the needs of Latino and linguistic-minority children in general. It is essential, however, for principals and teachers to realize that the concept of parental involvement is foreign to many Latinos, and effective ways to introduce them to and engage them in these new parental roles must be developed.

SOCIOECONOMIC FACTORS

Some of the obstacles to increasing Latino parental involvement are related to the low socioeconomic status of a large percentage of Latino families. Latinos in Boston comprise a largely poor, working-class population with a lower average household income than any other group in the city. The average Latino household income of $26,292 is only 56 percent of the white average household income of $46,676 (U.S. Bureau of the Census, 1992). Moreover, a significant percentage (34 percent) of Latino families live below the poverty line. The physical and psychological stresses of poverty, unemployment, dilapidated and overcrowded housing conditions, and other economic deprivations interact to limit many Latino parents' ability to be active collaborators in their children's education.

SOCIODEMOGRAPHIC FACTORS

Other factors that contribute to low Latino parental participation can be classified as sociodemographic. They include: low levels of parental education, a large number of single parents, a high percentage of families with children under six years of age, and many parents employed in marginal jobs.

More than 47 percent of Latinos in Boston over 25 years old have not graduated from high school compared to 33 percent of blacks and 18 percent of whites (U.S. Bureau of the Census, 1992). Thus, while many parents in Latino communities place a high value on education, they are often unable to translate that value into concrete help for their children. Montalvo (1984) states that:

> Middle class parents know how to do this. They can articulate the school's shortcomings, the ingredients of a good education, the steps they have to take to supplement their child's education, and even what attitudes and values can be contested as not being in the best interest of the child's development. These are knowledge and skills not readily available to many parents in Hispanic communities.

A large percentage of Latino families in Boston (33 percent) are single-parent families (U.S. Bureau of the Census, 1992). With only one adult present to juggle the multiple responsibilities of work, childcare, and school matters, single-parent families will encounter greater difficulties arranging and maintaining interactions between school and home than two-parent families. Without special attention and support from the school system, Latino single parents will inevitably find parental involvement trying and burdensome.

In addition, a significant percentage of Latino families in Boston have children under six years of age. Young children clearly make it more challenging for a parent to leave the home to visit a school.

Many Latinos in Boston work in secondary labor market industries that not only offer low wages (Boston Foundation, 1989) but provide very limited time off. Many Latinos actually work two jobs to make ends meet. Therefore, it is very difficult, if not impossible, for them to take time off to visit their child's school or even find time to help their child with schoolwork at home.

Models of Successful Programs

There are programs that have been implemented in the Boston public schools by teachers and other professional staff designed primarily to promote Latino parental involvement in their children's education. The following three programs are considered successful by some of the individuals interviewed, and they exemplify creative, practical approaches to engaging Latino parents in the specific roles of "collaborators and problem solvers" in their children's academic work. The first two programs have been run successfully at the elementary school level, while the third program was instituted at the high school level.

The first program, entitled "Helping Parents to Help Children to Learn," was coordinated by Ellen Folsom Goodale, a teacher at the Agassiz Elementary School in Jamaica Plain. This program, directed at a Spanish, bilingual, kindergarten class, seeks to find meaningful homework that parents can help their children with while trying to reduce excessive television watching at home.

Monthly educational units consisting of words to songs, poems, and task sheets were developed and sent home in an effort to get parents to read to their children and build up a home library during the school year. The teacher contacted every parent personally or by telephone to explain the homework project. Many parents were not accustomed to reading to their children, and some parents who were not meeting the objectives of the project were visited at home as a followup.

Parents and their children filled out a form that showed they had read a book together. Some children had as many as 30 and 40 books read to them over the course of the project. The homework assignment was a positive way for the teacher to relate to the parents, and a strong parent-teacher relationship was established through the meetings and the home visits related to the project.

Another successful program is the "Parent's Activity Center and Training Program" coordinated by Ana R. Muñoz, a teacher at the Blackstone Elementary School in the South End. In this project, classroom-based parent activity centers were created in classrooms to "develop parent's ability to work with their children in academic areas as well as to instill mutual respect among parents, students, and teachers" (Parent's Activity Center and Training Program, 1988).

A major premise of this program was that parents' trust in the teachers would be enhanced by their observing the teachers and their children working together. Furthermore, it was assumed that children would be positively influenced by seeing their teachers and parents working together with mutual respect.

Parts of the classrooms were sectioned off to create space for the centers involved in this project. Parents were invited to use materials developed by the teachers with their children in these centers. Once they had mastered these materials, parents could continue working on the assignments with their children at home. Some parents were even able to identify learning difficulties their children had and work with the teacher to address these. In addition, each teacher prepared a packet of educational activities for each parent to use over the summer. The exercises applied activities most families would engage in outdoors over the summer to the learning process.

Another aspect of the Parent's Activity Center project involved arranging for Spanish-speaking professionals to talk to parents about a variety of topics such as parental stress and the growth and development of children. Part of this effort entailed having a Latino male psychologist work specifically with Latino fathers on issues related to their children's education.

The third example project is called "Good Beginnings/Un Buen Comienzo" and was coordinated by Julia Ojeda, a parent coordinator and outreach counselor at what was the Jamaica Plain High School (now the English High School) in Jamaica Plain. This program targeted Latino students entering the ninth grade at the high school. The program sought to get Latino parents to assist their children in succeeding academically. The program also proposed "to make positive connections between home and school, [and] to make the school a more welcoming place for Hispanic parents ..." (Good Beginnings, 1988). Finally, the program sought to sensitize school personnel to the strengths and needs of Latino students, as well as to maximize the resources of Latino parents.

The two major components of this program were an outreach effort and a summer orientation. The orientation program sought to inform parents of the resources and expectations of the high school and included workshops on topics including assisting adolescents to achieve academically and parenting issues. A dinner for all parents and students was also organized to encourage participation. A penpal component matching upper-level Latino students to the incoming students was implemented to encourage their correspondence throughout the summer.

The outreach effort involved a Latino parent who visited and called all of the Latino parents of incoming ninth graders during the summer to recruit them for the program. Once Latino parents joined the program, the outreach coordinator made followup phone calls and home visits, and organized open houses and workshops for parents throughout the school year.

Engaging Latino Parents

According to most of the key informants interviewed, an increase in Latino parental involvement in the Boston public school system requires an authentic commitment to this task. All school personnel, from the superintendent to school office staff, must understand the importance of parental involvement in increasing student motivation and achievement. The following general recommendations for promoting Latino parental participation are based on the experience of the individuals interviewed and on existing literature on the subject (previously cited). These recommendations foster Latino engagement in all five of the parental roles identified by Henderson (1986) earlier.

An open-door policy for schools and classrooms should be maintained. Latino parents must feel welcome at their children's schools. Posting signs to entrances of the school building in Spanish, keeping the doors to the school unlocked, and making principals and teachers available for impromptu meetings can foster this goal.

Principals and teachers should make personal contact with Latino parents a priority. Outreach efforts such as home visits and phone calls are significantly more effective in engaging Latinos than written notes.

Teachers should be required to meet with parents at least three or four times a year to discuss their child's overall academic progress. It is important for teachers to avoid holding meetings exclusively to discuss problems that children are having. Efforts should be made to provide parents with positive feedback on every student.

The Boston public schools should hire Latino staff for all levels and programs of the school system and avoid isolating and limiting Latino personnel to the bilingual program. Mainstreaming bilingual staff will improve the school system's access to Latino parents. (Over 50 percent of Latino students are not in the bilingual program.)

All materials sent home to Latino parents should be translated into Spanish.

Schools should conduct workshops and training sessions in Spanish for Latino parents on topics parents have identified, as well as on the importance of parental participation and concrete ways that parents can contribute to their children's academic achievement. When appropriate and possible, these training sessions should be coordinated with Latino community agencies, and the Latino press should be used to attract parents.

Schools should provide childcare during any parental activity.

Latino parent meetings and training sessions should emphasize less structured, informal, small groups that are less intimidating. Efforts should be made to allow everyone an opportunity to participate in the discussion.

Cultural and social events that tend to attract more Latino parents can be combined with a training event in order to take advantage of the parents' presence at the school. For example, a play could be followed by a short workshop.

Schools should provide translators for all schoolwide parent meetings. Grouping Latino parents together in an area of the room and translating simultaneously is more effective and efficient than interpreting from the front of the room. For schools with large numbers of Latino parents, some meetings can be held in Spanish and translated into English. This will show Latino parents that their needs and concerns are being taken seriously by the school. Moreover, this approach will allow monolingual, English-speaking parents to experience a meeting the way it is experienced by monolingual, Spanish-speaking parents (or any other non-English-speaking parent), thereby potentially increasing their sensitivity to this latter group's needs.

The Boston public schools should conduct workshops for all school personnel on the value of parental involvement, cultural awareness, and sensitivity in order to improve their understanding of and ability to serve and work with cultural minorities.

Conclusions

The impact of parental participation on a child's academic achievement has been well documented. There is strong evidence that an effective partnership between Latino homes and school is a significant factor in improving the educational performance of Latino students. However, the interaction of factors mentioned earlier creates barriers that result in minimal Latino parental participation in the Boston public schools.

It is unrealistic to expect Latino parents to surmount these formidable obstacles by themselves. Overcoming these barriers will require an authentic commitment from the Boston public school system. This system's failure to make parental involvement a priority makes it very difficult for parents in general, and for Latino parents specifically, to fully participate in their children's education.

The Boston public school system's central administration, school principals, and teachers, working with the Latino community, must develop and replicate innovative, culturally-sensitive models to engage Latino parents in the education of their children. Particular attention must be given to the development and growth of Latino parents as "collaborators and problem solvers" and "advisors and/or co-decision makers." The three relatively simple programs described above required small financial investment to implement and yet have extraordinary potential to significantly increase Latino parental involvement in the Boston public schools. It is hoped that they will be seen as models to be supported and expanded in their respective schools as well as across the school system.

References

ASPIRA Institute for Policy Research. (1987). *Northeast Hispanic Needs: A Guide for Action.* Vol. 2. Washington, DC: Author.

Boston Public Schools. (1986). *The Boston Educational Plan Parent and Community Support Report.* Boston: Boston Public Schools.

Crespo, O., and Louque, P. (Comp.) (1985). *Parent Involvement in the Education of Minority Language Children: A Resource Handbook.* Rosslyn, VA: National Clearinghouse for Bilingual Education.

Goldenberg, A. (1987). *Success in Bilingual Education Programs.* Washington, DC: National Center for Bilingual Research.

Henderson, A. T. (1981). *Parent Participation? Student Achievement: The Evidence Grows.* Columbia, MD: National Committee for Citizens in Education.

Henderson, A. T., Marburger, C., and Ooms, T. (1986). *Beyond the Bake Sale: An Educators Guide to Working with Parents.* Columbia, MD: National Committee for Citizens in Education.

Hispanic Development Training Project. (1988). *Good Beginnings/Un Buen Comienzo.* Washington, DC: Author.

Hispanic Development Project. (1988). *Parent's Activity Center and Training Program.* Washington, DC: Author.

Montalvo, F. (1984). Making Good Schools from Bad. In *Make Something Happen: Hispanics and Urban School Reform.* Vol. 1. Washington, DC: National Commission on Secondary Education for Hispanics, Hispanic Policy Development Project.

Simich-Dudgeon, C. (1986). *Parent Involvement in the Education of Limited English Proficient Students.* Washington, DC: ERIC Clearinghouse on Language and Linguistics.

The Boston Foundation. (1989). *In the Midst of Plenty: A Profile of Boston and Its Poor.* Boston: Persistent Poverty Project.

U.S. Bureau of the Census. (1982). *Census of the Population: 1980, Volume 1, Characteristics of the Population, Part 23, Massachusetts.* Washington, DC: U.S. Government Printing Office.

U.S. Bureau of the Census. (1991). *Census of Population and Housing, 1990: P.L. 94-171 Data File.* Washington, DC: U.S. Government Printing Office.

U.S. Bureau of the Census. (1992). *1990 Census of the Population and Housing.* Massachusetts Summary Tape File 1A. Washington, DC: Government Printing Office.

Glenn Jacobs

Latinos and Educational Reform: The Privatization of the Chelsea Public Schools

Over the past few years the premier case of privatization of a complete public school system in a worn-out industrial suburb of Boston has catapulted that city and its Latino community into metropolitan and national headlines.[1] Prior to the Boston University takeover of the public schools in 1989, Chelsea's Latino community was more a hapless supplicant to the powerful than a respected player in city politics. The coming of Boston University has stirred an apathetic, poor Latino population caught in the thickets of survival into a community striving for greater self-determination.

The city of Chelsea has the third highest percentage of households in the Commonwealth with an annual income below $10,000, and the highest percentage of residents living below the poverty line. Within this context, Latinos fare the worst, as we learn from the foreword of a recent survey sponsored by Chelsea's Commission on Hispanic Affairs:

> By almost every economic and social indicator, Chelsea Hispanics fare poorly — not only in relation to non-Hispanics, but also in comparison with Hispanics in Boston. On average, Chelsea Hispanics are poorer, are more likely to be employed in declining sectors of the economy, have higher rates of unemployment, are more likely to be employed part-time or only part of the year, have lower levels of formal education and have lower levels of facility in English. Furthermore, by most of these indicators, the gaps between Chelsea Hispanic women and other women are wider than the gaps between Hispanic men and other men (Kennedy and Stone, 1990, p. ii).

In addition to their depressed economic conditions, Chelsea's Latinos are a diverse population. According to the 1990 U.S. Census, approximately 9,000 Latinos (31 percent of a total population of 28,700) (Massachusetts Institute for Social and Economic Research, 1991, p. 28) live in Chelsea, but researchers using additional data have estimated the actual Latino population as upwards of 46 percent of the total population. Puerto Ricans constitute about one-half of the Chelsea Latino population, with the remaining portion consisting of a large

Central American admixture (El Salvadoreans, Guatemalans, Hondurans, and Costa Ricans), Colombians and other Caribbean Latinos.[2] Despite their poverty, their educational underpreparedness, their diversity and, in many respects, their political inactivity, segments of this population have been aroused to fight for their children's educational rights and to engage in other community issues.

The arrival of Boston University and the novel legal, political, social, and civic implications of educational privatization and resistance to these implications by Latinos in Chelsea are revitalizing the meaning of citizenship. Similar struggles by minorities and women worldwide are transforming the meaning of citizenship (Turner, 1986; 1990). As Katznelson and Weir (1985) and others (Fuentes, 1984, p. 127) observe, this transformation is no accident. Minority struggles over education are societally transformative: They have never succumbed to the historical split between the politics of residence and the politics of work in the United States. Denial of educational opportunity always represents a more global assault on the exclusion of minorities from *all* sectors of public life.

Chelsea's Latinos are passing through the three stages of educational struggle Clara Rodriguez identifies as (1) examination of the problem, (2) development of community agencies to address school difficulties, and (3) litigation (1989, pp. 139-140). The reverberations of this movement are broad, encompassing complex strategies on a range of community issues. As a result, the Latino population of Chelsea, which typifies other recently formed barrios in small- and middle-sized cities, is exhibiting civic and political behavior typical of older eastern Latino populations (Borges-Méndez, 1992; Baver, 1984; Uriarte-Gaston, 1987; Rodriguez, 1989, pp. 139-143; Jennings, 1984a; Jennings, 1984b). Conflict with Boston University has resulted in a change of the social organization — the transmutation of "patron-recipient" minority politics into autonomous, popular politics (Jennings, 1984b, p. 92). It is the acceleration of a pattern seen in older, more established minority communities and identified as "institution building" (King, 1986, pp. 23-26).

Privatization Comes to Chelsea

In a recent essay on the privatization of public services Al Bilik notes that, "privatization leads to a loss of control and a decline of citizen participation in government" (1990, pp. 7-8). He goes on to identify the Chelsea project as an example of the danger privatization schemes hold for democratic accountability:

When Boston University was negotiating to run the Chelsea School District in Massachusetts, the University, a private institution, demanded exemption from state laws requiring open meetings and public records.

The university also insisted that it could not be held liable for any lawsuits brought against the district.

Bilik insists that public administration is "integral to our system of checks and balances" and that privatization — relying on the motives of private gain — compromises democracy.

Thus when the Chelsea project was announced, the reservations of eminent educators gravitated toward issues around educational rights. Harold Howe, former U.S. Commissioner of Education under President Johnson, later a member of the governor's appointed State Oversight Panel for the Chelsea project, speaking about the delicate balancing of power in Boston University's relationship with the city said:

> That's a tricky business because the citizens of a community have a right to ask questions about the operations of their school system....If the school board contracts away their authority, that leaves citizens without recourse (Fulham, 1988, p. 34).

Similarly, Charles V. Willie of Harvard University noted that the undertaking:

> has serious implications for the concepts of self-determination and accountability which go to the heart of the development of public education in this country....Boston University as a private institution with a self-perpetuating board of trustees is simply not accountable to the citizens of Chelsea as a school board would be (Daniels, 1988).

These qualifications echo a theme intoned in thoughtful discussions of privatization. As the sociologist Paul Starr says, privatization can diminish "the sphere of public information, deliberation, and accountability — elements of democracy whose value is not reducible to efficiency" (1987, p. 132). Along these lines, lawsuits that would be filed by Chelsea's Commission on Hispanic Affairs and the Chelsea Teachers' Union in the spring of 1989 addressed in detail the issues of accountability, openness of meetings, legal susceptibility, and the University's record-keeping in connection with the Chelsea project (*Devlin v. School Committee*, 1988; *Fifty-One Hispanic Residents v. School Committee*, 1990). The Commission on Hispanic Affairs suit challenged the basic structure of the contractual agreement between the city and Boston University, contending that "important constitutional safeguards of public accountability and public control over public education had been abrogated." The Chelsea Teachers' Union suit contended that violation of the state constitution had occurred, to wit, that public money should not be used to subsidize any primary or secondary school not publicly owned or exclusively controlled by officers or public agents authorized by the Commonwealth or federal government.

When enabling legislation, exempting the new arrangement from the strictures of state law, was introduced under a cloud of cautionary criticism by the Massachusetts Department of Education, the governor created a blue ribbon committee to oversee the University's mandated consultation with community representatives for the ten-year duration of the contract.

The Chelsea project grew out of school committee member and publisher of the *Chelsea Record* Andrew Quigley's request (in 1985) to John Silber for Boston University to manage the Chelsea schools after Silber's offer had been refused by the city of Boston. The Management School commenced the project rather than the Education School, according to Dean George McGurn, because U.S. business was worried about "our global competitiveness and schools of education were part of the problem."[3] Moreover, Silber and McGurn desired "a broad spectrum on management's impact on society" (George McGurn, Interview, May 3, 1990). The University's criticism of the Chelsea schools in its report (1988) was an expected response to substandard educational conditions and reflected the Management School's and President Silber's business-oriented disdain of national and local educational conditions. The would-be caretakers saw the city, its school committee, and administrative complement as bereft of educational resources (Interviews with Dean George McGurn, May 3, 1990; Chris Allen, first Chelsea project manager, May 3, 1990; and Robert Sperber, member of management team and Silber advisor, April 27, 1990, May 11, 1990).

Fealty to this premise prompted Boston University's insistence on virtual absolute contractual authority. As Dean Peter Greer, School of Education, put it: "We were going to take all the risks. Why shouldn't we have full control?" (Interview, February 16, 1990). This statement is nearly identical to Dean McGurn's earlier pronouncement, "We want the control, the responsibility and the accountability, and that's what management is all about" (Fulham, 1988, p. 34). Presumably, wanting the accountability meant control of information and immunity from disclosure. In addition, McGurn, alluding to the pantheon of urban problems, observed that "Chelsea is on top of every list you don't want to be on" (Bering-Jensen, 1988, p. 15), and delivering a back-handed complement, exclaimed, "The brilliant thing about Chelsea...is they recognize failure when they see it, even if they're responsible" (Fulham, 1988, p. 34).

Taken with the small size of Chelsea, McGurn exclaimed, "It was so small you could wrap your arms around it. It was microcosmic. Frankly, if you were to take over the Boston system, who would ever know?" (Interview, May 3, 1990). Elsewhere, such paternalism waxed unfettered, when McGurn stated:

We have to remember that Boston University is larger than the population of Chelsea. We can't be like Lenny in John Steinbeck's *Of Mice and Men*, who breaks the neck of the puppy (Bering-Jensen, 1988, p. 17).

Clearly this was to be no "experiment," as it has often been characterized. The University president and all who have administered it intended the project to be a precedent-setting solution to the ills of urban education. "I hope to change the national view on education," Silber is quoted as saying (Radin, 1988, p. 2). The *Boston University Report* asserts: "Boston University is willing...to assume the authority and responsibility to assure that Chelsea's public schools become a national model of urban education...." (1988, pp. I-2). The goals of the project transcend education and are traceable to John Silber's vision of wider social reform conceived in the 1960s when his "Proposal for a Measure Attacking Poverty at Its Source" was entered in the *Congressional Record* (U.S. Congress, 1965, pp. 7352-7353). A program for preschool education, it contained the premise that "Children born into Negro families and families whose native language is other than English are not sufficiently stimulated verbally or are insufficiently trained in English to compete successfully in the public school whose programs are designed for English-speaking children" (Ibid, p. 7352). The proposal provided for education "of mothers of slum children," provision of schools in "renovated slum houses," tutoring, remedial summer schools, and, presciently, "a massive crash program in one or two communities of a moderate size" (Ibid, p. 7352). Glimmers of this paternalism surface occasionally, as when management team members Carole Greenes and Peter Greer underscore the effects of "the moral climate of a school...on learning," with one major agenda item of the Chelsea project being that "character formation will be stressed and civic virtue reaffirmed" (Greenes and Greer, 1989, p. 15). That civic virtue might be conceived differently by Latinos and other dissenters has been anathema to Boston University and speaks to the issue of why there is a complete absence of University-sponsored evaluation of the Chelsea project.[4]

As soon as they entered the fray, the Latinos found their legitimacy questioned. In the School Committee's deliberations over the impending contract in 1988, Latinos were largely absent from public hearings, but in early 1989 they turned out in force, contending that virtually no information had been disseminated to the Latino community in English or Spanish and that the Latino leadership was ignored by the School Committee, the Aldermen, the Mayor, and the PTA.

While the topic was aired in *The Chelsea Record* for some time, the newspaper's well-known antipathy to and stereotypic depiction of Latinos preempted their readership and promoted their civic apathy. Latinos only made headlines in the police report of the *Record*; otherwise there was virtually no reporting of events and achievements of Latino individuals and organizations (Neidthart, 1990). No outreach had been done by the city government because there was no felt need to do so. Thus the strong protest that appeared in March, 1989, after the placid hearings of July through November, 1988, came as a shock to Chelsea's Anglos. It was, indeed, as if it had come *ex nihilo*.

The meager showing of Latinos at school committee meetings and hearings prior to 1989 and their subsequent heavy turnouts to demand inclusion and time to consider the impending contract is, with a few exceptions, viewed by proponents of the contract as a forfeiture of the prerogative of Latinos to influence the course of the negotiations. Mayor Brennan, School Committee member, Andrew Quigley, Alderwoman Marilyn Portnoy, and Rosemarie Carlisle, president of the Parent Teachers Association (PTA), among others I have interviewed, feel that "they [Latinos] had their chance" and flubbed it by not taking enough interest and participating actively early in the debate when the time came for community input. On the Boston University side the Latino activists are characterized as obstructive impostors. The response of Rosemary Carlisle, formerly president of the PTA, Andrew Quigley's replacement on and re-elected member of the School Committee, is instructive. Asked if she thought that Latinos had been excluded from the process of installing the contract, she briskly replied:

Hispanics were never excluded — and I don't know where you got that information. They had all the rights as I did as a citizen of Chelsea to be active in the B.U. partnership .... I attended numerous open meetings, I went to the statehouse. I was aware of the contract and of the problems that were in the contract and I voiced my opinion. So the Latino community were never deleted from any of it as far as I'm concerned (Interview, April 10, 1989).

When I asked, "So why do you think they were so upset at the time?" she skirted the issue by saying they entered the process late:

Because they came in too late in the process. If they had come out when Boston University first came here a year and a half ago and kept on track on top [sic] of everything, they would have been able to voice their opinion like all of the other citizens. I have no idea why it took them so long to voice their opinions. They should have voiced them earlier like we [i.e., the rest of the community] did (Interview, April 10, 1989).

On the national scene Latinos "have not been passive recipients in the educational process" (Rodriguez, 1989, p. 139). The polarization in Chelsea over the presence of Boston University and the perception of Latinos' resistance to privatization as bald obstinacy or incompetence bespeak the tendency of political and social establishments to view Latino struggles as a "disinclination to assimilate" (Rodriguez, 1989, p. 139). If school reform proceeds top down, then assimilation will be its goal and resistance to it will be construed as a block to progress. If we conceive of school reform preferably as a bottom-up affair, or a negotiable one, then we may view the Latino struggle in Chelsea as a search for a solution instead of a problem (Rodriguez, 1989, p. 139).

What is/are the agenda(s) of the supporters of Boston University's "experiment?" Answering this question requires at least an allusion to the history of Chelsea's school system. Along with its municipal government, the contours of Chelsea's school system, originally designed to provide limited education for its first- and second-generation, immigrant, factory labor (including intensive English-as-a-second-language instruction), has not changed appreciably for better than a half century (Peterson, 1990).[5] By the 1970s urban "blight" (the depletion of its industry and more mobile white populations) had made inroads into all of Chelsea's public institutions, and by the mid-1980s the "boodle" had run out for Chelsea's patronage-driven city government.[6] The school system, originally designed to prepare a white, ethnic, working class for local industrial employment, in tandem with the other municipal institutions, appears to have been in crisis, but this "crisis" had been going on for more than a decade when in 1985 Boston University's president John Silber was asked to intervene.[7]

The real crisis was that of the white-dominated political machine and its voter base, which was threatened by a burgeoning Latino and Southeast Asian population. It may be more useful to call the crisis a "moral panic" wherein a cry for help was issued to Chelsea's new Great White Hope for gentrification and dilution of its minority population.[8] As Mayor John J. Brennan. Jr., explained in an interview (January 22, 1990):

> All of your middle-class, middle-aged people are going....There's no more children of the white middle-class. That's what I honestly see. I think with B.U. here and a new school that we hope to build, I believe then that we'll draw people in a financial bracket that can pay for a good home and not be able to pay for private schools.

Thus the halcyon dream of Chelsea's earlier white working class for middle-class respectability would now be vouchsafed in the post-industrial age. As for the growing minority populations, their invisibility was transformed into the blur of an advancing wave of color and culture that could only be stemmed by forceful intervention, in this case, in the school system. On the other hand, with renewed vigor, a larger population, and a new crop of young leaders, Chelsea Latinos found in the school question all of the material they needed to launch a revitalized organization and an electoral campaign destined to change the contours of Latino politics.

Marta Rosa, president of Chelsea's Commission on Hispanic Affairs and member of the Chelsea School Committee, recalls that 1988 and 1989 were watershed years for the Commission, for they mark a kind of "changing of the guard of the Latino leadership" (Interview, February 8, 1990). It was a time when people were ready for new leadership and more influence on civic affairs. Her recollection is that there were many veteran activists on the Commission:

> People who had been around a long time, had worked in the community with ... different organizations — LUCHA and Comité Latinoamericano (LACC), people who had given a lot already .... They wanted to be involved but were really burnt [out] at the time. A core group of those people, people like Ceferino [Rosa], Elma Richard, Pat Vega, stayed with the Commission...Aperícia Rodriguez .... These are people who had been working in the community for years .... When I was in high school these people were working. People were ready for something (Ibid).

As she says, Rosa herself had not been an activist long enough to be burnt out, so when she and others such as Juan Vega came along, new blood blended with the old and reinvigorated activism in the city.

The year 1989 also was important because of the confluence of events surrounding Chelsea's contract with Boston University and the Commission on Hispanic Affairs' alliance with Multicultural Education, Training, and Advocacy, Inc. (META), an organization that had achieved national recognition for its advocacy work with linguistic minorities. Rosa became acquainted with META through Felix Arroyo, a prominent Puerto Rican educational activist and later-to-be Boston School Committee member, who suggested a meeting with the Chelsea Teachers Union. At that meeting toward the end of January 1989, Rosa met Javier Colon, a lawyer from META, and several meetings ensued between the two organizations (Ibid).

As the Commission on Hispanic Affairs became allied with META, Boston University was getting help from the conservative New England Legal Foundation, which joined the legal battle presumably to determine the constitutional constraints of the case (Morrison, 1989). As the conflict grew more intense, the Commission found itself casting an eye toward elective office. To accomplish this the arousal of the Latino electorate was necessary. Voter registration would be required.

Voter registration added grit — toughness and tension — to the process of acquainting Latinos with their prospective representatives and themselves. It became an important agent of politicization in the community. Resistance to voter registration was high within and outside of the Latino orbit, but this resistance provided a current for change agents to work with: pushing it here, guiding it there, and navigating its currents to achieve greater empowerment.

Angel (Tito) Rosa (Marta's husband) organized the voter registration drive.

According to him, in the spring of 1989 Chelsea contained only 650 registered Latinos (Interview, January 18, 1990). "We had to figure out why these people did not want to register and why they didn't want to vote." Apathy, ignorance, timidity greeted him in the trenches. "I had to develop a strategy," Tito confesses. He had no prior political experience and found himself thrown back upon his own personal and cultural resources. He would knock on a door and ask, "Would you like to register?" The reply might be, "Why do I have to register; what do I get out of it?" Tito would reply, "It's your right to be a registered voter. How do they know you live here?" The reply might be "I pay the rent." "No!" says Angel, "If your name is not found on that census, you don't live here, my friend. You're invisible. How do they know José Gonzalez lives here?" By now, interest would be aroused and his interlocutor in disbelief would exclaim, "What do you mean?" "That's how it works," he might say. "It's not only to register for government, it's to show the city that you *occupy* a place in Chelsea!" By now, recovering composure, the person might parry, "So you are a politician and want my vote." Not to be undone, Tito would reply, "How many Hispanics are representing us in City Hall?" and the reply would be "None." "Do you like that?" Tito would ask. "Don't you think one of us could be up there?" And so it would go.

The registration drive was punctuated with incidents of racist resistance at City Hall including intimidating clerks and dematerializing registration cards where people who had been registered for fifteen years were unknowingly removed from lists. "We had a whole family living in Chelsea for twenty-eight years and voting every two years and their name was taken right out," Rosa reports. "No reason; we could never find out a reason!" People coming into City Hall who did not speak English would be intimidated by the clerks. The clerks would make an issue of listing political party affiliation, which for Anglos is of minor consequence, but for Puerto Ricans or Central Americans can be a life-threatening declaration. Advocates like Tito Rosa were reprimanded for coaching them.

Voter registration offers talented citizen-activists like Tito Rosa the opportunity to expand their own awareness of the issues and obstacles to political participation in the community. It brings activists and residents face-to-face with each other and city officials, and it fosters an important dialogue about citizenship among all concerned.

The election of Marta Rosa in 1989, among a slate of School Committee candidates cosponsored by the Chelsea Commission on Hispanic Affairs, the Chelsea Teachers Union, and its parent, the American Federation of Teachers, evidently represented a victory for a popular front against the long arm of privatization and white supremacy. It fits an emergent trend (Jennings, 1984b, pp. 80-81): the appearance of independent grassroots leaders. Lyn Meza, a veteran Chelsea activist who served as Marta Rosa's campaign manager in 1989 and 1991 elections, noted that the time was ripe for change: "The reason why I couldn't say no [to serving as Rosa's campaign manager] was that this was something that we had been waiting for, working for, hoping for years in this community — for responsible leadership to develop" (Interview, April 24, 1990).

While election of minority leaders is a source of strength and pride to these groups, it is a threat to established interests. In an article in *Education Week*, management team chair Peter Greer (May 16, 1990) complained about citizen groups in Chelsea who "see the university's presence as a grand opportunity to gain power — even at the expense of students" through a "vote counting back door." Marta Rosa had already been elected (November, 1989) and the reference to a "vote counting back door" implied that her election somehow was underhanded.

From the very beginning of the controversy concerning Boston University's entrance into the community, the University evinced stubborn resistance to community involvement in educational policy making. Indeed, the management team line has been tenaciously held, including insistence on the purely advisory power of the Chelsea Executive Advisory Committee (CEAC). In the spring of 1990, CEAC's chair was reprimanded for speaking out on *any* policy issue, including support for bilingual education.

The management team has insisted from the outset that the community was wasting its time demanding inclusion instead of allowing the team to carry on its business. During the contract dispute of spring 1989, the Chelsea's Commission on Hispanic Affairs and META attempted to carry on negotiations with Boston University on bilingual education, parent participation, and other matters. The University would relay signals of willingness to talk and then balk. Finally in April 1989 the management team issued a memorandum saying that "The University is unable to make agreements on behalf of the Chelsea school department until the University is officially managing the Chelsea schools on behalf of the Chelsea School Committee (Management Team, 1989)." The University never again showed willingness to negotiate with the community.

Thereafter the University intoned a "troublemaker" theme, casting the Latino leadership as obstructionist. At the height of debate over the contract, an *Education Week* article quoted Greer as saying, "The Hispanic community happened to gear up at an untimely moment — the very moment when the agreement was about to be signed" (Snider, 1989). While Greer thought that it was "really healthy" that Latinos were forming to fight for education, he preferred "to see them expend their energies on implementing the project rather than trying to hold it up." Only one month earlier Boston University's President Silber accused the discontented Latinos of being manipulated by the Chelsea Teachers Union, implying they lacked the autonomy and judgement to act on their own (Sleeper, 1989). The Latinos protested Silber's comments as demeaning (*Boston Globe*, April 2, 1989).

Almost a year later the accusation of obstructiveness and opportunism would be levelled again, this time in response to Chelsea activist Tito Meza's charge that Silber was making premature and false claims about the project's success in his gubernatorial campaign propaganda and that the project was an exercise in government by secrecy. A diatribe from Greer, in the Boston University student *Daily Free Press*, asserted that, "I don't really take that criticism seriously .... The Hispanic leaders are just trying to get more power, and I think it is totally unfair to use John Silber as a means to gain power" (Benson, 1990). Moreover, claiming color blindness, Greer asserted, "Our view is that students are students, not Hispanics, whites, or blacks." He criticized the Latino leaders for wanting a majority of members on the Chelsea Executive Advisory Committee (CEAC) "because the council is supposed to represent all of the groups in Chelsea...not just the Hispanics." Therefore, "Instead of fighting, we decided to work with the people through other groups and simply bypass the leaders."

I have suggested that Boston University employs a "revolving door" strategy of community relations, typifying the manner in which dominant power holders seek to manipulate minority group organizations (Jacobs, 1990). When minority leaders do not fall into line with majority group strategies, the former are discredited as not being truly representative of their constituencies. Majority leaders and caretakers then threaten to work around these "false" leaders, that is, to work with the "true" community.

Members of the Boston University team are chagrined at the resistance put up by Latino community representatives; when they cannot keep the representatives in line, they strive to discredit them and support other leaders they considers more worthy. In 1991 the management team strove to insinuate themselves into the Latino community by offering blandishments to El Centro Hispano and frequently alluded to their harmonious relations with El Centro when the issue of the team's poor record of community relations was publicly raised. El Centro's current director, José Fernandez, has been trying to navigate an autonomous course for the organization and has assiduously steered it away from the shoals of internecine conflict while resisting the seductions of the University to render material aid and other support.

The University's aggrandizement of power obviates the pursuit of an enlightened community relations policy. An example of this is its hiring of a Latino superintendent of the Chelsea schools, Diana Lam, which was intended to score points with the Latino population. Lam needed all the courage and risk taking she proffered for the job because she was not welcomed with open arms by Chelsea's Latinos. Claiming to run an open superintendency, she acquired a reputation for stubbornness and resistance to unsolicited community input that marked her as a Boston University functionary. At the end of January, 1990, intending to forge a consensus, Lam convened a meeting with the Latino leadership. However, she became evasive and defensive at the leaders' insistence that she respect their grievances with the University, with the result that the boundaries remained drawn as before. A disappointed Lam lamented, "'It looks like what we're going to get out of this meeting is another meeting'" (Fieldnotes, January 24, 1990; January 25, 1990). Having already been reprimanded by Boston University vice president Westling for her admiration of Nelson Mandela, Diana Lam's position, no matter how competent and feisty she seemed, was structurally compromised (Belser, 1990; Robbins, 1990). She was, after all, the University's employee and throughout her stay, until the spring of 1991 when she declared her ill-fated candidacy for the mayoralty of Boston, walked a tightrope (Schattle, 1990).

Having completed the third year of its management of the Chelsea public schools, the University's stance toward the Latino community has not changed. At a talk given at a National Education Association Higher Education Conference (1991) during the second year, Marta Rosa characterized Boston University's management of Chelsea's schools as an "arranged marriage." Others, suggesting that "the proper role of a major university would be to offer to direct its resources...in an open accountable manner," have called it a "leveraged buyout" (Fine, 1989). The residents of Chelsea feel "taken over." Rosa asserted, "My greatest criticism of the project is that there is a lack of understanding on the part of B.U. of the culture of the community." She reported that her constituents feel ignored, frustrated, and apprehensive and are confused over the roles of parents in the project. Criticizing the management team's eagerness to score public relations points in the name of hastily conceived programs, she asked, "Is this so-called partnership empowering the community? Is it addressing the causes of the downfall of public education in urban communities?" (Rosa, 1991).

In answering these questions, the literature on educational partnerships is instructive. Those partnerships between universities and school systems that work best eschew corporate models, hierarchical and elitist arrangements, and favor participational/egalitarian ones (Goodlad, 1987, p. 1; McGowan and Powell, 1990). A recent appraisal of university-public school partnerships, categorizing these arrangements into three models (university control, allied elite and participational), fits the Chelsea project into the first — university control — and concludes, after examining this conflict-ridden arrangement, that "While we vigorously applaud Boston University's vision, boldness, and comprehensiveness, we have several concerns about the appropriateness and feasibility of the Chelsea project — especially as a model for other universities to emulate" (Harkavy and Puckett, 1990, p. 12). Their concerns "are directed primarily toward the *style* of the reform — the structuring of roles and relationships of the Chelsea project," which in the context of a "privatized ... urban school district ... is expert-driven, unidimensional, and only marginally participatory." Finally,

There is persuasive documentary evidence...that the University has exacerbated the tensions that would normally be expected in the kind of change proposed for Chelsea. Rather than build alliances with teachers, administrators, and parents, Boston University officials have ignored the concerns of these groups at critical junctures, eschewed their participation in significant planning and decision-making, imposed the University's agenda as a set of non-negotiable demands, and reacted indignantly to criticism from these quarters (Harkavy and Puckett, 1990, p. 13).

Privatization Is Not Partnership

It has been suggested that school reform might be a proxy for societal reform. The recurrence of educational reform often reflects "economic instability, shifts in population, and social change [which] uncover[s] tensions." Media and other groups "translate the unrest into recommended policies for schools to enact" (Cuban, 1990, p. 9). Social concerns "overflow" during times of economic and social crisis into the most vulnerable institutions capable of eliciting the *appearance* of change — schools. No matter that educational institutions cannot by themselves solve or resolve social, political, and economic problems; these socializing institutions become the screens for our projected fantasies of how we would like to have grown up and for how we wish society to work — mock societal reform.

On the other hand, when minorities and the poor struggle in the educational arena for their communities' educational rights, reform holds real promise because the struggle for schooling is central to bringing minorities together "as a group with particular political demands and a distinct history of political practice centered around education issues" (Katznelson and Weir, 1985, p. 190). In Chelsea, educational privatization catalyzed a community struggle whose educational horizons transcend the narrow and self-serving designs of the privatizers.

It is tempting to merely portray Boston University as a villain, but it is more fruitful to understand events in Chelsea as a struggle against privatization. In impugning the legitimacy of the Chelsea Commission on Hispanic Affairs and in casting aspersions on the political purity of Marta Rosa's election, the management team is enacting an erstwhile scenario of privatization: discrediting the public sphere (Starr, 1990, pp. 43-44) and substituting, i.e., inverting, the inviolability of one realm (the public) by another — the private. In this case, it is the *public forum as well as public service that is discredited.*

The University's strategy may be summarized as follows: (1) to maintain primacy in public opinion and mass communications by privatizing public opinion, i.e., pressuring dissenters to keep their opinions to themselves; (2) to ideologically redefine the standards of proper conduct of individuals and groups, i.e., to redefine civic roles in Chelsea; (3) to seek political advantage in the local and national arenas for the University's dominance and for Silber's designs on public office; and (4) to blur the boundaries between the public and the private realms in order to serve the University's private interests.

Some of Boston University's tactics look like sophomoric debating team maneuvers, but with its considerable resources and sizable public relations machinery, it has controlled the public image of the project. In attempting to shift the center of gravity for the standard of appropriate individual and group behavior from the public forum to the private sphere, the University pretends to decide when, where, and how discourse on public issues shall be framed. Yet, the University's attempts to vitiate Latino community empowerment have had the opposite effect, boosting morale and increasing animosity toward its attempts at defining participational legitimacy in Chelsea. The challenge to Chelsea's Latinos is to maintain the momentum in their efforts to secure self-determination while contending with a myriad of political, economic, and social forces sweeping through their neighborhoods. The Chelsea experience contains apt lessons for other Latino communities and may, indeed, provide leads for resistance to the even more massive assaults on the public weal lying in store for our society.

Notes

The author would like to acknowledge the following for their aid in facilitating this research: Marta Rosa, Tito Rosa, Don Menzies, Susan Clark, Juan Vega, Lyn Meza, Elizabeth McBridge, Kathy Kratz, and Gwendolyn Tyre.

1. The data used in this paper were collected over the past two years, commencing January 1991. The author's participant observation in Chelsea includes community organizations, civic groups, and public meetings (school committee, management team, state oversight panel, etc.). About 90 interviews have been completed. A large amount of documentary materials, including municipal documents, reports and proceedings, materials from voluntary associations, personal papers, and records, have been gathered, and voluminous newspaper files have been assembled. The work herein reported draws on a sizeable subset of this data pertinent to the Latino community.

2. Extrapolating from the Saint Rose Parish (now estimated to contain 88 percent of the total city population, including 51 percent of the city's total Latino population) survey of 1989, the University of Massachusetts research group estimates the Latino population to constitute between 42 percent and 46 percent of the population (Kennedy and Stone, 1990, pp. 1, 5-8). As to the size of the undocumented population, some say it ranges upwards of 50 percent (i.e., approximately 4,300) of the total Latino population (Sokol, 1990, p. 4).

3. According to Dean McGurn (Interview, May 3, 1990), when the University was invited to talk to the Chelsea School Committee, he and Silber "were not Johnny-Come-Latelies. We talked about the underclass," implying they were willing to face facts and to take action.

4. Peter Greer's reply to Fine's charges that "little has been made public about who

will evaluate the project" is instructive (Greer, March 9, 1990). He attempts to create the impression that there was near unanimous support for the project and bends Fine's question regarding evaluation into an issue of popularity. During the controversial preliminary period of approval for the contract, Greer said that the need to hire an outside evaluator for the project was critical (Cohen, 1989). The University has never sponsored evaluation from within or outside of the Chelsea project.

The State Oversight Panel has underscored the need for evaluation. For example, at the panel meeting/hearing in Chelsea on December 12, 1990, after the management team made their presentation, panel member John T. Dunlop commented: "Someday down the road somebody in the state or federal government is going to write this story. Was it good, or how good? And I regret to say, whether you like it or not, putting together a set of numbers is going to be a large part of the story. There ought to be one or two people developing *indices* on a time series basis....One of these days somebody's going to want to look back and measure the change. I would feel more comfortable if somebody was devoting some time to that. I know one or two people in your establishment who are competent to do that" (Field notes, December 10, 1990). Lam excused the lack of such data on technical grounds because there has been no computerization of records prior to the coming of Boston University (Field notes, December 10, 1990).

The absence of an evaluation component on the project has had a deleterious effect. An example of this effect is the Early Learning Center, the crown jewel of the project, which contained problems ranging from poor supervision to lack of a curriculum to overcrowding. Asked by a reporter by what means the operations of the center were evaluated, Silber, who touted the center extensively during his campaign for governor, replied: "By just going in there and watching those children" (Keller, 1991).

5. For a perceptive detailed analysis of the Chelsea schools, see Peterson (1990). For an ethnohistorical study comparing recent educational and earlier educational policies in Chelsea, see Montero-Sieburth and Peterson (1991). And for analysis placing Chelsea education institutions and the Boston University Chelsea project in social context, see Jacobs (1991).

6. For example, in 1985 the state had to bail Chelsea out of financial distress with a $5 million "cherry sheet" loan, safeguarded with the creation of a financial control board whose powers were basically limited to oversight. More recently, with impending receivership, expansion of this board has been considered in addition to other measures.

7. James O'Connor's little known but useful volume, *The Meaning of Crisis*, makes the point that the word "crisis" is ideological when it is "inappropriately substituted for...social movements seeking forms of self-management and democracy," that is when it is used as a ploy to facilitate "restructuring" (1987, p. 125). Used in this way "it legitimates demands by capital and state for the top-down reorganization of the economy, political system and state, and social life." Privatization has come upon us at such a time of "crisis."

8. Similar ground is covered by the evaluation of the State Oversight Panel in its report on the project's first year, which underscored the need for the University to improve its community relations, abjured the management team's "arrogant" manner in dealing with minority parents and the team's advisory committee, and emphasized the need to "create an atmosphere of inclusion for community groups and others in school policy decision making" (Chelsea Oversight Panel, 1990, p. 2). Boston University's reply to the report contends that the panel's criticisms overstep the boundaries of the legal contract,

i.e., "the Panel has no mandate to redo the agreement between the school committee and the University" (November 20, 1990). Technically correct, this argument holds serious implications for the privatization of government services.

References

Baver, S. (1984). Puerto Rican Politics in New York City: The Post-World War Two Period. In J. Jennings and M. Rivera (Eds.), *Puerto Rican Politics in Urban America*, pp. 43-59. Westport, CT: Greenwood Press.

Belser, A. (1990, February 2). Mandela Reference Causes Lam-Westling Disagreement. *Chelsea Record.*

Beltran, X., Roriguez, M., Straussman, J., and Zweig, E. (1976). *A View from Under the Bridge: A Plan for Hispanics in Chelsea.* Chelsea, MA: Care About Now, Inc.

Benson, A. (1990, January 19). Chelsea Committee Blasts BU's Treatment of Hispanics. *The Daily Free Press*, p. 1.

Bering-Jensen, H. (1988, August 15). A Last-Ditch School Remedy Gets a Go-Ahead Near Boston. *Insight*, 14-17.

Bilik, A. (1990, Spring). Privatization: Selling America to the Lowest Bidder. *Labor Research Review, 9*, 1-13.

Borges-Méndez, R. (1992). Migration, Social Networks, and the Regionalization of Puerto Rican Settlement Patterns: Barrio Formation in Lowell, Lawrence, Holyoke, Massachusetts. Paper presented at Conference on Puerto Rican Poverty and Migration, May 1, 1992, New School for Social Research.

Boston University. (1988). *Boston University's Report on the Chelsea Public Schools: A Model For Excellence in Urban Education.* Boston, MA: Boston University.

Chelsea Oversight Panel. (1990, November 20). *Report on the First Year of Implementation of the Chelsea School Committee-Boston University Agreement 1989-1990.* Chelsea: Author.

Cohen, M. (1989, August 13). While Pupils Play, BU Plans for Chelsea Schools. *Boston Globe*, Metro/Region.

Cuban, L. (1990, January). Reforming Again, Again, and Again. *Educational Researcher, 19*, 3-13.

Daniels, L. A. (1988, August 10). Doubts Abound on Boston U. Plan to Run Schools. *New York Times,* Education.

Devlin v. School Committe City of Chelsea. (1988). Civil Action 88-6634-D. Superior Court, Suffolk County, Massachusetts.

Dumont, M. P. (1989, September). An Unfolding Memoir of Community Mental Health. *Readings: A Journal of Reviews and Commentary in Mental Health, 4*, 4-7.

Fifty-One Hispanic Residents of Chelsea v. School Committee City of Chelsea. (1990). Civil Action 90-7273-D. Superior Court, Suffolk County, Massachusetts.

Fine, B. J. (1989, November). BU 'Takeover' of Chelsea Schools. *Science, 246*, 984.

Fuentes, L. (1984). Puerto Ricans and New York City School Board Elections: Apathy or Obstructionism? In J. Jennings and M. Rivera (Eds.), *Puerto Rican Politics in Urban America*, pp. 127-137. Westport, CT: Greenwood Press.

Fulham, D. (1988, July 31). BU-Chelsea School Plan Criticized: Specialists Cite Loss of Local Control as One Potential Problem for City. *Boston Globe*, section 2.

Goodlad, J. I. (1987). Linking Schools and Universities: Symbiotic Partnerships. Occasional Paper No. 1. Center for Educational Renewal, College of Education, University of Washington, Seattle, WA.

Greenes, C., and Greer, P. (1989, July-August). A Private Approach to Public Schools. *Philanthropy*, 14-15.

Greer, P. R. (1990, March 9). Boston University/Chelsea Project. *Science 247*, 1167.

Greer, P. (1990, May 16). Boston University and Chelsea: First Lessons. *Education Week, 32*, 24.

Harkavy, I., and Puckett, J. L. (1990). *Toward Effective University-Public School Partnerships: An Analysis of Three Contemporary Models*. Unpublished manuscript.

Harrison, B., and Bluestone, B. (1988). *The Great U-Turn: Corporate Restructuring and the Polarizing of America*. New York: Basic Books.

Jacobs, G. (1990, November). Education or Manipulation? What Boston University Needs to Learn about Community Relations. *El Faro*, 4-7.

Jennings, J. (1984a). The Emergence of Puerto Rican Electoral Activism in Urban America. In J. Jennings and M. Rivera (Eds.), *Puerto Rican Politics in Urban America*, pp. 3-12. Westport, CT: Greenwood Press.

Jennings, J. (1984b). Puerto Rican Politics in Two Cities: New York and Boston. In J. Jennings and M. Rivera (Eds.), *Puerto Rican Politics in Urban America*, pp. 75-98. Westport, CT: Greenwood Press.

Jennings, J. (1984c). Puerto Rican Politics in Urban America — Toward Progressive Electoral Activism. In J. Jennings and M. Rivera (Eds.), *Puerto Rican Politics in Urban America*, pp. 139-143. Westport, CT: Greenwood Press.

Katznelson, I., and Weir, M. (1985). *Schooling for All: Class, Race, and the Decline of the Democratic Ideal*. New York: Basic Books.

Keller, J. (1991, August 16-22). Child-Care Hype: Internal Turmoil Slows Down BU's Chelsea Program. *Boston Phoenix*, 16-17.

Kennedy, M. and Stone, M. (1990). *The Hispanics of Chelsea: Who Are They?* Boston, MA: Center for Community Planning, College of Public and Community Service, University of Massachusetts.

King, M. (1986). Three Stages of Black Politics in Boston, 1950-1980. In J. Jennings and M. King (Eds.), *From Access to Power*. Cambridge, MA: Schenkman.

Lee, A. M. (1970). On Context and Relevance. In G. Jacobs (Ed.), *The Participant Observer: Encounters with Social Reality*, pp. 3-16. New York: George Braziller.

Lucas, I. (1984). Puerto Rican Politics in Chicago. In J. Jennings and M. Rivera (Eds.), *Puerto Rican Politics in Urban America*, pp. 99-113. Westport, CT: Greenwood Press.

McGowan, T., and Powell, J. (1990, Spring). Understanding School-University Collaboration through New Educational Metaphors. *Contemporary Education, 61*, 112-118.

Merced, N. (1989). *The Hispanic Community of Chelsea: Discussion On Its Organization Direction*. Brookline, MA: Levine Associates.

Montero-Sieburth, M., and LaCelle-Peterson, M. (1991). Linking Critical Pedagogy to Bilingual Education: An Ethno-Historical Study Contextualizing School Policies in an Urban Community. In *Critical Perspectives on Bilingual Education Research*. Tempe, AZ: Bilingual Review Press, Hispanic Research Center.

Morrison, C. (1989, April). Foundation Lawyer Fights for School Takeover. *Lawyers Monthly*.

Neidhardt, F. S. (1990). *Chelsea's Hispanic Community: How Is It Served by the Local Print Media?* Boston, MA: Center for Community Planning, College of Public and Community Service, University of Massachusetts.

O'Connor, J. (1987). *The Meaning of Crisis: A Theoretical Introduction.* Oxford: Basil Blackwell.

Peterson, M. L. (1990). *School Policies and Immigrant Incorporation: An Historical Case Study from Chelsea, Massachusetts.* Unpublished manuscript.

Portes, A. (1990). *Immigrant America: A Portrait.* Berkeley, CA: University of California Press.

Radin, C. A. (1988, August 17). Silber Plan Takes Aim at Poverty. *Boston Globe, 1.*

Rivera, M. (1984). Organizational Politics of the East Harlem Barrio in the 1970s. In J. Jennings and M. Rivera (Eds.), *Puerto Rican Politics in Urban America*, pp. 61-72. Westport, CT: Greenwood Press.

Robbins, D. (1990, February 22). Dispute Over Mandela Creates a Stir in Chelsea. *Weekly News*, p. 1, 3.

Rodriguez, C. (1989). *Puerto Ricans: Born in the U.S.A.* Boston, MA: Unwin Hyman.

Rosa, C. (1984). Written Testimony to the Massachusetts Commission on Hispanic Affairs, June 21, 1984, Boston, MA.

Rosa, M. (1991, March 2). The Boston University/Chelsea Project: A Community's Response to Change. Talk given at National Education Association Higher Education Conference.

Schattle, H. (1990, March 1). Acting BU President Backs Away from His Remarks about Mandela. *Boston Globe.*

Sleeper, P. B. (1989, March 31). Silber Hits Union Foes of Chelsea School Takeover. *Boston Globe.*

Snider, W. (1989, April 5). Management Plan for Chelsea Schools Is Approved. *Education Week, 5.*

Sokol, N. (1990). *Undocumented Hispanic Immigrants in Chelsea.* Boston, MA: Center for Community Planning, College of Public and Community Service, University of Massachusetts.

Starr, P. (1987). The Limits of Privatization. In S. H. Hanke (Ed.), *Prospects For Privatization*, pp. 124-137. New York: Academy of Political Science.

Turner, B. S. (1986). *Citizenship and Capitalism: The Debate Over Reformism.* London: Allen and Unwin.

Turner, B. S. (1990, May). Outline of the Theory of Citizenship. *Sociology 24*, 189-217.

Uriarte-Gaston, M. (1987). *Organizing for Survival: The Emergence of a Puerto Rican Community.* Doctoral dissertation, Boston University, Boston, MA.

U.S. Congress. (1965, April 9). Senator Ralph Yarborough Entering John Silber's Proposal for a Measure Attacking Poverty at Its Source into the Congressional Record. *Congressional Record*, 7352-73553.

James Jennings

Latino Experiences in Vocational Technical Education: Implications for Educational Policy and Reform in Massachusetts

As the Commonwealth of Massachusetts enters the twenty-first century it is encountering major social, economic, and demographic transformations. The demographic transformation is witnessed in the rapid growth of communities of color at a statewide level and in some cities and towns of Massachusetts. As Latinos, blacks, and Asian-descent people continue to grow in numbers the economy of the Commonwealth must be able to provide opportunities for their social mobility, but this will not occur if these groups do not have the necessary education and training to respond to the economic needs of Massachusetts.

The educational and employment status of young Latinos in many of the larger American cities, including those in Massachusetts, suggests that significant numbers of this group are not being equipped with the necessary job-related skills to realize meaningful socioeconomic mobility as they grow older. Many social scientists, educators, and demographers have discussed the potential social, economic, and perhaps even the political crisis that this situation presents for all Americans.

Due to rapid impoverization and growth in the number of Latinos, it is especially critical for the social and economic well-being of the Commonwealth of Massachusetts that this group be provided with quality education. As stated in a report by Jobs for the Future, an increasing number of public policy analysts, civic leaders, and governmental officials are now insisting that effective strategies for economic development must reflect "genuine linkages between social deficiencies (poor education, family instability, poverty) and deficiencies in economic competitiveness" (Jobs for the Future, 1991, p. 2). Providing and guaranteeing educational opportunity for citizens of color can be one effective tool for economic development.

The fact that Latinos in vocational technical education generally have a lower high school dropout rate than Latinos in academic programs has started to motivate interest in expanding access for Latinos in vocational technical education (Alston, 1991). For example, the National Center for Research in Vocational Technical Education cites as "an exemplary program" a vocational technical education program to discourage bilingual students from dropping out of the Cambridge Rindge and Latin High School. The effort at this school has been effective as evidenced by a major decline in the dropout rate of Latinos enrolled in the Rindge Technical Vocational Program. In addition to its positive impact in terms of dropout rates, vocational technical education can be an effective way to equip Latino youth with the training and skills necessary to acquire jobs that pay relatively high and stable wages. Despite precipitous downturns and fluctuations in the economy of Massachusetts, there will still be a need for an increasing number of workers with appropriate training and skills to work in the construction, health, and manufacturing sectors.

There is another important reason for examining the status of young Latinos in vocational technical education in Massachusetts. New federal regulations now require states to examine and document the extent of access to vocational technical education for "special" or disadvantaged populations. The Carl D. Perkins Vocational and Applied Technology Education Act of 1990 was signed into law on September 28, 1990. This act calls for an expansion of efforts to reach "special populations including the poor, the handicapped, economically disadvantaged, disabled, single parents, foster children, women and the limited English proficient" populations (Coyle-Williams, 1991). As reported by the Center for Law and Education in Washington, DC, states must assess and develop plans to address the "capability and responsiveness of programs to meet the needs of special populations for access to, and services in, vocational technical education, including students who are: disabled, limited English proficient, in programs designed to eliminate sex bias, or in correctional institutions" (Center for Law and Education, 1991).

A first step in developing an understanding of how Latinos might better utilize the system of vocational technical education in Massachusetts is the generation of a status report on this topic. Such a first step should give some indication of the status of information regarding the experiences of Latinos in Massachusetts vocational technical education. Furthermore, it should begin to identify the sources and strengths or weaknesses of the available data for assessing Latino participation patterns in the state's vocational technical education system. A preliminary study should also begin to identify methods to overcome obstacles that prevent greater participation on the part of Latinos in vocational technical education in Massachusetts. The information and conclusions offered in this chapter give some indication of the policy issues that we must raise and resolve in order to encourage a greater participation of Latinos in vocational technical education.

Methodology

A thorough study of Latino experiences in vocational technical education in Massachusetts, as well as a content analysis of the available and germane literature, has not yet been produced. This chapter begins to respond to this need by reviewing the reported participation rates and status of Latinos in vocational technical education programs approved by the Massachusetts Board of Education. These approved programs are referred to as Chapter 74 programs.[1]

This study is restricted to persons in grades nine through twelve during the school year 1990 to 1991. There are two reasons for this restriction. The first is that the framework for this research, in terms of time and scope, is limited. The second reason is that the Latino presence as officially reported in postsecondary vocational technical education programs is minuscule and reflects a major decline in Latino participation from their participation rates in vocational technical education programs in grades nine through twelve. The findings in this study are based on data provided by the Division of Occupational Education, Massachusetts Department of Education; the data have been aggregated and organized in several tables.

Since information was collected for only one year (1990-91), the status reported for Latinos represents only a snapshot of the actual situation. The purpose of this snapshot is not to make definitive conclusions regarding the status of Latinos in vocational technical education, but rather to raise questions and point to the kind of research that we need in Massachusetts regarding this topic. Hopefully the snapshot provided here suggests the general framework that is necessary for more extensive and expanded studies of the experiences of Latinos and other people of color in vocational technical education.

In addition to an examination of data for the 1990-91 school year, the investigators of this inquiry relied on a panel of 15 interviewees[2] familiar with various aspects of public schooling and vocational technical education. The members of this panel were interviewed regarding their understanding of Latino experiences in the state's vocational technical education system. These individuals are directly or indirectly familiar with various aspects of the policies and delivery systems of vocational technical education in Massachusetts.

The interviewees were asked about possible sources of information regarding Latino participation in vocational technical education and to provide information about what they perceive as major obstacles to greater participation in vocational technical education on the part of Latinos. Interviewees provided some information about the following open-ended queries:

How can the status of Latinos in vocational technical education in Massachusetts be generally characterized or described?

What are major obstacles to greater participation on the part of young Latinos in vocational technical education in Massachusetts?

Has vocational technical education worked effectively for Latinos in terms of preparation for occupations and jobs?

What works to involve and attract Latinos into vocational technical education programs?

What are some of the similarities and differences between the experiences of blacks and Latinos in vocational technical education in Massachusetts?

Findings

Table 1 shows the total reported number of students enrolled in vocational technical education in Massachusetts during school year 1990-91 in grades nine through twelve, by race and ethnicity. As this table illustrates, Latinos comprised 8.4 percent of all enrollees in approved Chapter 74 vocational technical education programs. This figure is significantly higher than the statewide proportion of black students (5.9 percent) in vocational technical education programs. This is an interesting finding in that it indicates that, at least for the 1990-91 school year, Latinos are the largest minority group in Massachusetts vocational technical education.

Another related finding is that a higher proportion of Latino students are enrolled in vocational technical education programs compared to academic or general programs in Massachusetts public schools. For example, in the 1990-91 school year, 8.4 percent of all students in grades nine through twelve enrolled in vocational technical education programs were Latino, but only 6.8 percent of all students in these same grade levels who were enrolled in academic or general programs in public schools were Latino.

Nationally, there are more Latino and black students enrolled in vocational technical education programs than in academic programs. According to the Center for Educational Statistics, 51.5 percent of all Latino high school students were enrolled in vocational technical education programs in 1987 and 30.5 percent were enrolled in academic programs; the remainder were found in programs of general study. For black high school students, the enrollment figures were 51 percent in vocational technical education programs and 34.5 percent in academic programs. But only 37.4 percent of all white high school students across the nation were enrolled in vocational technical education programs, while 45.1 percent were enrolled in academic programs in 1987 (O'Malley, 1987, p. 73). These numbers further substantiate the important role of vocational technical education in addressing the educational needs of these groups.

Latino students enrolled in vocational technical education programs in public school systems in Massachusetts are concentrated in ten of the largest school systems (see Table 2). The total number of Latino students attending these ten school systems is 906. This represents 30.8 percent of all Latino students in vocational technical education programs throughout the state in grades nine through twelve.

A majority of all Latino enrollment for 1990-91 is found in 22 vocational high schools throughout the Commonwealth as illustrated in table 3. Altogether these 22 vocational technical education high schools enrolled 1,596 Latino students or more than half (54.4 percent) of all Latinos enrolled in vocational technical education throughout the state. These same schools enrolled a total of 19,296 white students or nearly 66 percent (65.9 percent) of all white students enrolled in vocational technical education schools in Massachusetts.

The largest vocational technical education program in terms of white enrollment in 1990-91, discounting Chapter 74 Exploratory, is carpentry followed by electrical (see table 4). This is different for Latinos; auto mechanics is the largest enrolled program for this group, followed by electronic technology. The two largest enrolled programs for blacks are food management and cosmetology. It is important to find out how and why young people individually decide to pursue a vocational technical education career; but, it is also important to know if various career tracks are, in effect, chosen for particular groups. A few interviewees expressed a concern, for example, that students of color are referred or tracked into the lower-skilled curriculum paths.

What actually motivates or steers Latino and black students to opt for career tracks that are different than those selected by white students? This kind of information could assist educators in developing strategies to encourage youth of color to seek out those occupations and careers currently not reflecting diversity or that have been traditionally inaccessible to underenrolled students.

There are some program areas in vocational technical education where black enrollment is more similar to white rather than Latino enrollment. In computer programming Latino students had a higher enrollment in percentage terms (4.1 percent) than either blacks (2.3 percent) or whites (2.1 percent). But the black student enrollment in community health work was insignificant at less than 1 percent (0.08), while the Latino enrollment (2.2 percent) was similar to the white enrollment (2.5 percent).

Several vocational technical education programs have a relatively high proportion of Latino students. Some of these programs, however, are small in total size and have less than 50 Latino students enrolled. Table 5 shows, for instance, that the heavy equipment, maintenance and repair program has a small statewide enrollment. The 36 Latino students enrolled in this program comprise almost two-thirds (63.6 percent) of all students enrolled. More than half (53.5 percent) of all students in radio and T.V. repair are Latino. This program enrolls 38 Latino students statewide.

The Latino enrollment in postsecondary and postgraduate vocational technical education programs is greater than black enrollment, but the proportion of total students is very small for both groups. Latino students comprise nearly 4 percent (3.9) of all enrollment in postsecondary and postgraduate vocational technical education programs, while black students represent less than 3 percent (2.7) of the total enrollment. Thus, there are no major differences in the number of enrolled blacks and Latinos in postsecondary and postgraduate vocational technical education.

The very few Latino and black students who are enrolled in postsecondary and postgraduate vocational technical education programs are concentrated in two areas. For instance, there are 12 black students in the practical nursing program out of a total black enrollment of 27. Similarly, in the statewide pool of 49 Latinos, 12 are enrolled in electrical technology and 11 are in practical nursing.

One factor influencing the enrollment levels of Latino students in postsecondary and postgraduate vocational technical education programs may be the completion rates for this group in secondary programs. If a certain level of Latino students do not successfully complete the secondary programs, this could reduce the pool of potential Latino candidates for postsecondary and postgraduate vocational technical education. It is, however, difficult to determine or assess the completion rates of Latino students at this time. The reason for this is that the Division of Occupational Education does not currently report enrollment by grade level in the secondary vocational technical education programs. For instance, although total enrollment for a particular program is available, the actual number of twelfth graders cannot be determined since information about this kind of grade breakdown is not collected.[3] Furthermore, some vocational technical education programs are open for entry at any grade, thus some twelfth graders may not have received four full years of vocational technical education.

Recommendations

One major finding of this study is that a large number of Latino students are already enrolled in various kinds of vocational technical education programs and schools; therefore, this topic should be receiving as much attention from the educational and policy community as the status of Latinos in nonvocational education public schools and programs. Another finding is that the state of information, data, and analysis regarding the recruitment, participation, persistence, and success of Latino students in vocational technical education programs is lacking in many ways; furthermore, it now must be prioritized by the Commonwealth of Massachusetts. Very little is known about Latino students' experiences in vocational technical education at the statewide, local, school, or individual program levels; yet, as stated earlier, this group can play a critical role in the development of strategies to improve the economy and educational system of Massachusetts.

The interviewees reported a high degree of dissatisfaction regarding the number of Latino or bilingual personnel in the vocational technical education system. They identified this factor as an important element in guaranteeing the enrollment and persistence of Latino students.

The panel of interviewees and the analysis of the data that were collected suggest at least six queries and topics that we need to target for further and more detailed examination:

How can we promote recruitment efforts and retention of Latino students into a broad range of vocational technical education programs?

How can we improve recruitment of Latino and black students into postsecondary and postgraduate vocational technical education programs?

How can we increase the number of Latinos in staff positions in the vocational technical education system and then encourage them to be role models for young Latinos in vocational technical education?

How can we effectively measure the status and assessment of the educational needs of Latino students?

How can we increase and improve parental and community participation in vocational technical education?

How can we use the curriculum as a tool to improve vocational technical education and as a way to train teachers in vocational technical education regarding the importance of appreciating racial and ethnic diversity in Massachusetts?

These queries and topics are consistent with the findings of the literature on vocational technical education and Latino students nationally (State Department of Education, 1990).

It is important to target and more systematically discuss the successful ways in which young Latinos have been recruited into vocational technical education. Comparisons should be made between Latinos in vocational technical education and Latinos in nonvocational education programs. One interviewee, Therese Alston, suggested that we conduct several case studies of specific programs and schools across Massachusetts and compare the experiences of Latinos and non-Latinos. Such research might provide direction regarding effective strategies for increasing the participation of Latinos in quality vocational technical education programs.

The area of postsecondary and postgraduate vocational technical education programs also requires major attention. The number of Latinos and blacks enrolled in this level of vocational technical education is minuscule. Accordingly, this situation presents serious implications for the future availability of blacks and Latinos with higher skills in vocational technical education. Furthermore, a greater pool of Latinos and blacks with postsecondary training could be a potential source of new vocational technical education teachers. One interviewee commented that increasing the number of Latino role models is critical for helping Latino students succeed in vocational technical education: "Latino students need to see teachers of their own ethnic background to help give them a sense of trust and feel that someone understands them." Latino faculty and staff in vocational technical education are needed not only as role models for youth, but as advocates for access, equity, and excellence for all students in vocational technical education.

According to one interviewee, three major obstacles prevent the increase of Latino faculty and staff in the vocational technical education system: (1) language barriers, (2) lack of information about how to access professional careers in vocational technical education, and (3) discrimination. These obstacles must be addressed in order to develop realistic strategies for increasing the number of Latino vocational technical education personnel.

In a survey published by the National Center for Education Statistics, it was reported that for the 1979-80 school year there were only 31 Latino faculty working in Massachusetts vocational technical education programs out of a total faculty work force of 7,061. Although these figures are now more than ten years old and current figures are not available, there does not seem to have been much improvement in this area. The proportion of Latino vocational technical education teachers in this state may still be far less than even the dismal national figure for 1980 of 1.5 percent (Staff, 1982). At the time this report was prepared, there was only a small number of Latino teachers in vocational technical education in Massachusetts, even in those places with high concentrations of Latino students. As one interviewee pointed out, even in vocational schools like Holyoke where there is a large Latino population there is a very small number (two) of Latino teachers.

There are some efforts underway to improve this situation. For instance, the director of Bilingual Services at Greater Lowell Regional Vocational Technical High School is coordinating a project to produce a recruitment strategy manual for teachers of color, bilingual personnel, and women. Efforts of this kind should be encouraged. The findings and strategies of the report produced by the Statewide Committee on the Recruitment of Minority Teachers, entitled "The Recruitment and Retention of People of Color in the Teaching Profession in

Massachusetts" (Board of Regents of Massachusetts, 1990), may prove useful to those interested in developing effective strategies for the recruitment of Latino vocational technical education teachers.

Efforts to collect and periodically present data and analysis about Latinos in vocational technical education must be strengthened. As mentioned earlier, the new Perkins Act regulations require improvement in the systematic collection of data and information in order to assess how "special populations" are being served by vocational technical education. Most of the interviewees expressed the need to have a better understanding of enrollment and participation patterns of Latinos and blacks in vocational technical education.

Clearly there is a need for more effective ways of collecting, analyzing, and distributing information about the experience of racial and ethnic groups in vocational technical education. The Division of Occupation Education must play a major role in this effort, but it should do so in partnership with researchers who are familiar with the urban and educational experiences of students of color. Collaborative efforts could assist in developing a comprehensive data base for the Commonwealth, and perhaps even the region of New England. Such efforts could also generate germane policy discussions on this topic. Applied research projects could also be started to compare carefully the experiences of Latinos and blacks in vocational technical education with comparable groups in academic programs. Additionally, a collaborative effort could periodically issue brief reports highlighting the vocational technical education participation and completion rates and patterns according to race and ethnicity as well as by school systems in Massachusetts. This kind of project could also be charged with helping educators in vocational technical education to identify strategies and tactics that will improve learning for all students, particularly students of color.

The involvement of Latino parents in their children's vocational technical education programs is another issue that requires attention. Some of the interviewees suggested that Latino parents may not be well informed of the opportunities for students who have successfully completed a vocational technical education course of study. Furthermore, parents may not be equipped with the information needed to inquire about the quality of particular vocational technical education programs. One interviewee responded that "a lot of people in the Latino community still feel you have to be a slow learner to go into vocational technical education." This was reiterated by another interviewee who stated "in general vocational technical education [is] viewed as less valuable than a college track — the sense is that if my child is not performing well then he might go into vocational technical education."

The interviewees also reported a community perception that vocational technical education is a "dumping ground." This is similar to a finding in a study investigating the experiences of black students in a vocational technical education in Massachusetts. Jennings and Moore (1988) reported that many black parents in Boston would opt for vocational technical education for their children if they could be convinced that this kind of education provided quality schooling. But vocational technical education has a poor history in many school districts with large numbers of black students. These issues require further investigation in order to understand how to develop effective strategies to improve the community's perception of the Massachusetts vocational technical education system.

The lack of bilingual vocational technical education personnel, and particularly native-language speaking individuals, makes reaching out to Latino parents difficult. The lack of materials written in Spanish is another obstacle. If we are to increase parental participation and community awareness of opportunities in vocational technical education, then we must expand outreach. We must target Latino parents in this outreach by using information and language that will effectively reach Latino parents. One interviewee, who works in a district with a large Latino public school enrollment but a very small Latino enrollment in vocational technical education programs, stated that this also means "Having information in Spanish; workshops for parents about what vocational technical education is and educating them about viable programs for their kids; word of mouth — if one student has a good experience, it will spread; use of community access channel and Spanish radio stations."

Finally, several interviewees noted that the lack of an appreciation for the importance of a multicultural learning environment is a serious and systemwide problem. We must direct efforts toward reviewing the curriculum utilized by vocational technical education programs and ensure the curriculum makes students aware of the importance of racial and ethnic diversity in our society. A curriculum that does this can be an important tool not only in attracting greater numbers of Latino students into vocational technical education, but in helping to prepare all students for the increasing racial and ethnic diversity that is characterizing the American work force, especially in Massachusetts.

Conclusions

There are several areas and problems that we should target for attention and reform at the national level in order to enhance the quality of vocational technical education for all students and to increase educational and economic opportunity for Latino students. We should direct efforts toward increasing the participation of Latino youth in vocational technical education in ways that do not reflect segregated tracks of learning. It is especially important that vocational technical education not be a dumping ground, or dead-end, for any student. Furthermore, it is possible to offer high-quality vocational technical education to growing numbers of Latino students in ways that open the door to other kinds of advanced and technical educational programs.

Racial and ethnic diversity represents an important potential strength for the Commonwealth. The field of vocational technical education and its leaders have an opportunity to play an important national role in showing that the Commonwealth can respond to its growing diversity by bringing excluded groups into the economy productively. This can only happen, however, by encouraging, inviting, and allowing large numbers of Latino youth to fully participate in high-quality vocational technical education.

This leads to the last important point. It concerns the role that employers can play in making important contributions to the economic well-being of the Commonwealth. This chapter has focused on a "supply" question regarding vocational technical education and the employment of Latino youth. In other words, the investigation explores whether or not the system of vocational technical education is working effectively for Latino youth. Since this is probably the first study of its kind, the conclusions and recommendations remain tentative until further study. However, we do not want to imply that the "demand" side of this question is insignificant. The attitudes of employers and labor leadership are also critical to ensuring that Latinos become skilled and employed members of the Commonwealth's work force. We cannot assume that even if Latinos were receiving the most effective training and schooling in vocational technical education that this would automatically lead to productive employment paying decent living wages. While there are many reasons why the Massachusetts economy is not as healthy as it should be, or perhaps could be, employers must examine their own roles and leadership regarding the preparation of Latinos, *in addition* to examining access that this group has to quality vocational technical education.

Notes

1. Chapter 74 programs are those programs that meet state regulations and that have been reviewed, evaluated, and approved by the Massachusetts State Department of Education's Division of Occupational Education.

2. The interviewees included the following persons: Theresa Alston, Educational Specialist, Division of Occupational Education, State Department of Education (Boston, MA); Pablo Calderon, Developer and Construction Contractor (Boston, MA); David Cronin, Associate Commissioner, Division of Occupational Education, State Department of Education (Boston, MA); Clifford Flint, Principal, Putnam Vocational High School (Springfield, MA); Herberto Flores, Executive Director, New England Farm Workers Council (Springfield, MA); Frank Lamas, Coordinator, Massachusetts Vocational Technical Teacher Testing Program (Amherst, MA); Modesto Maldonado, Assistant Super-

intendent of Education, Greater Lawrence Regional Vocational Technical High School District (Lawrence, MA); Anna Mangual, Former Director, Massachusetts Action Project (Springfield, MA); Mary Ellen McDonough, Educational Specialist, Division of Occupational Education, State Department of Education (Boston, MA); Starr Pipelas, Director of Bilingual Services, Greater Lowell Regional Vocational Technical High School (Lowell, MA); Edgar Rodriguez, Instructor, Deen Technical High School (Holyoke, MA); Marta Rosa, Member, Chelsea School Committee (Chelsea, MA); Jaime Talero, Director, Oficina Hispana (Boston, MA); Anne Wheelock, Policy Analyst, Massachusetts Advocacy Center (Boston, MA); Beatriz Zapater, Education Director, Hispanic Office of Planning and Evaluation (Boston, MA).

3. Chapter 74 enrolls ninth graders; therefore, the number of students in this grade level can be determined.

References

Alston, T. (1991, Spring). Personal interview. Education Specialist, Massachusetts State Department of Education.

Board of Regents of Massachusetts. (1990). *The Recruitment and Retention of People of Color in the Teaching Profession in Massachusetts, Report of the Statewide Committee on the Recruitment of Minority Teachers.* Boston: Authors.

Center for Law and Education. (1991, April 1). Alert — Your State's Vocational Technical Educational Plan. *Newsnotes.* Washington, DC: Author.

Coyle-Williams, M. (1991, September). *The 1990 Perkins Amendments: No More "Business as Usual,"* Technical Assistance for Special Populations Brief, Vol. 3, No. 1. Urbana, IL: National Center for Research in Vocational Technical Education, University of Illinois at Urbana/Champaign.

Jennings, J., and Moore, W. J. (1988). *Vocational Technical Education in Massachusetts and the Future of Young Minority Students.* Boston, MA: University of Massachusetts at Boston, William Monroe Trotter Institute.

Jobs for the Future. (1991). *Pioneers of Progress: Policy Entrepreneurs and Community Development.* Somerville, MA: Author.

O'Malley, J. M. (1987, March). *Academic Growth of High School Age Hispanic Students in the U.S.* Washington, DC: Center for Educational Statistics.

Staff. (1982, November). Sex and Racial/Ethnic Characteristics of Full-Time Vocational Technical Education Instructional Staff. *National Center for Education Statistics Bulletin.*

State Department of Education, Division of Vocational Technical Education. (1990, July). *Hispanic Youth — Dropout Prevention: Report of Task Force on Participation of Hispanic Students in Vocational Technical Education Programs.* Bosie, ID: Author.

Table 1

Vocational Technical Education Enrollment in Massachusetts, Grades 9 to 12, by Race and Ethnicity, School Year 1990-91

Race/Ethnicity	Number Enrolled	Percent
White	29,248	83.9
Black	2,088	5.9
Latino	2,938	8.4
Asian and Pacific Islander	462	1.3
American Indian	106	0.3
Total	34,842	

SOURCE: Division of Occupational Education, Massachusetts Department of Education. (1991, March 8). *Chapter 74 Enrollment by Race/Sex, Grades 9-12, School Year 1990-1991*. Boston, MA: Author.

Table 2

Ten Public School Systems in Massachusetts with Largest Enrollment in Vocational Technical Education Programs, Grades 9 to 12, by Race and Latino Origin, School Year 1990-91

School System	Total Enrolled	White		Black		Latino		Other	
		#	%	#	%	#	%	#	%
Boston	1,411	141	9.9	877	62.1	115	8.2	278	19.7
Springfield	1,074	379	35.3	336	31.3	314	29.2	45	4.2
Lynn	911	682	74.9	79	8.7	96	10.5	54	5.9
Holyoke	684	350	51.2	25	3.7	300	43.9	9	1.3
Quincy	442	416	94.1	6	1.4	5	1.1	15	2.5
Somerville	436	369	84.6	20	4.6	40	9.2	7	1.6
Newton	408	362	88.7	21	5.1	13	3.2	12	2.9
Chicopee	373	347	93.0	1	0.3	20	5.4	5	1.3
Pittsfield	318	296	93.0	21	6.6	1	0.03	0	0.0
Fall River	297	284	95.6	9	3.0	2	0.7	2	0.7
Total	6,354	3,626	57.0	1,395	22.0	906	14.3	427	6.7

SOURCE: Division of Occupational Education, Massachusetts Department of Education. (1991, March 8). *Chapter 74 Enrollment by Race/Sex, Grades 9-12, School Year 1990-1991.* Boston, MA: Author.

Table 3

Independent Vocational Technical Education Schools in Massachusetts with Enrollments of 500 or More Students, Grades 9 to 12, by Race and Latino Origin, School Year 1990-91

Vocational Technical Schools	Total Enroll	White #	White %	Black #	Black %	Latino #	Latino %	Other #	Other %
Greater Lowell	2,090	1,655	79.2	43	2.1	244	11.7	148	7.1
Greater New Bedford	1,632	1,501	92.0	90	5.5	31	1.9	10	0.6
Greater Lawrence	1,525	887	58.2	24	1.6	595	39.0	19	1.2
Worcester	1,446	1,199	82.9	67	4.6	144	10.0	36	2.5
Southeastern	1,339	1,153	86.1	97	7.2	62	4.6	27	2.0
Greater Fall River Regional	1,153	1,137	98.6	6	0.5	4	0.03	6	0.5
Northeast Metro	1,092	1,033	94.6	7	0.6	50	4.6	2	0.2
Shawsheen Valley	1,067	1,051	98.5	9	0.8	3	0.3	4	0.4
Montachusett	1,046	937	89.6	22	2.1	63	6.0	24	2.3
Whittier	973	900	92.5	13	1.3	55	5.7	5	0.5

Table 3 (Cont)

Assabet Valley	915	885	96.7	8	0.9	17	1.9	5	0.5
Blackstone Valley Regional	907	861	94.9	22	2.4	14	1.5	10	1.1
South Worcester County	902	824	91.4	3	0.3	66	7.3	9	1.0
Bristol-Plymouth	798	753	94.4	11	1.4	19	2.4	15	1.9
Minuteman	727	700	96.3	15	1.6	6	0.8	6	0.8
Tri County	697	683	98.0	5	0.7	8	1.1	1	0.1
Essex Agricultural	691	667	96.5	9	1.3	9	1.3	6	0.2
South Middlesex	684	483	70.6	19	2.8	179	26.2	3	0.4
Old Colony	503	493	98.0	9	1.8	0	0.0	1	0.2
Pathfinder	520	513	98.7	2	0.4	4	0.8	1	0.2
Morthampton-Smith	526	502	95.4	6	1.1	13	2.5	5	1.0
Cape Code Regional	518	479	92.3	26	5.0	10	1.9	3	0.6

SOURCE: Division of Occupational Education, Massachusetts Department of Education. (1991, March 8). *Chapter 74 Enrollment by Race/Sex, Grades 9-12, School Year 1990-1991*. Boston, MA: Author.

Table 4

Vocational Technical Education Programs in Massachusetts with Largest Enrollments, Grades 9 to 12, by Race and Latino Origin, School Year 1990-91

Programs	Total Enroll	White		Black		Latino		Other	
		#	%	#	%	#	%	#	%
Chapter 74 Exploratory	5,064	3,869	76.4	506	10.0	573	11.3	116	2.3
Carpentry	2,625	2,396	91.3	90	3.4	116	4.4	23	0.9
General Marketing	1,724	1,564	90.7	78	4.5	68	3.9	14	0.8
Computer Programming	809	628	77.6	50	6.1	123	15.2	8	0.9
Cosmetology	1,269	1,032	81.3	104	8.1	119	9.3	14	1.1
Electronic Technology	1,366	1,089	79.7	65	4.7	172	12.5	40	2.3
Community Health Work	826	738	89.3	18	2.1	66	7.9	4	0.4
Food Management	2,175	1,844	84.7	178	8.1	130	5.9	23	1.2
Electrician	2,211	2,017	91.2	82	3.7	88	4.0	24	1.0
Plumbing and Pipefitting	907	828	91.2	42	4.6	27	2.9	10	1.1

Table 4 (Cont)

Automotive Body Repair	1,279	1,063	83.1	63	4.9	132	10.3	21	1.6
Automotive Mechanics	2,212	1,881	85.0	93	4.2	181	8.1	57	2.5
Drafting, General	1,070	939	87.7	30	2.8	87	8.1	14	1.3
Graphic and Print Communications	1,334	1,106	82.9	64	4.7	135	10.1	29	2.1
Machine Tool/Shop	1,279	1,085	84.8	50	3.9	96	7.5	48	3.7
Metal Fabrication	812	687	84.6	33	4.0	80	9.8	12	1.5
Total	26,692	22,766	85.2	1,551	5.8	2,193	8.2	182	0.6

SOURCE: Division of Occupational Education, Massachusetts Department of Education. (1991, March 8). *Chapter 74 Enrollment by Race/Sex, Grades 9-12, School Year 1990-1991*. Boston, MA: Author.

Table 5

Vocational Technical Education Programs in Massachusetts with Latino Enrollment of 15% or More, Grades 9 to 12, School Year 1990-91

Programs	% Latinos Enrolled	# Latinos Enrolled
Heavy Equipment Maintenance and Repair	63.6	36
Marketing, Distribution and Other	63.2	12
Radio and T.V. Repair	53.5	38
Upholstering	50.0	10
Medical Secretarial	32.0	8
Radio, T.V. Production and Broadcasting	25.7	9
Financial Services Marketing	25.3	21
Clothing Management, Production and Services	22.3	62
Hotel/Motel Management	20.2	18
Nursing Assisting	19.0	87
Institution and Home Management and Service	18.0	60
Renewable Natural Resources	17.9	7
Agribusiness and Agricultural Products and Other	16.7	11
Computer Programming	15.2	123
Major Appliance Repair	15.2	23
Total		525

SOURCE: Division of Occupational Education, Massachusetts Department of Education. (1991, March 8). *Chapter 74 Enrollment by Race/Sex, Grades 9-12, School Year 1990-1991.* Boston, MA: Author.

Part III
Research and Policy Implications

Antonia Darder and
Carole Christofk Upshur
What Do Latino Children Need to Succeed in School? A Study of Four Boston Public Schools

What do Latino children need to succeed in school? Despite almost 30 years of educational research, liberal reforms, and compensatory programs, academic achievement by Latino children has improved only marginally and remains poor. A publication by the Children's Defense Fund, entitled *Latino Youths at a Crossroads* (Children's Defense Fund, 1990), states that the proportion of Latino students who are two or more grades behind their age group has increased since 1981 and that the achievement scores of Latino students have shown only modest increases overall. These facts represent a most sobering reality for the Latino community of Boston — one of the most impoverished and least educated in the city.

According to a paper published by the Boston Persistent Poverty Project, entitled *In the Midst of Plenty* (Boston Foundation, 1989), 75 percent of all Latino children in the city of Boston live in poverty, and 90 percent of all Latino families send their children to the public schools. That is, the majority of Latino parents depend on the public schools for their children's formal education, despite the tremendous difficulties many of their children face in the Boston schools.

Many of the academic difficulties experienced by Latino children have been associated with traditional school policies and practices that tend to undermine student motivation and participation, alienate parents, and hinder community involvement — factors shown to contribute to low academic achievement of Latino students (Cummins, 1986; Rivera, 1988). These traditional policies and practices include tracking and ability grouping, mainstreaming, grade retention, achievement testing, the hidden curriculum, meritocracy, and teacher expectations (Darder, 1991). These are practices that shape the daily lives of the 11,267 Latino students currently enrolled in Boston public schools.

A report compiled by the Massachusetts Advocacy Center, entitled *Locked In/Locked Out* (Massachusetts Advocacy Center, 1990), speaks to the impact of these educational practices as reflected by high dropout, retention, and truancy rates as well as poor achievement test scores. In Boston public schools, for example, the 1988 dropout rate for Latino students was 19 percent, while cohort dropout rates[1] for the graduating classes from 1983 to 1988 ranged from 42 percent to as high as 54 percent. In addition, the Boston public school district has one of the highest overall retention rates (10 percent) in the Commonwealth of Massachusetts.

Grade retention is a major educational concern, particularly given the findings of numerous studies that the experience of grade retention is a significant factor in increased school dropout rates among Latino students in public schools (Children's Defense Fund, 1990; Fernandez and Shu, 1988; Fernandez and Vélez, 1989; Vélez, 1989). In relation to these findings, it is significant to note that retention rates for Latino students in the Boston public schools drastically increase when they enter the middle school (sixth grade). The retention rate for Latino children in the sixth grade (9.0 percent) is approximately four times greater than that in fifth grade (2.3 percent), while the retention rate for seventh graders (17.2 percent) increases to over seven times that of Latino children in the fifth grade (Wheelock, 1990).

Latino children in Boston public schools are at the highest risk for educational failure of any ethnic group enrolled in the system. Latino youth have the highest high school dropout rate of any ethnic group. In the 1989-1990 school year, 13.1 percent of Latino youth dropped out of high school in Boston (High School Zone Office, 1990). It is important to note further that 16.6 percent of Latino youth in mainstream[2] educational programs failed to graduate, while a smaller percentage, 11.0 percent, of Latino youth who were in bilingual education programs in high school did not graduate (Massachusetts Advocacy Center, 1990).

The differences in these dropout rates provide clues as to what can assist Latino youth to be more successful in school. In addition, examination of reading and math achievement scores from grades one to twelve reveal that Latino youth generally have the lowest scores of any ethnic group across all grade levels. A higher percentage of Latino youth also fail the degrees of reading power test compared to other groups. However, Latino youth have consistently higher math scores than reading scores throughout all grades, and their math scores are higher than some other groups in elementary grades. The discrepancy between math and reading scores is quite large during the elementary grades, ranging from 8 to 17 points in the 1987-1988 school year (Boston Public Schools, 1990). In all grades, Latino youth scored 60 or above in math in this year, while scoring in the 40s or 50s in reading. Again, these data point to areas to explore in terms of the strengths of the system.

Another key issue identified when looking at where the system has strengths to build on is the contrast between achievement scores of Latino youth in elementary grades (first through fifth) compared to middle school and high school grades. There is a precipitous drop in scores in math for Latino sixth graders (scoring 49) compared to fifth graders (scoring 63). There is also a drop in reading scores, from the high 40s and 50s in elementary school, to the low 40s and 30s in middle school, and to a continuing decline in high school. Thus, something key seems to be happening between the elementary grades and middle school for Latino children. These puzzling findings, along with the overall poor performance of Latino children on the system's traditional measures, became the impetus for this study.

The study was designed to identify the significant themes and issues associated with school achievement for Latino children in four Boston elementary schools. The study was driven by the increasing sense of urgency on the part of many Boston parents, community leaders, and education professionals, who feel that urban schools in general, and Boston schools in particular, have failed to address the changing needs of today's public school population adequately. In 1991, the Boston public school population was 80 percent children of color, yet the school district's statistics on the culture of origin of their teachers indicate that less than 30 percent were teachers of color. In addition, classroom materials, books, curricula, and teacher training barely began to address the cultural needs of the children.

The study was designed to obtain more specific information about school life from the most direct and immediate sources: the firsthand experiences of children, parents, and teachers in the classrooms. The goal was to identify specific attitudes, practices, activities, teaching approaches, and uses of classroom materials that were viewed positively by Latino children and their parents, and to make recommendations as to how these practices might be expanded to increase the chances for academic success for Latino children.

In an effort to assess the pre-middle-school experience of Latino students, the study focused on fifth graders. The primary rationale for studying the fifth grade was that it constitutes a critical developmental period, immediately preceding the major academic transition of students to middle school. Studies suggest (Gardener and Carpenter, 1985; Alexander, 1987; Simmons, 1987; Fenzel, 1989) that difficulty in making this academic transition smoothly and effectively, as a consequence of poor academic and social preparation, might be related to the dramatic increase in middle-school retention rates for Latino students. Hence, this study sought to assess the conditions and relationships present at the end of the elementary school experience through an investigation into the descriptions and perspectives provided by administrators, teachers, parents, and students regarding the preparation of fifth graders for the middle-school transition. Data already cited about dramatic changes in the school performance of Latino students between fifth and sixth grades reinforced the importance of studying this transition.

The major research categories examined in this study were derived from factors previously cited by other researchers in the field as significant to the academic achievement of Latino students (Lucas, Henze, and Donato, 1990; Moll, 1988; Garcia, 1988; Carter and Chatfield, 1986; Cummins, 1986; Cardenas and First, 1985). These factors include (1) school leadership, (2) teacher morale,

(3) teacher preparation, (4) school environment, (5) curriculum, (6) instructional approaches and teaching strategies, (7) meaningful use of Spanish, (8) teacher expectations, and (9) future expectations.

The link between educational attainment and economic success is another important concern of this study. A high school graduate has been shown to have lifetime earnings triple that of a nonhigh school graduate (Bowles and Gintes, 1976). The relationship between educational level and income has also been shown to depend on gender, age, race, and physical ability. Notably, a higher percentage of Latinos (65 percent) in Boston who do not have a high school diploma live in poverty than do either African Americans (42 percent) or whites (30 percent) (Boston Foundation, 1989). In other words, without adequate education and training for the new jobs of the future, Latinos will continue to be disproportionately represented among the disenfranchised.

Studies across the country have shown that Latino students who have been delayed in their schooling as a result of grade retention are far more likely to drop out of high school (Velez, 1989). Thus, it is important to identify school relationships and conditions that can serve to reduce grade retention rates in the middle schools.

If we can identify the variables that can positively impact the academic achievement of Latino children, we may also assist in improving their economic conditions in the future. It is thus vitally important for researchers to help identify the variables that contribute to the effectiveness of public schools mandated by law to meet the educational needs of Latino children. It is particularly important to the development of public policy on educational instruction and school criteria — these are the policies that will improve the status of Latino students living in poverty in Boston, as well as in other cities across the country.

Lastly, this study is particularly timely, given the numerous struggles taking place between educators, school officials, and the Latino community at large to bring about educational reform that will improve the academic achievement of Latino children attending Massachusetts public schools.

Methodology

The study was designed specifically to determine what principals, teachers, parents, and children identified as the educational requirements and resources necessary to promote the educational success of Latino children. Four elementary schools with large Latino student enrollments (45 percent to 55 percent) were selected for the purposes of this study. The principals were invited to participate, and the study was approved by the Boston Public Schools Office of Research and Development. Information was gathered from principals, teachers, parents, and children through interviews, questionnaires, and classroom observations.

An interview was completed with each principal. The principals were asked to assist in scheduling a time when the research team could meet with all the teachers in their school together to discuss their perceptions of the needs of Latino children and to distribute a two-page questionnaire for all teachers to return. Next, permissions were obtained from one bilingual and one regular-education, fifth grade teacher in each school to observe one full day or two half days of class activities. Letters were sent to children's parents, informing them of the study and requesting permission to have a group discussion with their children on the topic of "what is a good teacher and a good school." Letter were also sent home to arrange for a parent meeting at the school for a similar discussion.

The manner in which the study was actually conducted in the four schools differed slightly depending on the level of receptivity by the principals and teachers. For example, in one school the principal stated it would not be possible in the four to six weeks to arrange for a meeting with all teachers. In this school, we had to depend on distributing our questionnaire in teacher mailboxes with a stamped, self-addressed, return envelope to obtain teacher comments. In another school, only the bilingual teachers were invited to speak with us, despite the fact that we had made it clear to the principal we were interested in talking with all teachers. In a third school, the principal called a mandatory all-school meeting for us to talk with teachers, and about 35 attended. In the last school, the principal invited us to attend the regular weekly team meetings, and we had a receptive welcome and a good discussion with about 28 teachers at that school.

In order to ensure the return of as many teacher questionnaires as possible, the questionnaire with a cover letter and a stamped, return envelope was distributed to all 189 teachers at the four schools. An indicator of the level of interest in the study by the teachers is that only 16 percent (31) of the questionnaires were returned. On the other hand, many teachers were quite willing to share their thoughts when we were in the schools, and only one of the nine teachers asked for permission to observe their classroom declined.[3]

In an effort to reach parents, letters in Spanish and English, with stamped, return envelopes were sent out indicating a choice of dates for an evening meeting. The letter asked parents to return their telephone number to us if they wished to talk with us but could not attend the meeting. Despite repeated efforts to make letter and phone contact with parents and to elicit the teachers' assistance in contacting parents, only 19 percent (17) of the parents contacted chose to participate in the study.

Despite the varying degree of receptivity among teachers, and parents in particular, over 200 school personnel, children, and parents participated in this study, and over 100 hours of school observations and visits were completed.

Summary and Analysis of Results

The following is a summary and analysis of the information gathered from principals, teachers, students, and parents. The discussion will specifically address the major research categories posited in the scope of this study.

SCHOOL LEADERSHIP

When asked specifically to examine the particular needs of Latino students, the four principals interviewed, while reticent, tended to give responses that can best be described as passive or ambivalent. The four principals tended to universalize the academic needs of all children and reduce the discourse to an emphasis on "the basics" and on oversimplified psychological notions of "self-esteem." By so doing, these principals were inadvertently ignoring or overlooking their own particular leadership responsibilities in ensuring that effective strategies are in place to meet the educational needs of Latino children, especially those in poverty.

While some parents felt the principal played an important role in welcoming them to the school, others interviewed felt that there was inadequate contact concerning ways to become involved in their child's school. The importance of a "good" principal to having a "good" school was mentioned by some of the students as well.

Rather than acts of bad faith or ill-will on the part of the principals interviewed, the lack we saw among school administrators of consistent leadership in meeting the needs of Latino students and their parents is most likely the result of inadequate knowledge or lack of professional preparation in pedagogical concepts related to culture, cognition, literacy, bicultural development, and bilingualism, as well as a lack of the necessary practical tools. Nonetheless, it is unfortunate that the principals seemed so ill-prepared to provide teachers with the educational leadership and institutional support required to effectively run their programs and to contend with the major deficits in Latino parent involvement.

TEACHER MORALE

The consequences of inadequate administrative leadership and institutional support for teachers were reflected in signs of poor teacher morale. This is not to suggest that the teachers who participated in this study did not like their work, but rather that many of the teachers expressed great frustration with the inadequacies of the system in providing them with educational resources, professional development opportunities, and administrative support. It appears that the current educational policies and structures have had a detrimental impact on teacher effectiveness and creativity. This was reflected in feelings of despair and disempowerment voiced by many of the teachers at the four schools.

A major source of frustration expressed by the teachers is the discrepancy between the way the administrators view the needs of the teachers and of their students, and the way the teachers themselves experience these needs in the classrooms on a daily basis. This dynamic was demonstrated in one school where the principal stated that the school had adequate bilingual materials and textbooks, and the bilingual teachers strongly repudiated this claim. Observation of the bilingual classrooms supported the teachers' views.

Overall, teachers expressed much distress over the inability to obtain adequate materials, equipment, and resources from the school district. Many teachers spent money out of their own pockets in order to provide the children with needed textbooks and materials. Further, teachers expressed dissatisfaction with the perfunctory nature of faculty meetings and the lack of effective and productive communication between the district and school administration and the teachers; between mainstream teachers and bilingual teachers; and between parents and the school.

TEACHER PREPAREDNESS

Although a significant number of teachers who participated in this study had obtained graduate degrees, most of them felt that they did not have adequate preparation with respect to the educational needs of Latino children. As a consequence, teachers considered themselves to have many in-service needs, particularly with respect to (1) the history and culture of different Latin American countries, (2) theoretical and practical understanding of the nature and impact of culture on learning, (3) second language acquisition skills, (4) multiculturalism, (5) conversational Spanish instruction, and (6) knowledge of the purpose and goals of bilingual education.

In general, principals did not acknowledge the wide-ranging in-service needs of the teachers and did not emphasize this area as significant to strengthening the school. Parents noted the need for teachers to understand them and their children, while children were most concerned with how teachers talked to them, particularly in terms of discipline (not to "yell"). The information obtained indicates that there is a great need for in-service educational opportunities that are responsive to the identified needs of teachers, parents, and children.

SCHOOL ENVIRONMENT

The overall environment in most of the schools observed can generally best be described as deficient. The physical environment of the four schools is very unattractive and functionally lacking in many respects. The building walls, the halls, the playground, auditorium seats, libraries, and bathrooms often were dirty and poorly maintained. The outside of the buildings were reminiscent of old warehouses with a grave, institutionalized appearance that conveyed neither warmth nor welcome.

Despite the ugliness of the school architecture, many of the teachers managed to maintain clean and orderly classrooms. In these classrooms, the seating and activity centers were well-organized; books, equipment, and other materials were readily accessible for use by the children; and bulletin boards were attractive and colorful. Nevertheless, most of the classrooms were small and consequently tended to appear somewhat cluttered and crowded. Still, a number of the classrooms observed did generate a warm and welcoming feeling.

When the children spoke about changing the school facility, they most often mentioned building a swimming pool, getting hall lockers, putting in air conditioning, painting the school, fixing the seats in the auditorium, getting larger windows and larger classrooms, putting doors on the toilet stalls, and generally cleaning up of bathrooms, playground, and surrounding neighborhood.

It is interesting to note that although the children placed great emphasis on and expressed much concern about the physical environment of their schools, principals, teachers, and parents seldom mentioned the physical characteristics of the school as important to children's learning. The children seemed to experience the negative impact of the physical environment more directly and concretely and seemed to see the implicit message of their environment as that they do not deserve anything better.

CURRICULUM

The curriculum, materials, and textbooks found in the classrooms observed, including the bilingual classrooms, were described by principals and teachers as essentially the same as those utilized throughout the school district. The major areas of instruction observed included language arts, social studies, science, and mathematics.

For the most part, the curriculum did not reflect a significant inclusion of Latino cultural values, history, or the realities experienced by the Latino community today. Although there was some effort made by a few teachers to integrate the experiences of their Latino students into the curriculum, this appeared to be more as a result of an extra individual effort on the part of these teachers than any institutionalized effort by the system to meet the needs of the children in the curriculum. The most extensive inclusion of Latino culture was in the bilingual classrooms where a part of the academic instruction was done in

Spanish. But even in some of these classrooms, students were often encouraged to speak exclusively in English.

Teachers, students, and parents all agreed that there was a great need for materials and textbooks that not only reflected the history and culture of Latinos in this country but that were written in Spanish.

Although some classrooms had educational equipment such as computers, microscopes, and cable television, these resources were very limited. Principals, on the other hand, did not indicate teaching materials and other educational resources as a high priority need. Instead, they stressed the need for more outside support services and social services for children and families.

INSTRUCTIONAL APPROACHES AND TEACHING STRATEGIES

The instructional approach of the teachers observed in this study varied considerably. While some teachers preferred a more dialogical, collaborative, and egalitarian approach in their teaching and interaction with the children, others functioned in a more formalized, individualized, and authoritarian manner. From the interviews with Latino children, it was quite evident, however, that they preferred learning in group activities and enjoyed teachers who communicated with them in more personalized and informal ways, praised their accomplishments openly and exhibited their work.

In addition, few situations were observed in which Latino children themselves functioned in specific leadership roles with respect to instruction. Despite this observation, it was also evident that children who worked consistently in small groups appeared to have more opportunities to experience a sense of personal empowerment through their active dialogical participation and that it provided purpose and meaning to their learning.

Teaching strategies identified by many of the teachers as effective with Latino children included making lessons concrete and personalized, using literature texts directly instead of using the summaries provided in the basal readers, providing immediate feedback so that children could see their mistakes and correct them, involving children in cooperative learning and group activities where they can assist one another, and giving project-oriented assignments.

Latino parents also expressed a preference for project-oriented work and for seeing their children's work displayed in the classroom. Parents also noted that there was a need for more computer and math work and for career guidance. They frequently stressed the need for individualized attention for their children, smaller class sizes, and more reinforcement for achievement. While the principals varied in their emphasis on issues of curriculum, two of the four did express interest in promoting instructional approaches — for example, cooperative learning and more integration of bilingual and mainstream programs — to enhance the achievement of Latino children. Thus, a number of concrete and positive themes were raised by all groups concerning effective teaching strategies for Latino children.

Another area of concern in effective instruction and teaching strategies is the utilization of teaching assistants in the classroom. Only four of the nine classrooms had teaching assistants. All were Spanish-speaking. For the most part, the teaching assistants were not well integrated into the instructional process and functioned predominantly as passive agents rather than active members of the teaching team. As a consequence, their interaction and connection with the children was limited and their role tended to be more custodial than that of a significant human resource in the instructional dimension of the classroom and the academic development of the children.

MEANINGFUL USE OF SPANISH

The findings of this study clearly indicate that the meaningful use of Spanish in the school and classroom occurs only where there are principals and teachers who are committed to this practice. Whenever Latino children were in classrooms where English functioned as the preferred language for communication, instruction, and constructing meaning, their use of Spanish was observed to be more limited or almost nonexistent. This was even observed during recreational activities and in conversations with other Spanish-speaking children. In contrast, wherever the principal and teachers encouraged and legitimated the use of Spanish by actively conversing with Latino children in their native language, the children were more apt to respond and converse actively in Spanish in the classroom, in peer interactions, and on the playground.

Some Latino children expressed ambivalence about speaking Spanish in school because of the manner in which they felt perceived or treated by teachers and students who do not speak Spanish. This seems significant considering that in no instances were teachers observed to make any concerted effort to prevent the development of negative biases or prejudices regarding the use of Spanish by Latino children among monolingual English-speaking students.

The most meaningful use of Spanish was found, almost exclusively, in bilingual classrooms where at least 50 percent of the instruction took place in Spanish. Not surprisingly, most Latino parents interviewed preferred classrooms where their children were able to continue learning in Spanish as well as English. Most of the principals, on the other hand, seemed to be oriented toward integration and mainstreaming rather than promoting full literacy and competency for children in both languages.

TEACHER EXPECTATIONS

Although some teachers expressed high expectations for all the children in their classrooms, the general expectations for Latino children held by most teachers cannot be considered sufficient to promoting academic success. The findings of this study (see table 1) are that the teachers placed greater emphasis on such expectations as "learning to think," "improving English," "trying their best," while "mastery of the material" was placed at the bottom of the list. There are several problem with this rank ordering by the teachers in this study of their expectations for Latino children:

Generally, all children in normal physical condition participate in the act of thinking;

Studies indicate that English language development is facilitated for bilingual children when they have mastered the language principles in their native language;

The children themselves expressed the desire to learn and to do their best;

Academic achievement is, above all, measured in the Boston public school district through children's performance on standardized testing that is designed primarily to measure their mastery of the material; and

Most disturbing of all, teachers were unable to suggest strategies for intervention when a child is failing to live up to their expectations.

Thus, teacher expectations are at odds with educational research, with the stated goals of the Boston school system, and with the inherent motivation and desire to learn expressed by the children who participated in this study.

FUTURE EXPECTATIONS

Although Latino children and their parents expressed many future professional and vocational aspirations, outside of a few individual efforts by particular teachers, this study did not find a consistent orientation toward college or professional careers reflected in schools and classrooms observed.

In terms of the near future, only perfunctory or scattered efforts were mentioned by teachers and principals with respect to preparing of low-income Latino children for the transition to middle school. This is particularly of concern given the abrupt transition of bilingual students into nonbilingual classrooms, the pedagogical shift in instructional approach, and the high retention rates and low test scores documented for Latino students during the middle school grades.

PARENT INVOLVEMENT

Parents interviewed for this study strongly emphasized the importance of teachers maintaining contact with parents. The parents expressed appreciation for teachers who took time to explain how their children were doing and also felt more inspired to encourage their children's efforts when they were in consistent contact with the teacher. It is also interesting to note that a number of the children interviewed felt that it was helpful when parents came to school.

Despite these findings, several of the principals as well as teachers complained about the difficulty of communicating with Latino parents and getting them to participate in school meetings and activities. Only on two occasions during the study was there any direct evidence of parent participation in the classrooms. Although a number of the parents interviewed did mention their participation in a variety of school activities, most of the principals estimated that less than 5 percent of all parents in the school participated on any consistent basis.

Other difficulties that surfaced with respect to Latino parent participation included the lack of transportation, parents working outside of the home and arriving very late or tired in the evening, and the inability of parents to assist their children with their homework. It is also significant to mention here that parent involvement was highest in classrooms where the teacher consistently communicated with parents through telephone conversations.

DIFFICULTIES FACED BY LATINO CHILDREN

Parents, teachers, and principals perceived the difficulties faced by Latino children in poverty in very different ways. Most of the principals and teachers tended to view the source of the problems faced by Latino children as either originating in the environment or in the child. Principals mentioned home problems related to the effects of poverty, tough neighborhoods, family violence, drug use, cultural isolation, lack of parental supervision, or the parents' inability to support or assist in their children's education. This view tends to place the need for change outside of the general domain of the public school.

On the other hand, most teachers defined the problems in terms of the child's lack of conceptual understanding in English, lack of motivation, lack of enthusiasm for learning, boredom, or to the difficulties associated with children not retaining what they learned. This view places the blame or responsibility primarily on the individual child. Only on a few occasions did teachers mention the inadequate curriculum, textbooks and materials, negative views towards bilingual education, or the prejudices and inadequate crosscultural understanding of teachers as a difficulty faced by Latino children, especially those in poverty, in the public schools.

In contrast, parents tended to see the problem as related to the conditions their children face in the schools or parents' own inadequacy and inability to assist their children. Hence, parents generally described the school problems in terms of the teacher's inability or unwillingness to work and communicate more effectively with Latino parents, the lack of value placed on Latino culture, and the negative impact experienced by the children when they made the transition from bilingual to mainstream classrooms.

With respect to themselves, parents expressed regret that they were unable to help their children with their homework because they did not have the necessary language or educational skills, or that they were unable to participate more actively in school activities because their work schedules did not permit them to do so. Parents felt that these inadequacies on their part contributed to some of the difficulties their children faced in the public schools. That is, while Latino parents see the need for the schools to be more responsive to their children, they also acknowledge their own responsibilities.

The findings highlight the need for schools to recognize their role not only in meeting the unique needs of Latino children, but also in responding to the needs of low-income Latino parents in their efforts towards greater participation in their children's educational process.

NEEDS OF LATINO CHILDREN

More often than not, when principals were questioned directly as to the needs of Latino children, they addressed the issue by emphasizing that what all children need is "a good education" and "to feel good about themselves." In addition, they stressed the need for addressing broader social and community resources. Teachers, on the other hand, noted that Latino children needed to improve their language skills in both English and Spanish. The majority felt this goal was best achieved through a whole language approach and the use of Spanish in content learning. In addition, they felt that Latino children needed to develop better test-taking skills, build greater self-esteem and self-confidence, and gain more exposure to mainstream culture.

Parents saw the needs of their children tied to the classroom environment. They emphasized the need for smaller classes, more individual attention for their children, increased awareness and understanding of Latino culture by the teachers, and more rewards and incentives to support their children's academic successes. A few parents mentioned the necessity for their children to be more invested in their own learning.

When children were asked about their needs, they responded concretely. The children stated that they needed more sports activities, more field trips, better food in the cafeteria, new and interesting books, more computers, more teachers who were humorous and friendly and did not yell at them, more group activities and projects, to be safe at school, a more relaxed dress codes, better school facilities, and school jobs where they could earn some money. The impact of such basic, day-to-day, physical and educational resource deficits on children should not be underestimated.

The major contrasts in the ways that needs of primarily low-income Latino children are perceived among the participants of this study suggest that the schools have failed to be "child-focused." If only the specific needs identified by the children in this study were fulfilled, the goals of parents, teachers, and principals could be more easily fulfilled as well. For example, children expressed the desire for more field trips, while teachers affirmed the need for children to be exposed to more mainstream cultural activities. The children's desires for new and interesting books and more group- and project-based activities are very compatible with teachers' advocacy for whole language instructional approaches and development of self-esteem in their students. Most importantly, the overall results of this study indicate that there are a number of easy-to-implement, concrete changes that could be made within the Boston public schools to increase the system's responsiveness to the educational needs of Latino children. Given these findings, the school system can no longer simply point to the social and economic problems found in the community as the primary reason for the lack of educational achievement among low-income Latino children.

Conclusions and Recommendations

Several important issues and themes emerge from the data collected from this study. Summarized below, they serve as a foundation for recommendations on educational policies and practices that could significantly enhance the academic achievement of Latino students and positively impact their performance beyond the elementary-school experience into the middle-school years.

Teachers have a range of expectations of Latino students, and these expectations serve to reinforce a school culture. This is particularly apparent in schools where teachers do not have high expectations of academic achievement and critical thinking skills for Latino children, especially those in poverty. Given what we know about the influence of teacher expectations on achievement, this is an important finding.

The separation of bilingual children from others in the building, and their segregation for most of the school day, appears to set up a dynamic and perception of stigma. Further, this stigma often was found to extend to relations between bilingual teachers and mainstream teachers. Lack of positive attitudes about bilingualism and denial by non-Latino teachers that Latino children or families have any unique needs work against the interests of the children they teach. These attitudes emerged in a range of issues from a lack of recognition of the substantial Latino enrollment, to the introduction of French rather than Spanish as an enrichment activity for advanced work classes. This form of educational denial and neglect in place of recognizing and working to meet the actual needs of Latino children functions as a detriment to academic achievement.

Little thought has gone into incorporating education about future careers or academic expectations of college attendance into the elementary school curriculum. It would seem appropriate to begin to instill dreams and visions early in children with respect to the possibilities for the future. This seems particularly important by fifth grade. The lack of attention to assisting children in thinking constructively about their futures is of major concern, particularly for Latino students from low-income families.

Although, the middle-school years (11- to 14-years-of-age) represent a period of great social, cognitive, and physical change in the child's life and can be substantially affected by the external forces at work in the school environment, little planning and preparation for the transition to middle school seems to be the norm. The drop in achievement levels noted in the first section of this paper indicates that Latino children seem to flounder and are particularly at risk in middle school. The risk is compounded if they move directly into monolingual classes after spending all of their elementary years in smaller, bilingual classrooms. An effective and supported transition from elementary to middle school seems crucial to the long-term educational success of low-income Latino children and must be planned carefully. Further, there is some agreement among educators that shifting of children out of bilingual education should not be done at the same time they change schools and are expected to begin a different form of academic program.

Successful strategies identified in the study for working with low-income Latino children included the use of cooperative learning, activity-based learning, use of group work, integration of Spanish language use across classrooms, and opportunities for integration of bilingual and monolingual classrooms. While these strategies may work particularly well for Latino children, they have also consistently been identified in recent education research as common approaches to improving the educational achievement of all children. Given their noted success, these strategies should be uniformly adopted by school districts and fully implemented in all classrooms.

The lack of adequate teaching materials in Spanish and of texts reflecting the different cultural histories and realities of the low-income Latino children who attend the Boston schools surfaced as a major concern. The Spanish basal readers were described by several Latino teachers as poorly written translations and difficult to read. The lack of other literature in Spanish and of Latino authors was notable, as was the absence of reference materials such as encyclopedias, dictionaries, maps, and films in Spanish. The children talked about the poor condition of their books and described the quality of most of these texts as boring. Inadequate teaching materials and textbooks obviously limit the opportunities and ability of Latino children to excel academically.

The need emerged for very specific in-service training for teachers on a variety of topics, as did some excellent ideas for improving the teachers' ability to meet the needs of Latino students, especially those in poverty. Teachers themselves consistently expressed a desire to become more knowledgeable and proactive in their interactions with Latino students, whether in mainstream or bilingual classrooms. The need for in-service training is not limited to non-Latino teachers; Latino teachers themselves expressed the need for support, for instance, to learn about Latino cultures other than their own. All teachers need opportunities to grow and learn in their jobs and to develop skills for meeting the challenges of a changing student population and changing world. The public school system must actively facilitate and provide access to in-service training that can meet the specific epistemological and pedagogical needs identified by teachers.

It is important to stress that the manner in which the teaching assistants function in the classroom is clearly the responsibility of the master teachers. If teachers do not integrate the assistants actively into the pedagogical process or do not know how to create partnerships with their assistants, this issue must be addressed by professional development. This is of particular concern in meeting the need of Latino children who can well benefit from the additional individual attention in the classroom.

Both observation and Latino children's comments indicated the need for improved school facilities. Children complained repeatedly about the conditions of the bathrooms, the playgrounds, the walls, and the auditorium. From observation, it was quite obvious that the physical environment of the schools studied were in dire need of remodeling and rehabilitation. This seems particularly important given the evidence of how the well-being of children and adults is affected by the physical environment of where they must learn and work on a daily basis.

Without question, the role of the principal is paramount in providing leadership within the school. Interview data with the principals seldom reflected the solid theoretical understanding of the pedagogical and cultural issues essential to developing or supporting educational programs to meet the academic needs of Latino children who live in poverty. Hence, most public school principals could benefit from a professional development program geared to strengthening their understanding of Latino children and their educational needs. Such a program could greatly enhance their ability to provide effective leadership in their schools.

The issue of parent involvement must be seriously addressed by public schools at all levels. That is, efforts must be made to look at and restructure the traditional approaches to parent involvement so as to promote greater participation by Latino parents. The current approaches limit which parents can participate and the manner in which parents can be involved, and a greater sense of school-parent partnership may also help overcome children's issues of embarrassment or worry about parent visits to the school.

The issue of homework surfaced in interviews with parents, teachers, and children. Although homework assignment has traditionally been seen as a way to build study habits and promote parents' participation in children's education, the data suggests that these are unrealistic expectations given the economic, educational, and social realities that exist for Latino children who live in poverty. Inadvertently, traditional use of homework appears to exacerbate stress between students and teachers, teachers and parents, and parents and their children. Hence, the issue merits greater consideration and possibly even efforts to restructure the homework policy to conform more realistically to the lives of Latino children who live in poverty.

It is strongly recommended that further research and intervention be undertaken in the following areas, with specific emphasis on their relationship to the academic achievement of Latino children. These areas include: (1) school leadership; (2) teacher in-service; (3) curriculum development; (4) transition into middle school; (5) homework policies; (6) retention practices; (7) parent participation; and (8) the rehabilitation of the physical environment.

While these recommendations are based on a small sample from four Boston elementary school communities, it is felt that genuine, concrete, and meaningful issues were raised by all groups that cannot be ignored. The issues raised do not constitute insignificant nor marginal views. On the contrary, strong themes arose across the different schools and among the constituency groups, lending validity and strength to the findings. Direct contact was made with over 200 children, parents, teachers, teaching assistants, and school administrators during the course of this study. The voices address clearly many specific, basic, and inexpensive activities that could improve the achievement of Latino children in the Boston public schools.

The goal of this project was to surface issues and identify activities associated with positive results that could be replicated and strengthened in order to be of immediate benefit to Latino children. In many ways, the possibilities for success already exist in the system, but need to be better reinforced and more systematically implemented. Moreover, the children, parents, and teachers — those with the most day-to-day investment in the classroom educational process but with the least resources for reform — need to be heard and assisted to participate in the improvement of the schools and the academic success of Latino children who live in poverty.

Notes

1. Cohort rates reflect the number of youth who enter ninth grade who do not graduate with their class four years later, dropping out in any one of the four years.

2. Mainstream, here and throughout this chapter, refers to a setting in which the emphasis is placed on traditional educational approaches and curriculum, and where English is the language of instruction.

3. The one teacher unwilling to participate in the study was in a school where there were only two fifth grade classrooms. As an alternative, a fourth grade classroom was observed at this school.

References

Alexander, W. (1987). Toward Schools in the Middle: Progress and Problems. *Journal of Curriculum and Supervision, 2*(4), 314-329.

Boston Foundation Report. (1989). *In the Midst of Plenty.* Boston, MA: Boston Foundation.

Boston Public Schools. (1990). *School Profiles 1988-89.* Boston, MA: Boston Public Schools Research and Development Office.

Bowles, S., and Gintes, H. (1976). *Schooling in Capitalist America.* New York: Basic Books.

Cardenas, J., and First, J. M. (1985, September). Children at Risk. *Educational Leadership.*

Carter, T., and Chatfield, M. (1986, November). Effective Bilingual Schools: Implications for Policy and Practice. *American Journal of Education.*

Children's Defense Fund. (1990). *Latino Youth at a Crossroads*. Washington, DC: Children's Defense Fund.

Cummins, J. (1981). The Role of Primary Language Development in Promoting Educational Success for Language Minority Students. In Office of Bilingual Education, California State Department of Education, (Eds.), *Schooling and Language Minority Students: A Theoretical Framework*, pp. 2-49. Los Angeles: California State University, Evaluation, Dissemination, and Assessment Center.

Cummins, J. (1986). Empowering Minority Students: A Framework for Intervention. *Harvard Educational Review, 56*, 18-36.

Darder, A. (1991). *Culture and Power in the Classroom*. Massachusetts: Bergin and Garvey Press.

Fenzel, M. (1989, April). *An Ecological Study of Changes in Student Role Strains During the Transition to Middle School*. A paper presented at the Biennial Meeting of the Society for Research in Child Development, Kansas City, MO.

Fernandez, R., and Shu, G. (1988). School Dropouts: New Approaches to an Enduring Problem. In L. A. Valverde (Ed.), *Education and Urban Society*. Beverly Hills, CA: Sage Press.

Fernandez, R., and Velez, W. (1989). *Who Stays? Who Leaves? Findings from the ASPIRA Five Cities High School Study*. Washington, DC: ASPIRA Association.

Garcia, E. (1988). Attributes of Effective Schools for Language Minority Students. In L. A. Valverde (Ed.), *Education and Urban Society*. Beverly Hills, CA: Sage Press.

Gardener P., and Carpenter, R. (1985, April). *A Needs Assessment for Transition from Elementary Schools to Middle Schools*. Report No. 85.05. Vancouver: Educational Research Institute of British Columbia.

High School Zone Office. (1990). *High School Restructuring and Improvement Plan*. Boston, MA: Boston Public Schools.

Lucas, T., Henze, R., and Donato, R. (1990). Promoting the Success of Latino Language-Minority Students: An Exploratory Study of Six High Schools. *Harvard Educational Review, 60*, 315-340.

Massachusetts Advocacy Center. (1990). *Locked In/Locked Out*. Boston, MA: Massachusetts Advocacy Center.

Moli, L. (1988). Some Key Issues in Teaching Latino Students. *Language Arts, 56*(5).

Odlin, T. (1989). *Language Transfer: Cross Linguistic Influence in Language Learning*. Cambridge: Cambridge University Press.

Ramirez, M., and Castaneda, A. (1974). *Cultural Democracy, Bicognitive Development, and Education*. New York: Academic Press.

Rivera, R. (1988, June). *Latino Parental Involvement in the Boston Public Schools: Preliminary Notes from the Field*. Boston, MA: University of Massachusetts, William Monroe Trotter Institute.

Simmons, R. (1987). Social Transitions and Adolescent Development. *New Directions for Child Development, 37*, 33-62.

Velez, W. (1989). High School Attrition Among Hispanic and Non-Hispanic White Youth. *Sociology of Education, 62*, 119-133.

Wheelock, A. (1990, October). *The Status of Latino Students in Massachusetts Public Schools: Directions for Policy Research in the 1990's*. Boston, MA: University of Massachusetts, Mauricio Gaston Institute for Latino Community Development and Public Policy.

Table 1

Rank Order of Teacher Expectations of Latino Children*

Expectation	Rank Order
Learn to think	1
Improve English	2[†]
Try their best	2[†]
Ask questions	3
Learn to cooperate	4
Be responsible	5
Improve Spanish	6
Organize work	7
Behave appropriately	8
Attend regularly	9
Master material	10
Complete homework	11

N=21
*Not all respondents filled this part of questionnaire.
[†]Tie for second rank

Manuel Frau-Ramos and Sonia Nieto
I Was an Outsider: An Exploratory Study of Dropping Out among Puerto Rican Youths in Holyoke, Massachusetts

Introduction

The high school dropout phenomenon has long been viewed as a serious social and educational problem. It is well documented that leaving high school without a diploma has negative individual and social costs (Levin, 1972) and is associated with occupational opportunities that limit economic and social well-being. Because of their relatively low educational levels, many high school dropouts lack the academic skills that enable them to secure steady employment and adequate income. This disadvantage is shown not only when these students first leave school, but over time, as dropouts have fewer opportunities to upgrade their academic skills and cannot remain even relatively competitive in the rapidly changing labor market (Rumberger, 1987).

Leaving high school prematurely affects not only individuals but society at large. To cities, states, and the federal government, the high school dropout rate is associated with increased expenditures in social welfare and costly employment and training programs (King, 1978; Levin, 1972). According to Fine (1985), "dropouts are more likely to be in prison, to have multiple pregnancies and children, to be on welfare, unemployed or in dead-end jobs than high school graduates. This is particularly true for girls: a diploma means the difference between being a domestic and being a clerical worker."[1]

While over the past four decades the nation's high school dropout rate has decreased substantially, Latinos have not shared proportionately in this improvement. Latino students continue to have the highest dropout rate among all major racial groups. According to the National Center for Educational Statistics (NCES, 1990), while non-Latinos' annual high school dropout rate declined in the last decade, the rates for Latinos have not declined.

As is well documented by the National Council of La Raza (NCLR), Latinos not only have higher dropout rates but also tend to leave school earlier than any major population group (NCLR, 1990). By the age of 17, almost 20 percent of Latino students leave school without a diploma. In 1988, only 51 percent of all Latinos 25 years old and over were high school graduates, compared to 63 percent of African Americans and 78 percent of whites.[2]

What is true at the national level is also true in Massachusetts. Of all the major racial/ethnic groups in the state, Latinos have the highest dropout rate. According to a recent report, the annual dropout rate for Latino students from 1987 to 1989 remained higher than that of any other group: the current yearly dropout rate of Latinos is 14.1 percent, while it is 9.2 percent for African Americans, 7.8 percent for native Americans, and 4.0 percent for whites (Massachusetts Department of Education, 1990).[3]

Review of the Literature: Why Latinos "Leave" School

Many studies have documented an array of factors identified with the likelihood of dropping out of high school. These factors are primarily related to student and family characteristics and can be sorted into six major headings: demographic, family related, economic, individual, peer, and school related (Rumberger, 1987). Unfortunately, most analyses of school dropouts tend to treat these factors as if they exist in isolation from the social and political contexts in which students live and go to school. Few attempts have been made to analyze how such characteristics are related to larger societal, economic, and political contexts. For example, poor facilities and inadequate teaching staff (Fine, 1986), discrimination, racism, and low expectations (Miller, Nicolau, Orr, Valdivieso and Walker, 1988), lack of Latino role models among school personnel, inadequate resource allocation, and the lack of appropriate programs to meet language needs and involve parents (NCLR, 1990) are also factors that contribute to students leaving school. More recently, research on school dropouts has been more comprehensive in explaining why many students leave school (Wehlage and Rutter, 1986; Wheelock, 1990; Fine, 1991).

In traditional research on dropouts, the demographic factors most frequently associated with leaving school prematurely are race and ethnicity. Dropping out of school has been shown to occur more often among members of racial and ethnic minorities, especially Latinos, than among white youth (Rumberger, 1987). Dropping out also occurs more often among Puerto Rican and Mexican-American students than among other Latino groups (NCLR, 1990). Attending public schools in urban areas in the Southwest, where large concentrations of Mexican-Americans are found, is another demographic factor associated with dropping out (Ekstrom, Goertz, Pollack and Rock, 1986).

Race and ethnicity characteristics cannot be separated from the sociopolitical context in which they are found. It is the way in which students' race and ethnicity are valued or devalued in society, not students' race and ethnicity in themselves, that puts students at risk. In fact, it has been argued that institutional racism, classism, and ethnocentrism are major underlying causes of students' failure in American schools (Bowles and Gintis, 1976; Persell, 1989; Fine, 1991;

Nieto, 1992). Claiming that race or ethnicity per se are risk factors shifts the blame of school failure solely to students and their families.

In addition to demographic characteristics, numerous studies have identified family-related factors that influence the dropout behavior of high school students. In this category the two most important factors are family socioeconomic status and family background and structure. Students from lower socioeconomic strata have consistently been shown to have higher dropout rates than their peers who come from higher socioeconomic origins, regardless of which variables or predictors are used to measure economic and social status (Rumberger, 1983). Low-level parental education (and income), sibling(s) who dropped out of high school, a single-parent family, language minority status, and lack of learning materials and opportunities in the home are other family-related risk factors linked to dropping out (Steinberg, Blinde and Chan, 1984; Ekstrom, et al., 1986; Vélez, 1989; Fernández and Vélez, 1990; and NCLR, 1990).

It is important to emphasize that these factors in themselves do not explain the root causes of dropping out, but rather seek to describe the conditions under which certain students leave school. For a more comprehensive explanation, we need to understand how family-related characteristics are viewed in schools. For instance, Anyon has documented that schools are tremendously affected by the socioeconomic status of the communities in which they are found (Anyon, 1981). Her ethnographic research illustrates how the quality of education in various schools, from those in poor and working-class communities to those in professional and upper middle-class communities, differs dramatically. The differences between these schools are seen in their curricular offers, instructional strategies, and teachers' expectations of students. This finding is corroborated by research in an Appalachian school that demonstrated that, in spite of a teacher's best intentions, instructional strategies are often driven by teachers' limited expectations of students because of their social class (Bennett, 1991). Persell (1989) echoes this finding by claiming that students are far different when they leave school than when they enter. This researcher finds that schools, rather than being "the great equalizer," tend to exacerbate even further the social and racial differences that children bring to school.

Blaming single-parent status on students' failure in school is also found in much traditional dropout research. Here too it is important to understand that single-parent status alone cannot be responsible for so many students dropping out. Research by Clark (1983) conducted in inner-city schools in Chicago, found that some Black students, even those from single-parent households where parents had a low educational level, can be extremely successful in school.

National data analyzed by the NCLR (1990) points out that a combination of the factors mentioned above put many Latinos in a "high risk" category and increase their odds of leaving school. The NCLR report also notes that selected factors have a greater effect than others on the probability of students leaving school. For instance, single-parent family status plus low family income, and low parental education in addition to limited-English-proficiency are reported as two significant combinations. The report shows that among eighth-grade Latino students, 36 percent tend to exhibit two or more of the risk factors, compared with 14 percent, of white students and 41 percent of African-American students. Among Latino subgroups, Puerto Ricans (40.8 percent) and Mexican Americans (39.3 percent) are most likely to have two or more risk factors than Cubans (23 percent).

Another study suggests that in addition to socioeconomic status and Latino origin, Spanish-speaking students have a higher dropout rate than either English-speaking students or those who have another language status. However, as the authors emphasize, "no analysis has independently examined ethnicity, language minority status, and socioeconomic status as contributors to dropping out" (Steinberg, et al., 1984). Other researchers who have looked into this issue in more depth pinpoint teacher attitudes and biases toward Spanish language use, rather than any inherent deficiency caused by speaking Spanish, as the real problem. For example, one study in Texas found that teachers repressed Spanish use by their students because they viewed it as a handicap and a "social problem." Teachers thought that continuing to use Spanish was a way for students to persist in being "foreign" and thereby refusing to become "American." In spite of the fact that most of their students were American citizens, teachers still viewed them as "outsiders" if they continued speaking Spanish (Hurtado and Rodríguez, 1989).

The use of Spanish at home alone cannot explain poor academic achievement or high dropout rates among students. For example, Cuban students have the highest educational level of all Latinos, yet they are also the most likely to speak Spanish at home. Their largely middle-class background has been shown to be a more salient factor in their relative success than their language use (Valdivieso and Cary, 1988). In fact, speaking Spanish has been found to be an asset rather than a handicap for students in a number of studies. Focusing on the relationship between Spanish-language background and achievement among first-, second- and third-generation Mexican-American high school students, one study found that, contrary to the conventional wisdom, Spanish is not an impediment to Latino students' success (Buriel and Cardoza, 1988). Another study focusing on academically successful students from a variety of racial, ethnic, linguistic, and social-class backgrounds found similar results: All of the students whose families spoke a language other than English were adamant about maintaining it. The same was true of culture. That is, cultural and linguistic maintenance, even if at times in conflict, had a positive impact on the academic success of these students (Nieto, 1992). Although there are certainly exceptions to this, the role of language and culture as mediating factors in educational success cannot be overlooked.

Another study of Latino high school students found that those who were highly proficient in Spanish performed better on achievement tests and had higher educational aspirations than those who were not (Nielson and Nielson, 1981). Furthermore, a long-awaited federal Education Department study concludes that although each of the three types of bilingual education methods used (English immersion; shifting to English over four years; and shifting to English over six years) is beneficial to native Spanish-speakers, *the more native language instruction students received, the more likely they were to be reclassified as proficient in English.* The study found that although English immersion programs may be effective in teaching children English, bilingual programs are even more effective (Ramírez, 1991).

Well-implemented bilingual education programs have been found to reduce the odds of Spanish-speaking students leaving school. This has been confirmed by a number of studies, including one conducted in Massachusetts that included Holyoke schools. In this study it was found that students enrolled in bilingual classes were less likely to be held back a grade and had a higher attendance rate than those not in the program (Walsh and Carballo, 1986). All of these data would suggest that issues of language use and proficiency, just as those of family and social characteristics, have to be understood within their social and political contexts. Speaking Spanish alone is not an adequate explanation for Latinos' high dropout rates, but the way in which Spanish use is viewed by teachers, schools, and communities could be a crucial consideration (Walsh, 1991).

Economic, peer, and personal factors have also been associated with the premature leaving of school. Getting a job to help the family finances is the most common reason given for dropping out of high school. Poor motivation, pregnancy, marriage, low self-esteem, and friends' educational and social expectations are also often associated with dropout decisions (Ekstrom, et al., 1986; Wehlage and Rutter, 1986; Rumberger, 1983). Yet different studies show that some of these factors are not really related to dropping out at all. For example, recent studies have pointed out that most teenage females who get pregnant do so after dropping out of school, not before. There may be structures within schools that push females to drop out, these studies imply; but it is only afterwards that many of them decide to become pregnant. Other factors associated with dropping out need to be challenged in order to get to the root cause, rather than the symptoms, of dropping out. For instance, poor motivation, rather than being the reason for dropping out, may actually be the result of poor schooling and lack of academic success.

Several school-controlled factors associated with the decision to leave school have also been identified. Among these are school policies related to students' behavior (discipline problems, cutting classes, and absenteeism that result in suspension from school) and poor academic performance (poor grades and grade retention). In mainstream dropout research, these factors, combined with individual and family social and economic characteristics, tend to blame students who drop out for their "failure." As Wehlage points out, "by focusing exclusively on personal and social characteristics shared by dropouts, this research makes it appear that dropouts are deviant, deficient, or negligent with regard to school" (Wehlage and Rutter, 1986).

Rather than blaming the victims who drop out, several researchers have focused on how school characteristics themselves may influence student academic achievement and behavioral problems and, consequently, school retention. It has been found that some school policies and practices may negatively influence Latino students' academic performance and behavior, and their decision to stay in or leave school. Fernández and Shu (1988), in analyzing data from the *High School and Beyond* study, reached a puzzling conclusion: Latinos had higher dropout rates even when their grades were higher than other students, they were in the academic rather than the "general" track, they were not from poor families, they did not have parents with less schooling, and they did not have problems with their teachers. The authors concluded that schools have been unsuccessful in holding onto Latino students even when they did not display any of the traditional "risk factors" associated with dropping out. A possible reason for these students dropping out came from the finding that many Latino students, both dropouts and graduates, expressed many more negative feelings about their schools than other students in the national sample.

These findings lead to the necessity of exploring conditions in schools themselves that may encourage some students to leave. These conditions are what Rutter and Wehlage have called the "holding power" of schools (1986). They conclude that it is the combination of certain student attributes and certain school conditions that are responsible for students' decisions to drop out. The school factors and a brief description of each follows:

> *Grade retention*: National data show that after native Americans, Latino students are more likely to be held back for two or more grades than any other racial/ethnic group (NCLR, 1990). In Massachusetts, the percentage of African Americans (8.5 percent) and Latinos (8.3 percent) recommended for grade retention for the 1988-89 school year was higher than for Asians (3.9 percent) and whites (2.7 percent) (Massachusetts Department of Education, 1990). In addition, in seven of ten districts with the highest Latino student population, grade retention rates among Latinos were higher than for other groups (Wheelock, 1990). Grade retention among Latino students is a major reason why they leave school and experience higher dropout rates (NCLR, 1990).

> *Over age*: Students who have been held back and put behind their age cohorts tend to experience higher dropout rates (Fernández and Vélez, 1990). School dropout among students ashamed for being older than their

classmates has been noticed. An explanation that focuses on economic reasons seems to be related. As Fernández and Vélez suggest, "given limited financial resources at home and doubts about the long-term benefits of a high school diploma, older students may decide that the personal costs of staying in school are too high."

Confrontation: Cutting classes, absenteeism, disciplinary problems and school suspension can be classified as "confrontational practices" by students. According to Kim (1985), students who feel alienated from the educational goals of the curriculum and school personnel become engaged in confrontational practices. Vélez (1990) point outs that "persistent confrontation can lead to official dismissal from school or to uncomfortable situations that cause the student to leave on his or her own." School suspension also increases the odds of dropping out for all Latino groups.

Placement practices: Enrollment in a precollege preparatory curriculum tends to decrease the likelihood of dropping out. This has been found to be the case among Puerto Rican students. As stated by Vélez (1990), enrollment in an academic curriculum is "a defense against dropping out." It is well documented that Latinos are overrepresented in "special" and nonacademic programs. In addition, Latinos are far more likely than whites to enroll in "special" and low-status courses, and far less likely to take advanced-level courses (Massachusetts Advocacy Center, 1990; NCLR, 1990; Wheelock, 1990).

Low participation in extracurricular activities: Although participation in extracurricular activities and its effect on dropping out has not been studied thoroughly, a few studies suggest that such participation may act as a buffer against dropping out. One study centering mostly on interscholastic athletics found that participation is more likely to enhance than interfere with high school students' academic achievement (Steinberg, et al., 1984). The previously cited research on academically successful students from a variety of backgrounds also found this to be true. In almost every case, academically successful students were far from the stereotypical "nerd" suggested by the conventional wisdom but were involved in a great variety of activities, from school clubs and sports to participation in community, cultural, and religious activities (Nieto, 1992).

Methodology

The research on Holyoke public schools reported in the next section of this chapter is based on a study done in 1991 to explore what factors may lead Latino youths in Holyoke, Massachusetts, to drop out of high school. Because of its large Puerto Rican school population and growing dropout problem, Holyoke provides an ideal setting for investigating the dropout problem of Latinos.

This research will: (1) compare students who complete high school with those who do not on a number of factors including race/ethnicity, socioeconomic status, age, and school-related experiences (such as nonpromotion, participation in bilingual education program, grades, and placement in a particular track); (2) explore possible reasons that account for Latinos in Holyoke dropping out of high school; and (3) recommend school policies based on an analysis of the dropout situation in the Holyoke public schools.

This research uses data provided by the Holyoke School Department. Data were drawn from the students' cumulative folder as well as from school district annual reports. These sources provided information on administrative practices and policies, and students' socioeconomic background and academic performance.

A student sample of 125 was drawn from the 273 students in the Holyoke High School graduating class of 1990. In addition, all students (82) from the class of 1990 who dropped out of school during their junior or senior high school year were included in the study. Among those students who did not graduate, 35 left school in the eleventh grade, and 47 left some time during their senior year (twelfth grade). Each one of these students was chosen because their cumulative school folders appeared to be complete and up-to-date regarding information required for the study. A sample of 12 Latino students that included both graduates and dropouts was drawn for personal interviews. Due to the students' frequent mobility, only three male students (two graduates and one dropout) were reached. These students were located and interviewed by telephone. Attempts to locate additional students from the 1990 cohort group were unsuccessful.

The racial/ethnic and gender distribution of the 125 graduating students sampled is as follows: 71 Latino students (38 female and 33 male); 50 white students (23 females and 27 males); 2 Asian male students; and 2 African-American students (one of each gender). The breakdown of the 82 students in the dropout group is as follows: 49 Latino students (28 males and 21 females); 26 white students (16 females and 10 males); 4 African-American male students; and 3 Asian students (1 female and 2 males).

A Profile: Dropouts and Graduates in Holyoke Public Schools

The number of Latinos in Massachusetts rose dramatically from 1980 to 1990. According to 1990 Census Bureau figures released by the Massachusetts Institute for Social and Economic Research (MISER), the number of Latinos living in Massachusetts grew 103.9 percent compared to a 2.4 percent increase for non-Latinos during this period.[4] Between 1980 and 1990, after Asian Americans (189.7 percent), Latinos became the second-fastest growing community, making them the largest minority group in the Commonwealth.[5]

During the last two decades, Holyoke has experienced a dramatic change in the racial/ethnic composition of its population. The Latino population within the city, which is 92 percent Puerto Rican, has increased significantly in the past decade. As the overall Holyoke population declined 2.2 percent between 1980 and 1990, the rate of Latino residents increased by 120 percent. In 1980, the white population was 38,276, the African-American population was 1,045, and the Latino population was 6,165. According to 1990 Census Bureau figures, the racial and ethnic population composition of Holyoke was most recently measured as 31,938 whites, 1,571 African Americans, and 13,573 Latinos (MISER, 1991).

The racial/ethnic student composition of the public schools shows the same demographic changes that can be seen citywide: declining white student enrollment and an increasing Latino student population. According to data published by Holyoke public schools in 1974, 80 percent (7,014) of the total school system enrollment was white, and less than 16 percent (1,414) was Latino (HPS, 1991). In 1985, these figures were 44 percent (3,030) for Latinos and 51 percent (3,481) for whites. One year later, the number of Latino students surpassed the number of white students. By 1990, while the rate of white students enrolled in the Holyoke schools dropped almost 32 percent from what it had been in 1980 (to 2,407), the enrollment of Latino students jumped 62 percent (to 4,711).

For the 1986-87 school year, the rate of Puerto Ricans and other Latinos who left high school in Holyoke was the highest among all racial/ethnic groups.[6] According to Holyoke public school annual dropout rate data, more than half (52 percent) of those youths who left school were white students, followed by Latinos (46 percent), and Asian Americans (2 percent). However, at the junior high school level, 64 percent of the total dropouts were Latino students, compared to 36 percent of white students (HPS, 1990).[7]

By the 1989-90 school year, Holyoke's Puerto Rican students were dropping out at a higher rate than whites. During this period, the dropout rate for Latino high school students was the highest at 68 percent, followed by white students at 25 percent. The annual dropout rate among Puerto Ricans students at the junior high school level rose from 64 percent to 69 percent between 1986-87 and 1989-90, while the dropout rate of white students decreased from 36 percent to 25 percent.

Forty-four percent of all students in the sample taken for this study (207) reported that they were born in the city of Holyoke. Among white graduates and dropouts combined (76), about three out of four students reported that they were born in Holyoke. In contrast, 22 percent of the Latino students (120) were born in Holyoke and 44 percent in Puerto Rico. Only three Latino students were born in South America. It is significant to note that the students born in Puerto Rico exhibited a disproportionately higher dropout rate than those born in Holyoke. Of those students in our sample, only 10 percent of Puerto Ricans born in Holyoke left high school compared to 42 percent of those born on the island.

Latino dropouts in Holyoke tended to live in a single-parent family, usually with a mother but no father. This study found that more than half of the Latino students lived with one parent at home. Fifty-one percent of these lived in families headed by a mother. Compared with their counterparts who left school early, Latinos who stayed in school were twice as likely to come from a family with two parents at home. Thirty (44 percent) of the Latino high school graduates in the sample lived in two-parent families, compared to 11(22 percent) of the dropouts.

When gender is taken into account, the situation changes dramatically. The rate of Latino females (graduates and dropouts) who lived in single-parent households was higher (58 percent) than that of Latino males (44 percent). However, the rate of Latino females who completed high school and lived in a single-parent family, in most cases headed by the mother, was higher (58 percent) than those high school graduate females who lived with both parents (37 percent). Male Latino students who came from two-parent families exhibited a higher rate of high school completion (53 percent) than their female counterparts (37 percent).

Self-reported data of parents' occupational status shows an unequal pattern between both white and Latino males and females. Forty-six percent of white male parents reported that they were employed in blue collar occupations (machine operator, tool maker) and 33 percent in professional jobs (teacher, lawyer, engineer), compared with 35 percent and 6 percent respectively for Latino male parents. On the other hand, 55 percent of Latino female parents identified their occupation as housewife, 12 percent as unemployed or on welfare, and 12 percent as a blue collar worker, compared with 30 percent, 3 percent, and 22 percent respectively for white female parents. In addition, 24 percent of the white mothers reported being employed as either a nurse, teacher or manager, compared to only 1 percent for Latino mothers. In the dropout group, a high proportion of Latino students' parents (64 percent) identified their occupation as housewife, unemployed, or on welfare, compared to 11 percent of white students' parents.

Data on the students' dominant language was available for 106 Latino students. Of all Latino students, 45 percent appeared to be Spanish dominant, followed by English-dominant speakers (36 percent), and speakers of both Spanish and English (19 percent). Data obtained regarding the students' language proficiency as determined by the home language survey and the Bilingual Syntax Measure (BSM), appeared to yield contradictory findings.

Spanish-language dominance appeared to be a factor for both those who dropped out and those who graduated. Among the Latino dropouts, the proportion of students whose dominant language was reported as being Spanish was higher (46 percent) than English-dominant students (38 percent). However, among graduates, the data indicates that the proportion of Spanish-dominant students was higher (45 percent) than English-dominant speakers (38 percent).

Among Latino students at the Holyoke public schools, those enrolled in mainstream programs were more likely to drop out than those enrolled in the Transitional Bilingual Education (TBE) Program. Sixty-nine percent of all Latino dropouts were enrolled in mainstream programs, compared to 31 percent enrolled in the TBE program. Of those students enrolled in mainstream programs, 65 percent reported English as their dominant language; 15 percent reported being bilingual; and 15 percent identified themselves as being Spanish-dominant. Among this last group, all of the students had attended the Holyoke public schools since the primary grades. Of the 15 students enrolled in the TBE program who dropped out of high school during either their junior or senior year, ten were Spanish-dominant. All of these students had transferred from various public schools in Puerto Rico one or two years prior to dropping out. In addition, all of them had obtained grades of C or lower in all academic subjects. Among Latino students in Holyoke public schools, 9 of 28 dropouts (32 percent) were enrolled in the TBE program at some time *prior* to entering high school, compared to 17 out of 38 (54 percent) graduates.

When asked why they left high school, "work" was the most popular reason reported by dropouts: 53 percent of all dropouts reported work as a reason for leaving high school. Among Latinas, both work (43 percent) and getting the GED (33 percent) were the most frequently cited reasons for dropping out. While no Latino males reported this reason for leaving school, at least in the sample obtained, data from *all* Holyoke High School dropouts for the 1989-90 school year shows that Latino students left school to get a job at a higher rate (35 percent) than white students (28 percent). However, 43 percent of all students reported leaving high school for reasons such as "dropout" and "other."

Information on advanced level courses taken by Latino and white students sheds light on Latino students' academic achievement and educational opportunities. This research shows that the gap between Latino and non-Latino students in Holyoke public schools is greatest in the areas of school performance (as measured by reported grades) and educational expectations (as measured by advanced courses taken and plans to attend college). Whites were shown in this study to be far more likely than Latinos to take advanced level courses.[8] Of the 104 advanced courses taken by the 1990 graduating class, 69 courses were taken by white students and 30 were taken by Latino students. Female students took 66 percent of the total advanced courses taken by Latino graduates. Among white students, by comparison, white males took more (55 percent) advanced courses than female students (45 percent). Six advanced-level courses were taken by Latino, white, Asian and African-American dropouts combined.

If taking the Scholastic Aptitude Test (SAT) is a good predictor of students' plans to attend college, the data in this study further illustrate differences in the educational opportunities between white and Latino students. Twenty of the 71 Latino graduates took the SAT compared to 36 of 50 white graduates. Among the dropouts, only five white students and no Latino students took the SAT. Latina students were twice as likely to take the SAT as their male counterparts: one out of three Latina female graduates took the test, compared to one in five Latino males.

When considering the grade point average of students who graduated, the data indicate that whites are far more likely to get As than Latinos. Eleven (66 percent) of the 14 A students were whites, while three (21 percent) were Latino. Nevertheless, Latino students on the average achieved higher grade point averages than either white graduates or dropouts. For example, 56 percent of Latino students graduated with a grade average of B compared to 39 percent of white students. In addition, the percentage of Latino students (67 percent) with a grade average of C by far surpassed the percentage of white graduates (31 percent).

In the Latino graduate group, two females were held back in the ninth grade as a result of poor academic performance. However, both completed high school with a grade average of B. Given the research on grade retention mentioned earlier, it is interesting to note a comment in another Puerto Rican student's cumulative record made in the second grade, stating that the student "should have repeated first grade (but parent insisted she be promoted)." Ten years later, this student graduated with a grade average of C+.

Twenty of the 33 graduates who entered Holyoke public schools at the high school level came from the public school system in Puerto Rico. Their grade point averages ranged from C to B. Of the dropouts who entered at the high school level, a high proportion came from the island's public school system (71 percent). This latter group tended to have lower academic grade averages. With the exception of one student with a B average, the group's grade average ranged from low Cs to low Ds. Grade distributions among eleventh and twelfth grade dropouts reveals that 35 percent reported a grade average of C, and 3 percent of B. Seventeen out of 37 Latino dropouts reported a grade average of C or higher, compared to six out of 20 (27 percent) white students.

A high proportion of white graduates and dropouts had been in Holyoke schools for most of their school life. Among graduates, 78 percent had attended Holyoke schools since prior to sixth grade, and 10 percent prior to ninth grade. The remaining 12 percent of white graduates entered the Holyoke schools at the high school level; all were previously enrolled in private schools. The percentage of Latino graduates who enrolled in Holyoke public schools prior to sixth and ninth grade was 42 percent and 13 percent respectively. The remaining 45 percent of Latino graduates enrolled at the high school level. Among Latino dropouts on the other hand, 49 percent and 8 percent had attended the Holyoke public schools since prior to sixth grade and ninth grade respectively.

The Latino students in this study can be clustered into two groups: those students who had been enrolled in the Holyoke schools since prior to high school, and those who enrolled at the high school level. Among the longer-term Holyoke students, the data indicate that Latinos who had been in the TBE program at some point in their schooling had a better chance of graduating than those who had never been in the program. A high proportion of longer-term students described themselves as Spanish-dominant; this could be a significant factor when considering their higher dropout rate. There are reasons, however, to consider these findings nonconclusive. The two methods the school uses for determining language dominance (the home language survey and the BSM) were administered to the students years prior to entering high school. It is important to note that the BSM, a screening instrument designed to determine "language proficiency," is not a comprehensive measure. Also, given the fact that the majority of these students had been Holyoke students since the primary grades, it is unlikely that Spanish continued to be their primary language for academic purposes.

On the other hand, the "early-exit" philosophy of TBE programs has been shown to disadvantage many students for future academic success. While no longer totally dominant in Spanish, many of these students are also not academically proficient in English. The result can be a disproportionately high number of students who are referred to special education services or who simply wait out their time in high school until they can drop out (Cummins, 1984).

When considering those students who moved from Puerto Rico and enrolled in Holyoke public high schools, analyzing the data is easier. There is no doubt that Spanish is their primary language, which may explain why a high proportion of Holyoke's Latino graduates are Spanish-dominant. The TBE program provides the means for those who come with a grade average of C or higher to attain graduation. Lack of graduation for the students who come from Puerto Rico at the high school level may be related to the quality of education they received in Puerto Rico.

The number of Latino students enrolled in advanced courses and those who took the SAT was significantly small. This might be due either to a lack of academic aspirations beyond the high school level or a lack of information and encouragement on the part of the school system. A high number of Spanish-speaking students found their field of choices in advanced courses limited because of their late enrollment at the high school and their apparent lack of English proficiency. This is also true for Latinos who are English dominant, although they have more curriculum choices in English. Low academic achievement as measured by grades and low self-expectations influenced by teachers' low expectations might be possible explanations that apply to this latter group.

The curriculum offered at the high school may shed light on the source of alienation described by the three Puerto Rican students interviewed for this study (and perhaps more implicitly reflected in their dropout rates). The Holyoke High School Course Selection Guide offers a complete listing of all the courses available at the high school. For a school system with a 62 percent Puerto Rican student body, there was only one course on Puerto Rican history, and it was found only in the bilingual program. For English-speaking Puerto Rican students in the mainstream program, who represented the majority, no equivalent course was available. Ironically, although the number of African-American and Jewish students in the school system was very small, a course on Apartheid and another on the Holocaust were available.

Some Thoughts from Students

Interviews with three students, one who had dropped out and two who had completed high school, revealed that additional school-related experiences may be implicated in students' decision to drop out. José, one of the students interviewed, explained how he felt at school: "I felt alone." After a brief silence, he added, "Tú sabes ... no son los míos" (You know ... they are not my people); "I was an outsider."[9] José was an eleventh grade dropout and had been a Holyoke school student since kindergarten. At the time of the interview he was living with both parents and three siblings and worked at a paper factory. José reported that he did not plan to go back to high school or get the GED. Because of his feelings of isolation, José implied that he was neither able to benefit from his educational and social experience in Holyoke nor build on his culture and language to help him succeed.

Pedro was a Holyoke High School graduate who lived with his mother. He worked as a machine operator in a local paper factory and was planning to attend college as soon as his mother was economically independent. A Holyoke school student since the seventh grade, Pedro described his overall school experience as "buena" (good) even though he made a point of clarifying that "algunas maestras yo no las entiendo" (I don't understand what some teachers say) in reference to the "americanas" (Americans). When asked if his level of English proficiency accounted for this lack of understanding, and if this discouraged him from taking advanced courses or the SAT, Pedro replied: "No mister ... no, no es el inglés...el problema es otro ... no sé explicarle, no sé." (No, mister ... no, it is not the English ... that's not the problem ... I don't know how to explain it, I don't know.)

When asked to make recommendations to the Holyoke School Department geared toward helping Puerto Rican students stay in school, Pedro answered: "Hacer algo para que los boricuas no se sientan aparte." (Do something so that the Puerto Ricans would not feel separate.) Although Pedro's experience was different from José's, it is quite clear that his educational experience was less than adequate.

Carlos, a Puerto Rican student who enrolled in the high school in eleventh grade and graduated a year later, described his experience by saying, "la pasé bien" (I had a good time). When reacting to the comment that he had been a student in Holyoke for only two years he said: "Sí, eso es verdad pero la pasé 'cool' ... porque yo no me meto con nadie." (Yes, that's true but it was 'cool' ... because I keep to myself.) This statement could indicate that in order to be successful in school, Carlos had to keep to himself. Carlos was working as a janitor and living with his mother and two siblings at the time of the interview. He reported that he finished high school so that his mother would be proud of him since he was the first one in the family to do so.

Discussion

It comes as no surprise that low socioeconomic status, measured through parental occupation and family structure, appears to affect a higher proportion of Latino students than white students and result in more Latino dropouts than graduates. Among dropouts, especially Latinos, living in a single-parent family, being overage for a grade by at least one year, and low family income increase the odds of leaving school. Because limited family income often means a family is dependent on a single wage, older students may decide that they are better off working than staying in school. As Vélez (1990) points out, "the lack of economic resources at home increases the costs of further education because the income that the student would receive if he or she was working would significantly improve the family's situation." This situation appears to be confirmed by the high rate of Latina students that report "work" as a reason for leaving high school.

The literature reviewed earlier in this chapter focuses on a number of factors related to dropping out. Some of these traditional studies point to family structure, socioeconomic status, and academic achievement as measured by grade average as factors explaining why some students drop out. However, such studies do little to provide definitive and clear-cut explanations for the dropout phenomenon among Latinos in Holyoke. In fact, these studies reveal contradictions and disparities when held up to the data from Holyoke public schools. For example, family structure — specifically female-headed households — might be a contributing factor for dropping out, but this does little to explain why almost half of Holyoke dropouts come from two-parent families. Likewise, both dropouts and graduates of Holyoke public schools were more likely to be Spanish dominant than English dominant, thus challenging the claim that English dominance inevitably leads to a higher rate of graduation. Also, while success in school as measured by average grades results in larger numbers of white students remaining in school, the same is not true for Latinos. Given their grades, we would expect that a much higher proportion of Latino students would graduate than do.

All of these factors suggest that dropping out cannot be explained by simply looking at socioeconomic status, family structure issues, or students' relative academic achievement. Although grueling poverty and attendant problems of unemployment, inadequate housing and poor health care, among others, certainly make academic success more difficult, these factors alone cannot account for the success or failure of students in the Holyoke schools.

Other conditions inside and outside of the school system may be equally important. As this particular study has focused on schools, we have not considered other societal factors that may be important in explaining school dropout rates. But because it is the schools' responsibility to educate all students regardless of their socioeconomic status, language ability, or family structure, schools need to review the impact that their policies and practices have on particular groups of students.

The research reviewed here has made it abundantly clear that a combination of teacher, school, and societal expectations of students based on their social class, race, ethnicity, and language are important factors to consider when looking at students' achievement. The curriculum also serves as a "risk factor" in that it is often unrelated to the experiences and background of many students. Given this, factors such as socioeconomic status and family structure cannot offer sole explanation for high dropout rates. Regrettably, it is students' race, language dominance, family structure, and social class that are often cited as the most important considerations in school failure. This focus of traditional research tends to dismiss the schools' obligation to educate all students. In the final analysis, this study shows with some certainty that while some factors (like female-headed households) may be a contributing factor, they are not the sole reason, by any means, for the wholesale dropout rate among Latinos.

A better way of understanding school dropout rates can be found by exploring factors that may influence different students in different ways. Factors beyond family characteristics and socioeconomic status need to be considered. This study's critique of traditional dropout research is based on the conclusion that contextual factors have to be included in any analysis of students' reasons for leaving school. These factors could include school policies and practices, including curriculum offerings and programs that build on students' language and culture, community and school expectations of students' achievement, teachers' interactions with students, and the general climate in schools that either encourages or discourages students from staying in school. By focusing on these factors, some insights regarding the disproportionately large number of Latinos who drop out of school in Holyoke can be identified.

Several existing conditions in the Holyoke public schools have shed light on why some of this school system's students are more easily retained than others. Spanish dominance, as mentioned above, was not a deterrent to students' school success. On the contrary, it was shown to be an asset if these students had the advantage of a bilingual program. Bilingual education, then, should be seen as an important way for schools to mediate students' experiences by helping them to acculturate to their educational environment while using the language and culture most familiar to them. As previous research has cited, the potential of bilingual education to help students successfully complete school by making them feel comfortable within the academic setting is noteworthy.

Holyoke students' own voices reinforce the importance of feeling comfortable in the school setting. Although the students contacted for this study are not meant to be representative of dropouts or graduates, the three students did offer cogent messages about their school experiences. All three, whether they had completed high school or not, described feeling alienated by their school experiences. "Fitting in" was an issue for all three students despite the fact that two had been in the school system for six years or more. The urge to belong and "fit in" cannot be overemphasized; it has also come up as a primary concern of Latino students in national studies (Miller, et al., 1988).

The rewards of staying in school, studying long hours, and graduating are also brought into question by this research. It is noteworthy that the two students interviewed who had completed high school were not necessarily better off economically than the one who had dropped out. All three were working in low-level and poor-paying jobs that offered little promise for the future. The advantage of a high school education may not be apparent to students, whether they are dropouts or graduates. It is no surprise that students may choose to drop out if they do not see the advantage of a high school diploma.

It is also important to mention that those students who had been in Holyoke schools since kindergarten or first grade had a significantly lower dropout rate than those who were not. In this case, it seems that the schools were more successful in helping these students feel more comfortable in school. Whether these Latino Holyoke high school graduates received any tangible benefits from their diploma is, however, unknown. The only data that we have concerning these students' plans to attend college (whether or not they took the SAT) are not hopeful. Although "fitting in" is an important first step in helping students succeed in school, it is by no means enough to encourage them to pursue a higher education or even to have higher expectations of themselves.

Implications of Research for School Policy and Practice

A number of implications for changing school policy and practice are suggested by this research:[10]

> *Maintain and strengthen bilingual programs*: Despite the limits of using primarily quantitative data, this study has provided some dramatic examples of programs and policies that are more successful than others. The Holyoke schools' bilingual program, for one, has proven to be substantially more effective at helping students stay in school than the mainstream program. The implications of this success for Holyoke and similar school systems could not be clearer: Continuing and strengthening the bilingual program is an important step to ensure that more Latino students receive a meaningful education and graduate from high school.

> *Reform the curriculum*: It is difficult to determine how the actual school curriculum affected students from the data reviewed here. However, we found that the stated curriculum was narrow in its focus and offered little relevance for the majority of students. The bilingual program offered no advanced courses, reinforcing the low status of the program. In addition, the complete absence of courses that focus on the background and experience of the majority of students in the Holyoke schools confirms the need for sweeping curriculum reform. The fact that so many Latino students were found in lower-level courses could offer some indication of the impact that curriculum can have on students' school experiences.

> *Rethink ability grouping*: This research has confirmed the problem with "ability group" tracking.[11] We found that Latino dropouts left the Holyoke schools with higher grade point averages than their white counterparts; those Latino students who graduated also did so with higher grades than their white peers. Yet Puerto Rican students were grossly underrepresented in college-preparatory classes. Ability grouping needs to be rethought if all students are to have access to the "high-status" education (courses for high achievers, college-level courses, etc.) that is necessary for academic success and college attendance.

> *Revise retention policies*: Previous research has demonstrated, and this study confirms, that retention as a policy simply does not work. Schools need to find alternatives to help students who are not succeeding in school.

> *Improve counseling practices*: The role of counselors in motivating students to stay in school cannot be overemphasized. Even among those

Latino students who graduated from high school, the notion of college as a real possibility was remote at best. This was clear from looking at the small number of Latinos who were in advanced level or college preparatory classes and those who took the SAT. In many high schools, counselors are assigned to perform scheduling, testing, and other activities unrelated to direct work with students. This situation needs to be changed in order to provide equal access to an excellent education for all students.

Maintain reliable records and accurate information on dropouts: It was clear from looking at students' records that students who drop out often do so without speaking to a counselor, teacher, or high school administrator. These students' records indicate such reasons for dropping out as "drop out," an explanation that does little to alert school personnel (or policy makers) to factors that may motivate some students to leave. Schools need to have systems in place that ensure that all students who are thinking of leaving school have the opportunity to speak with professional staff to explain their reasons for leaving. Interviewing each student carefully and thoroughly is a first step in understanding not only individual students, but also those policies and practices that help to push other students out.

Reform disciplinary policies: A review of the literature confirms the negative role that disciplinary policies can have, particularly when they are perceived as unfair by students. These policies include suspensions for absences and for other infractions. Students who are repeatedly suspended are more likely to drop out of school. Including students in reformulating disciplinary policies is one way to begin to reverse this process.

Investigate teacher-student interactions: Although little information about students' interactions with teachers was provided in Holyoke's records, the school climate in which teachers and students interact needs to be explored. The fact that the Holyoke public schools have changed from a predominately white to a majority Puerto Rican system in the past 20 years means that it has been through some tumultuous and dramatic changes. Some administrators and teachers may not yet feel comfortable or knowledgeable enough about their students to work effectively with them; others may be insensitive and expect little from their students. More data from in-depth interviews are needed to investigate this important issue further.

Develop a more welcoming school climate: Developing a more affirming school climate for all students is also indicated by this study. What became clear through the few interviews secured with former Holyoke high school students was that they did not feel comfortable in the school system.

Perhaps even more important than what can be accomplished at the classroom level is what can happen through the leadership of administrators. This administrative initiative could include the curriculum reform previously mentioned as well as outreach to encourage parental involvement, creating clubs that are of interest to a wider array of students, actively recruiting Latinos into existing clubs and teams, and developing a cadre of students to work with their peers in both academic and nonacademic endeavors.

Conclusions

The Holyoke schools are reflective of school systems throughout the country that have high Latino enrollments. Given the historic tensions, typical of our society, between the newest immigrants and other more established city residents, it is no surprise to see that racism and apathy are going hand-in-hand in the destruction of a school system. As a recent newspaper article on the crisis in the Holyoke public schools stated, "A factor in the system's problems, some say, may be racism. A number of teachers and principals said they believe an aging white community has abandoned the schools because of antagonism toward Puerto Rican children, who make up almost 63 percent of the student body here." (*Boston Globe*, 1991).

Traditional dropout research has focused on socioeconomic status and structural factors as major explanations of high dropout rates. Although these are certainly contributing factors to this problem, they fail to adequately explain the dropout rates of Latino students. Factors that focus on the social, cultural, and political contexts in which these students live and go to school need to be considered as well. These factors include school curriculum and climate, policies and practices that discourage students from staying in school, and the quality of interactions among teachers, students, and parents.

This research has made it clear that much more needs to be done by the school system to create environments that affirm all students. Nevertheless, there is some reason for hope. Bilingual education, in particular, is one program that is successful in holding onto students. Although the data from the school system shed some light on several factors that may contribute to the high dropout rate, other contextual information is hard to assess.

Given the limits of this study and the many questions that remain unanswered, the following queries need to be investigated more thoroughly:

What curricular changes might provide a more inclusive learning environment for all students?

What is the quality of interactions between students and teachers?

How is the school climate perceived by students?

What alternative activities within the school setting might attract a more diverse student population? How would these affect the dropout rate?

If students who have been in Holyoke since their early schooling are much more likely to graduate, how can we capitalize on this? What are the implications for policy and practice?

How does graduation affect students' choices for work or further education? Does high school graduation pay off for Latino students in Holyoke?

Notes

1. According to the Center on Budget and Policy Priorities (1988), poverty rates rose notably among Latinos without a high school diploma: In 1978, the poverty rate among Latinos age 35 and over who left high school before graduation was 25 percent; by 1987, the rate had reached 36 percent.

2. Although dropout figures vary from study to study depending on the definition and the computation of the dropout rate, Latinos continue to have the highest school dropout rates of any major group.

3. The Massachusetts Department of Education defines a dropout as a student 16 or older who leaves school prior to graduation for reasons other than transfer to another school. Annual dropout rates describe the percentage of students who drop out in a given year.

4. Persons of Latino origin may be of any race.

5. Persons of Asian and Pacific Island origin grew at a higher rate than any other racial or ethnic category, making them the fastest growing population in Massachusetts.

6. The Holyoke high school system consists of the Dean Technical High School and the Holyoke High School.

7. The Holyoke junior high schools included in this study were the Lynch and Peck Middle Schools.

8. Holyoke High School offers honors or advanced course sequences in language, mathematics, science, and English. Courses designated advanced placement are defined as those offering equivalent college credit and offering "a more significantly demanding pace and depth."

9. All of the names used are pseudonyms.

10. The majority of the policy implications that follow were suggested by Luis Fuentes during his response to our research at the "Conference on Latinos, Poverty, and Public Policy: A Researchers' Seminar", University of Massachusetts, Boston, 1991.

11. For a comprehensive study on the curricular tracking system in Boston, see

Massachusetts Advocacy Center, (March, 1990), *Locked In/Locked Out: Tracking and Placement Practices in Boston Public Schools.*

References

Anyon, J. (1981). Social Class and School Knowledge. *Curriculum Inquiry, 11*(2), 3-41.

Bennett, K. P. (1991). Doing School in an Urban Appalachian First Grade. In C. E. Sleeter (Ed.), *Empowerment through Multicultural Education.* Albany, NY: State University of New York Press.

Bowles, S., and Gintis, H. (1976). *Schooling in Capitalist America.* New York: Basic Books.

Buriel, R., and Cardoza, D. (1988). Sociocultural Correlates of Achievement among Three Generations of Mexican American High School Seniors. *American Educational Research Journal, 25*(2), 177-192.

Center on Budget and Policy Priorities. (1988). *Shortchanged: Recent Development in Hispanic Poverty, Income and Employment.* Washington, DC: Author.

Clark, R. (1983). *Family Life and School Achievement: Why Poor Black Children Succeed or Fail.* Chicago: University of Chicago Press.

Cummins, J. (1984). *Bilingualism and Special Education: Issues in Assessment and Pedagogy.* Clevedon, England: Multilingual Matters.

Ekstrom, R., Goertz, M., Pollack, J., and Rock, D. (1986). Who Drops Out of High School and Why? Findings from a National Study. *Teachers College Record, 87*(3), 357-373.

Fernández, R., and Shu, G. (1988). School Dropouts: New Approaches to an Enduring Problem. *Education and Urban Society, 20*(4), 363-386.

Fernández, R., and Vélez, W. (1990). Who Stays? Who Leaves? Findings from the ASPIRA Five Cities High School Dropout Study. *Latino Studies Journal, 1*(3), 59-77.

Fine, M. (1985). Dropping Out of High School: An Inside Look. *Social Policy, 16*, 43-50.

Fine, M. (1986). Why Urban Adolescents Drop into and out of Public High School. *Teachers College Record, 87*(3), 393-409.

Fine, M. (1991). Framing Dropouts. Albany, NY: SUNY Press.

Holyoke Public Schools. (1991). *Annual Dropout Rate by Race for the 1986/1987, 1987/ 1988, 1988/1989, and 1989/1990 School Year.* Holyoke, MA: Author.

Hurtado, A., and Rodríguez, R. (1989). Language as a Social Problem: The Repression of Spanish in South Texas. *Journal of Multilingual and Multicultural Development, 10*(5), 401-419.

Kim, S. K. (1985). Oppositional Practices among High School Boys: Their Expression, Determinants, and Consequences. Unpublished doctoral dissertation, University of Wisconsin-Madison, Madison, WI.

King, R. H. (1978). *The Labor Market Consequences of Dropping Out of High School.* Columbus, OH: Center for Human Resource Research, Ohio State University.

Levin, H. M. (1972). *The Costs to the Nation of Inadequate Education.* Washington, DC: U.S. Government Printing Office.

Massachusetts Advocacy Center. (1990). *Locked In/Locked Out: Tracking and Placement in Boston Public Schools.* Boston, MA: Author.

Massachusetts Department of Education. (1990). *Dropout Rates in Massachusetts Public Schools: 1989.* Quincy, MA: Author.

Miller, S., Nicolau, S., Orr, M., Valdivieso, R., and Walker, G. (1988). *Too Late to Patch: Reconsidering Second-Chance Opportunities for Hispanic and Other Dropouts.* Washington, DC: Hispanic Policy Development Project.

National Center for Educational Statistics. (1990, June). *The Condition of Education 1990.* Washington, DC: Department of Education.

National Council of La Raza. (1990). *Hispanic Education: A Statistical Portrait 1990.* Washington, DC: Author.

Nielson, F., and Fernández, M. (1981). *Hispanic Students in American High Schools: Background Characteristics and Achievement.* Washington, DC: National Center for Education Statistics.

Nieto, S. (1992). *Affirming Diversity: The Sociopolitical Context of Multicultural Education.* White Plains, NY: Longman Publishers.

Persell, C. H. (1989). Social Class and Educational Equality. In J. A. Banks and J. A. McGree Banks (Eds.), *Multicultural Education: Issues and Perspectives.* Boston: Allyn and Bacon.

Ramírez, D. (1991). *Final Report: Longitudinal Study of Structured English Immersion Strategy, Early-Exit and Late-Exit Transitional Bilingual Education Programs for Language Minority Children.* Washington, DC: Office of Bilingual Education.

Rumberger, R. W. (1983). Dropping Out of High School: Influence of Race, Sex, and Family Background. *American Educational Research Journal, 20*(2), 199-220.

Rumberger, R. W. (1987). High School Dropouts: A Review of Issues and Evidence *Review of Educational Research, 57*(2), 101-121.

Schmidt, P. (1991, February 20). Three Types of Bilingual Education Effective, E.D. Study Concludes. *Education Week,* 1.

Steinberg, L., Blinde, P., and Chan, K. (1984). Dropping Out among Language Minority Youth. *Review of Educational Research, 54*(1), 113-132.

Valdivieso, R., and Cary, D. (1988). *U.S. Hispanics: Challenging Issues for the 1990s.* Washington, DC: Population Trends and Public Policy.

Vélez, W. (1990). High School Attrition among Hispanic and Non-Hispanic White Youths. *Sociology of Education, 62*(2), 119-133.

Walsh, C. E. (1991). *Pedagogy and the Struggle for Voice: Issues of Language, Power, and Schooling for Puerto Ricans.* New York: Bergin and Garvey.

Walsh, C. E., and Carballo, E. (1986). *Transitional Bilingual Education in Massachusetts: A Preliminary Study of Its Effectiveness.* Bridgewater, MA: Bridgewater State College.

Wehlage, G., and Rutter, R. (1986). Dropping Out: How Much Do Schools Contribute to the Problem? *Teachers College Record, 87* (3), 374-392.

Wheelock, A. (1990). *The Status of Latino Students in Massachusetts Public Schools: Directions for Policy Research in the 1990s.* Boston, MA: University of Massachusetts, Mauricio Gastón Institute.

Virginia Vogel Zanger
Academic Costs of Social Marginalization: An Analysis of the Perceptions of Latino Students at a Boston High School

Introduction

Language issues overshadow all others in much of the research on the educational needs and experiences of Latino students in the United States. The ongoing political debate over bilingual education, fueled most recently by the assimilationist U.S. English movement (Crawford, 1992), has profoundly influenced the educational research agenda. Thus the majority of studies seek answers to the question: In what language do children from Spanish-speaking backgrounds learn best (Cummins, 1989)? Some research (Fillmore, Ammon, McLaughlin, and Ammon, 1986) looks at pedagogical methods, asking the question: Which teaching methods work best for Latino youngsters?

A newer area of research interest that is just beginning to be explored is the social context of schooling for Latino students. Inspired by Vygotsky's theories of learning as a socially constructed phenomenon, researchers are beginning to ask: What social conditions in the school provide the best learning environment for Latino students? Vygotsky (1978) theorized that, contrary to the tenets of behavioral psychology that shaped American educational research, animals and humans learn in profoundly different ways because of the social nature of human beings. Human learning is an interactive phenomenon according to Vygotsky. Internal cognitive development, he argued, is triggered "when the child is interacting with people in his environment and in cooperation with his peers" (1978, p. 90). Intellectual guidance provided by a teacher or peers and an environment conducive to mental risk-taking are necessary conditions for learning within a Vygotskian framework. Trueba (1989) and Abi-Nader (1990) used Vygotsky's theoretical work to explain academic failure and success respectively among linguistic-minority students.

To understand just how social factors influence the schooling experiences of Latino students, Moll and Diaz (1987) recommend studying the dynamics of social organization at the school level. Trueba (1989) also suggests "context-specific" investigations at the micro level in order to gain a more precise understanding of the social dynamics of learning for linguistic-minority students. The study described here looks at social relationships within one school from the perspectives of a group of Latino students. It seeks to illuminate the nature of the relationships between Latino and non-Latino students at the school, as well as relationships with teachers, by analyzing the perceptions of academically successful Latino students. Implications for the academic development of Latino students are also explored.

The Study

The data for the study reported here was collected as part of a larger action/ research project (Zanger, 1989).[1] Twenty academically successful, Latino students enrolled in college skills classes at a high school were asked to reflect on their experiences in school and suggest ways in which the school might be improved for students like themselves. Their responses were videotaped on two occasions: in a class discussion and at a panel presentation for teachers at the school.

The school in which the data was collected was a neighborhood high school in Boston that has since closed. At the time of the study, the student population of the school was 40 percent Latino; the majority of the remaining students were African American. The administration of the school was predominantly African American, while the teaching staff was predominantly white. The school employed a number of Latino staff members, but they taught only in the Spanish bilingual program.

The videotaped students are from diverse backgrounds. Approximately half are Puerto Rican and Dominican and half Central and South American. At the time of the videotaping, several were enrolled in the school's transitional bilingual education program, some were bilingual program graduates, while others were educated exclusively in all-English classrooms with Anglo peers. Some students were born in the United States to Puerto Rican or Dominican parents; others immigrated from Spanish-speaking countries as recently as three years before. Thus students fall into both categories of linguistic-minority literacy students identified by Weber (1990): those who had become literate in their native language as children and acquired English literacy later on, and those who first learned to read in English, along with their English-speaking peers. All the students are bilingual, though some are dominant in Spanish and others dominant in English. The videotaped discussions took place in English, since students were presenting or preparing to present to the monolingual English-speaking staff.

In spite of the variations among the students' educational, national, and linguistic backgrounds, all shared a commitment to finishing high school and going on to college. Their academic success and motivation was a prerequisite for admission to the college skills class. Their teacher was a bilingual, culturally sensitive Anglo as profiled by Abi-Nader (1987, 1990). The teacher understood the project to be an opportunity to engage students in transformative education (Freire, 1968), beginning with critical reflection and moving on to changing the social reality. First, he asked students to reflect on and write about their own experiences in school and on those of their peers and family members. Next, students shared these reflection in class. The class discussion, which was videotaped, focused on two main issues: reasons for the high dropout rate (over 45 percent) of Latino students at the school, and recommendations for improving the school for Latino students. Three students were selected to synthesize and give voice to the concerns of the group, as participants on the panel for teachers. These presentations were also videotaped. In the accounts that follow, students are given pseudonyms.

Students' Imagery of Marginalization

Students' descriptions of their experiences as Latinos in Massachusetts schools convey a strong sense of marginalization: They do not feel part of the social or academic mainstream in class or anywhere in school. "Just because we're Hispanics, we're left out," states a Central American girl, and this sentiment is echoed in the imagery chosen by her classmates to describe their experiences. These images of marginalization fall into three categories. One set of images revolves around students' sense of exclusion from the group by teachers and by their non-Latino peers. A second set of images refers to their subordinate status in the school's hierarchy. A third group of images conveys students' sense of cultural invisibility. Students' recommendations for ways to improve their marginalized status in the school share a common theme. They believe that for Latino students to "be joined in," the school community must recognize and validate their cultural identity as Latinos.

EXCLUSION

Students convey their sense of exclusion and isolation through a number of images, but the phrase "pushed out" recurs four times. Sandra, a Dominican girl, describes the pressure from African-American peers to assimilate or face rejection:

> They won't accept you if you're not like them. They want to monoculture [you]. If you don't do that, they just take you out of the group. Put you out.

Teachers, too, are perceived as contributing to the students' sense of exclusion.

Teachers are described as "pushing" students "right to the side," "right from outta the class," and "out to the edge."

The Latino students' desire to establish more caring, family-like relationships with teachers is clearly articulated. Several students contrast the nature of teacher-student relations in Latin countries with those they find here and express their yearning for relationships that are more familiar, in both senses of the word. Elsa articulates a preference for Latin-style support that she experienced after making the decision to study in the Dominican Republic. She made the decision as a result of feeling that in the United States her "opinions weren't worth anything" due to her minority status. She says:

> [In the United States] we're playing a game in school, it's just them [teachers] and us. Teachers don't get together with us. And in our countries, teachers are part of the students, they're part of the body of the students. They're friends, families to the students. I think teachers should open up to us, and try to be our friends and our parents. And then everything will be much better.

Students also express their desire for a change in attitudes among their peers. Sandra expresses the desire for acceptance this way:

> We want them [other students] to welcome us .... That's why we're trying and we're pushing hard so [that they will] understand that we're persons, that we're from another culture, but we understand them. We want them to understand us.

SUBORDINATION

Another distinct group of images depicts the low status position to which students feel themselves relegated. Here is Sandra's analysis of the hierarchical relations at the school:

> They [the other students] think that we're much, much under them. They want to step on us. And it shouldn't be like that. That's why some of students drop out of school, because they feel under them.

Students select these prepositions to describe their position in the school: "below," "under," "low," and "down."

Some students recount experiences with teachers who seem to be just as contemptuous of Latinos as the most racist of their peers are. It is the Puerto

Rican students who seem to have encountered the worst instances of racism on the part of teachers. One accuses her teachers of "treat[ing] us just like cats and dogs." A Puerto Rican boy describes his shock when a teacher called him a "spic" in class. He adds that the teacher was later suspended. Alicia, an outspoken Puerto Rican girl, tells of her teacher's habit of asking only white students to watch her purse for her, rejecting Alicia's offers to help. Alicia concludes: "They [teachers] think that just because you don't have blond hair and blue eyes you're not honest."

Students' accounts of their low status in the school reveal a sense of stigmatization for their Latino backgrounds and Spanish language, for their English skills, even for their accents. One Guatemalan boy describes his experiences as a new student this way:

> They [monolingual peers] use you as a joke. When you come in, and they hear you're Hispanic, the black kids and Americans they start making fun of you. They don't like the way you dress, 'cause if you're not wearing Adidas, you're not joined in, that's what they say. And some people can't take it. Some of them can't take that people laughing at them, but some of us have the guts to keep going.

A Guatemalan girl recounts a recent "terrible experience" that made her furious: A classmate told her, "You talk so funny, you have a funny accent."

The students suggest various remedies to raise the status of Latino students and improve intergroup relations at the school. Some voice the need for more interaction as a way of dispelling the racism of their peers. Sandra thinks:

> [Schools] should give us the opportunity to express ourselves, and to let them know that we can do as Americans do, that we can express ourselves and let them know that our culture is as good as their culture, let us unificate [sic] with them so they understand us and we understand them.

Elsa echoes this desire for unity by criticizing the tendency among all students to "group into different groups...and leave out the other groups." She thinks that the "separate parts of the melting pot" should "blend in more."

However, even among those who do articulate the need for more integration, there is tremendous vehemence against the idea of assimilating. Cultural pride is a strong current running throughout many of the students' comments, and the students are most adamant about their desire to be accepted for who and what they are. After calling for more blending, Elsa says in the next breath:

> Together, we have to learn to cooperate and live together. Learn a bit from each other. You can learn a lot from us and we can learn a lot from you. Try to learn from us, 'cause we can teach you a lot.

Her demand for respect from teachers and other students is predicated on their recognition of her cultural identity as a Dominican American. In her panel presentation, she tells the teachers:

> You can't succeed in a place where no one respects you for what you are .... I think Hispanic students should learn English, but not change their Spanish or change their culture. You don't need to change your culture to be American.

In this statement Elsa alludes to the assimilationist pressures on Latin students. At one point she calls upon her classmates to "defend our culture." Furthermore, she challenges the school's subtractive orientation with her vision of an additive pedagogy:

> I think we should try to learn English, but not lose our Spanish. They want us to learn English and lose our cultural backgrounds. And I think there's a way they can work up on our already [sic] culture. And build it to be strong and better than what they are and we are. Two things combined can be very good. I mean we take the Spanish culture and a little bit of the English culture, we can be great students, we can be great people, we can be great leaders of this country.

CULTURAL INVISIBILITY

A third set of images reflects the ways in which students feel ignored and left out, reinforcing further their position on the periphery. These images highlight the social distance that seems to separate them from non-Latin classmates and teachers. The failure of teachers and peers to acknowledge their cultural identity in a positive way communicates to these Latino students a sense of their own marginality, a feeling that teachers wished that they just were not there. Marla, a Bolivian girl, describes teachers as "looking away from us. They're saying 'Oh, they're Hispanics, they can't do as much as the other kids can do. They're saying that we're not good enough." Elsa, a Dominican-American born in the United States, contrasts the teachers' attitudes she found when she went to study in the Dominican Republic:

> [There] they related to us, they were like our second parents. They opened up to us .... Here, the teachers are just "open the book, read from page 20 to page 30, answer the question on page 35." They don't relate to us as much, they don't talk to us, they just shut us off. Some people say it's because we're Spanish, and I don't think it's just Spanish. I think it's all the students.

Ana, a Puerto Rican, echoes this feeling of abandonment by American teachers: "They don't try for us to learn anything .... They just leave us." Another classmate accuses teachers of failing to challenge Latino students for fear of pushing them "over the edge."

Students' perception of teachers' failure to "push them," the lack of support that they voice over and over, is experienced emotionally as abandonment. The disastrous consequences of neglect are spelled out by one student's description of what happens to many of her Spanish-speaking peers: "They just feel left out, they feel like if no one loves them, no one cares, so why should they care? No one wants to hear what they have to say, so they don't say anything." According to the students, the social dynamics of the school result in the alienation, the silencing, and decline in motivation among many of their peers. Dropping out is yet another consequence. According to Alicia:

> The reason why most Hispanics drop out of school is because we're very sentimental, we like people to think of us as human beings .... People say well most Hispanics have attitude problems, some of us do — why? Because we've been kicked around too many times, and we feel that we need to speak out.

Contributing further to students' sense of being ignored is the failure of the school to acknowledge students' cultural backgrounds, although more than one out of every three students at the school is of Latino origin. Marla offers the following analysis:

> I would put some of the blame on the school system because they say they have programs for ethnic backgrounds, for multicultural communities, but that isn't really true, all the way. It's true to some extent, [but] they only focus on certain ethnics, besides whites, but they don't really focus on ours. They ignore ours. They don't give us the respect that we deserve. They ignore our culture, our Hispanic culture.

Teachers' ignorance about their students' backgrounds also contributes to their alienation from their Latin students, according to a Puerto Rican girl who feels that teachers "should know about our ethnic backgrounds before they start judging us." If they did, she feels, teachers would "treat us the same as other people." Furthermore, several students assert that if teachers incorporated their cultures into the curriculum, it would help dispel some of the racist misconceptions of their classmates and raise the status of Latino students by legitimizing their ethnicity. Elsa calls for "put[ting] our culture into the curriculum, let it be enforced who we are, what we feel." She sums up the impact on students of the school's failure to do so: "It's real hard to be somebody in a place where they don't know who you are, they don't know what you feel."

As remedies, students suggest bringing in Latino role models, including Latin American cultures in the curriculum, instituting more cooperative learning in classes, and designing special extracurricular activities. These recommendations suggest that students would like to integrate more into the mainstream of the school, but that their fuller participation depends on a more welcoming environment and an acknowledgment of their distinct Latino culture.

What Can Be Learned from the Study

What can we learn from the pain, anger, and frustration expressed by these students? One lesson is a renewed respect for the courage and mental strength of those Latino students who do survive and succeed in such a hostile and alien school climate. Another is an appreciation of the eloquence and intelligence that these students display in their analysis of their own sociopolitical reality. Their reflections provide insight into the dynamics of schooling for Latino students. Further analysis of their data reveals three ways in which the social dynamics of the classroom and of the school undermine opportunities for Latino students to reach their full academic potential. First, the failure of the school to incorporate the students' language and culture frames learning in a subtractive context and denies students access to culturally meaningful activities to promote academic learning. Secondly, the racist climate described by the students drives some students to leave school and impedes the learning process for those who do stay. Third, the breakdown in trust between Latino students and many of their teachers denies them access to a central condition necessary for learning: teacher-student cooperation. This section will explore these themes further, drawing on research literature on linguistic-minority education.

"THEY IGNORE OUR CULTURE, OUR HISPANIC CULTURE"

The data in this study is quite explicit about the failure of the school to acknowledge and incorporate students' cultural background. "They're taking away our heritage" asserts Marla, while her classmates articulate the pressures on them to lose their Spanish language. One of their principal grievances is the failure of teachers to recognize and learn more about their cultural backgrounds. They resent efforts by teachers and other students to "monoculture" them, and they complain that the supposedly multicultural curriculum of the school fails to include their cultures. They believe that the school should provide an opportunity for Latinos to express their cultural identities and be respected for those identities:

What we're trying to say is that we're Hispanic and this is who we are and you have to accept that. You have to realize that we are here and you're going to have to deal with us all of your lives. (Marla)

Cummins' (1989) research on minority students' academic achievement identifies linguistic and cultural incorporation as one of four essential dimensions for empowering minority students. He asserts that failure to validate the home culture is one way in which schools reproduce the inequitable power relations between majority and minority groups in society, and that cultural hegemony contributes to the academic disablement of minority students. Cummins cites research data that suggests that cultural and linguistic incorporation in the school curriculum is a significant predictor of academic success, as measured by standardized tests of reading.

Data from the present study documents how the school's refusal to affirm Latino students' "already" culture, in the words of Elsa, contributes to feelings of isolation and alienation. Students sorely resent pressures to change their cultural identity to fit in. Their descriptions of the subtractive orientation of their school echo those of Rodriguez (1975) reflecting on his own experience as a Chicano student: "Education seemed to mean not only a gradual dissolving of familial and class ties but also a change of racial identity." Trueba (1989) asserts that second language development is contingent on some degree of acculturation into the second culture. Yet when acculturation is perceived to be such an either/or proposition, when cultural identity is seen as the price of academic success, it is not surprising that some students develop the "attitude problem" alluded to in the data. Nearly half of the Latino classmates of the students in this study had chosen to drop out of the school. According to some of those who have decided to stay, dropping out is a direct response to the school's attempts to "monoculture" them.

Other Latino students respond to the school's assimilationist pressures by mentally withdrawing. Recent research among younger linguistic-minority students labelled learning disabled identifies withdrawal as the response by some students to the stress engendered by the cultural demands of the American school (Trueba, 1989; Jacobs, 1990). Some students try to cover up their withdrawal with behaviors that often allow them to "pass" for competent students, while others simply give up "when the rewards of trying did not compensate for the pain" (Trueba, 1989).

Resistance is yet another student response to the failure of the school to incorporate students' language and culture. There is a growing body of literature linking Giroux's (1983) theories of resistance to schooling with the experiences of linguistic and racial minorities in U.S. schools (Erickson, 1987). This framework suggests that: "Consistent patterns of refusal to learn can be seen as a form of resistance to a stigmatized ethnic or social class identity that is being assigned by the school" (Erickson, 1987, p. 350). Matute-Bianchi identifies the ways in which some Chicano students resist adopting cultural behaviors dictated by the school because to do so is seen as undermining their cultural identity: "They must choose between doing well in school or being a Chicano" (1986, p. 254). Ogbu and Matute-Bianchi (1987) postulate the development of a collective oppositional identity among caste-like minorities, a way for minorities to protect themselves emotionally from the inequities of institutionalized racism. Similarly, white, working-class youth may also refuse to "enter the race" because they perceive that the achievement ideology of the dominant culture is a hoax (MacLeod, 1987). Walsh (1987, 1991) describes the struggles of Puerto Rican students to maintain their own voice in the face of the assimilationist demands of the school, a resistance manifested in their behavior and maintenance of Puerto Rican linguistic style and discourse forms. Student resistance is suggested in the data presented above in Alicia's discussion of Latino students' "attitude problems." In her remarks, she acknowledges the existence of her peers' negative attitudes toward school, the perception of those attitudes by the school authorities, and the justification of students' resistance as a legitimate response to being "kicked around too many times."

The research cited above suggests the damage that ignoring the home culture can do. There are also studies that clearly support Elsa's point that it makes pedagogical sense to build on students' "already" culture (Cummins, 1989). For example, a study (Malik, 1990) of English literacy acquisition among second-language learners supports the hypothesis that access to culturally familiar points of reference enhances literacy. A psycholinguistic analysis of the reading behavior of Iranian students at an American university was conducted, comparing reading strategies used with two texts: selections from the Encyclopedia Britannica on Japanese and Iranian belief systems. Iranian students' reading comprehension and reading strategies such as predicting, confirming/correcting, and integrating were significantly enhanced when given the text that was culturally familiar, compared to their performance when reading text about Japan. Malik cites the findings from other reading studies among both native and non-native English speakers that have concluded that culturally familiar text aids in reading comprehension, speed, and recall.

Culturally unfamiliar content is only one of the barriers that Latino students face in U.S. schools. Differences in sociolinguistic conventions, motivational strategies, and other aspects of cultural discontinuity can contribute to students' confusion, and these have been explored in a number of ethnographic studies (Zanger, 1991). Heath (1986), for example, has explored the impact of cultural differences in oral genres. Genres, such as stories, accounts, and recounts exist among all linguistic communities; however, their frequency and the language associated with them vary cross-culturally. Discrepancies in sociolinguistic conventions may confuse both students and teachers unfamiliar with each other's genres. Heath cites the example of a Mexican-born child in her study: "In Mexico, he had been a reader; in his community he knew what stories were and he could tell them. In his new school setting, definitions of reader and storyteller do not include his ways of recognizing or telling stories" (1986, p. 174).

Trueba points out, "The literacy problems faced by [limited-English-proficient] children are related to school personnel's inability to capitalize on children's different experiences, cultural knowledge, and values" (1989, p. 71). The failure of schools to acknowledge the background knowledge of all students is ultimately a political statement as well as an educational one. Social reproductionists theorize that a primary mechanism that enables school to reproduce the socioeconomic stratification of society along ethnic, class, and racial lines involves the validation of only the "cultural capital" that middle-class white students bring to school (Bourdieu, 1977). The corollary, of course, is the invalidation of the "cultural capital" of students from minority and working-class backgrounds. These students are made to feel that their life experiences, ways of speaking, and cultural knowledge do not count in school. By incorporating the cultural capital of some into the content of the curriculum, schools give these students a head start. When others fail to see their cultural capital legitimized by the classroom, it puts them at a distinct disadvantage. The students cited in our study were marginalized as learners because their background knowledge clearly did not count. This denial of access to a learning environment that is culturally congruent to the backgrounds of the students is highly political:

> Social/cultural control is tied directly to the structure of knowledge and symbols in schools and to the manner in which knowledge is presented in the schooling context. Schools, acting as agents for the culture, control the extent to which personal knowledge may enter into the public knowledge of school curriculum; they thus have a direct influence upon cultural continuity and change. (Roth, 1984, p. 303)

"WE'RE VERY SENTIMENTAL. WE LIKE PEOPLE TO THINK OF US AS HUMAN BEINGS"

Students' resentment about what they perceive as the racist treatment by their peers is another recurring theme in the data, and the racist climate of the school may be seen as a second factor contributing to the academic underachievement of many Latino students. Students in this study expressed anger at the racism of their classmates, at feeling "under them," and "pushed outta the group" because of their ethnicity and language. They are also resentful of being treated "like cats and dogs" by some teachers. Furthermore, adults in the school are seen as abdicating their responsibility by ignoring incidents of racism among students.

Similar accounts of stigmatization of linguistic-minority adolescents in public high schools in the United States appear in studies by Gibson (1987), Zanger (1987), Hoffman (1988), Margolis (1968), the Massachusetts Advocacy Center (1990), and the National Coalition of Advocates for Students (1988). The latter study, which was the result of a national two-year research project in United States public schools, reported "immigrant students in every part of the country facing harassment and intergroup tensions as part of their daily school experience" (1988, p. 60).

This climate of racism, of being treated "like cats and dogs," has devastating consequences for Latino students. One is that it drives many to leave school. One boy quoted above explains the high dropout rate among Latinos as the result of not being able to "take" the ridicule to which they are all subjected. He says that those who drop out lack the "guts" to stay in such a hurtful environment. Other students in the study cite feeling "left out" as the main cause of the high Latino dropout rate.

For those who do stay, what impact does the racist atmosphere they perceived have on their learning? An experimental study by a psychologist (Gougis, 1986) suggests that a climate of racism functions as an "environmental stressor" that can reduce motivation and interfere with cognitive processes. In an experiment with African-American subjects, those who were asked to perform a task of memorization in a situation where they were exposed to racial prejudice experienced more emotional stress, spent less time studying, and were less successful in recalling the assigned material than were a control group who were not exposed to racial prejudice.

In addition to undermining cognitive functioning, racist environments can also affect student motivation. Case studies of Puerto Rican and Vietnamese adolescents' acculturation experiences in a Boston bilingual program concluded that students' sense of stigmatization had a negative impact on the academic development of all the students (Zanger, 1987). For the more newly arrived Vietnamese students, racial hostility severely impeded their English-language development. Puerto Rican students in the study, who had spent more time in U.S. schools than the Vietnamese students, had internalized many of the negative messages of the school environment. Though these students had become quite proficient in English, their lowered expectations for themselves had decreased their academic motivation and resulted in significant academic underachievement. Trueba asserts that "the isolation of linguistic minorities had been highly instrumental in retaining low levels of literacy" (1989, p. 120). Sociolinguistic research on second-language acquisition further suggests just how such isolation limits students' access to the optimal conditions for learning English, one of the ingredients for academic success in the United States. Many sociolinguists believe that how well and how fast students learn a second language depends upon the social dynamics between language learners and the target language community (Schumann, 1978). Specifically, factors such as quality and quantity of contact, societal expectations, and attitudes such as ethnocentrism may be even more important than the quality of instruction or even intelligence of the language learner (Gardner and Lambert, 1972). This research has clear implications for understanding how the racist school climate depicted by the Latino students in our study may impede the acquisition of English literacy among Spanish-speaking students.

"TEACHERS DON'T GIVE US ENOUGH CONFIDENCE"

The third way in which the school described in our data fails to produce an environment conducive to the academic development of Latino students is through a breakdown in the mutual trust between students and teachers. The students quoted above depict relationships with teachers in which trust and cooperation appear to have eroded on both sides. The students feel betrayed by what they see as teachers' lack of "comprehension" (*comprensión*, understanding) and "confidence" (*confianza*, trust), the low expectations, and the blatant racism of many of their teachers. They cite several examples of behavior that they interpret to be racist, such the use of a racial epithet, differential treatment, and assumptions about students' dishonesty. Adding to the students' sense of betrayal by their teachers is the perception that the adults in the school have failed to use their position of authority to dispel the ignorant and racist misconceptions of the other students, which the Latinos perceive as an abdication of moral responsibility.

Other research studies suggest that the experiences of these students are not unique. Educational anthropologist George Spindler (1974) has done extensive research on the unconscious positive bias that teachers tend to display toward students most like themselves culturally and economically. Evidence of negative teacher bias is revealed in Ortiz's (1988) six-year study of 97 classrooms. She studied Latino students in both bilingual and in integrated, mostly suburban classrooms. The study documents repeated expression by teachers of negative attitudes toward Latino students' abilities. When children defied their teachers' expectations, the latter reacted with resentment and suspicion. In addition to negative comments, Ortiz records teachers' avoidance of interaction and eye contact with Latino students and their tendency to leave them out of classroom activities. An earlier report by the U.S. Commission on Civil Rights (1973) found similar bias in their study of 400 classrooms in the American Southwest. Mexican-American students were praised 36 percent less often, were 40 percent less likely to have their ideas developed, received positive responses from teachers 40 percent less often, and were asked questions 21 percent less frequently.

These findings are especially alarming because a healthy bond between student and teacher is so central to the learning process (Erickson, 1984, 1987; Vygotsky, 1978; Trueba, 1988). What might explain the disintegration of the bond described by the Latino students in our study? Three possible explanations are worth exploring: racist bias, cultural variations in interactional style, and the impact of a culturally inappropriate curriculum.

That some teachers hold racist attitudes cannot be disputed. Some of the evidence cited by the students, such as being called "spic" in class, is so shocking that it is a wonder that any of the Latino students witness to that event were ever able to regain trust in Anglo teachers. Such incidents damage the legitimacy of the authority upon which a healthy student-teacher relationship depends:

> Learning what is deliberately taught can be seen as a form of political assent ... Assent to the exercise of authority involves trust that its exercise will be benign. This involves a leap of faith — trust in the legitimacy of the authority and in the good intentions of those exercising it, trust that one's own identity will be maintained positively in relation to the authority, and trust that one's own interests will be advanced by compliance with the exercise of authority. (Erickson, 1987, p. 344)

Without denying the biased attitudes and behaviors on the part of some of the teachers alluded to in this study, it is possible to also argue that the Latino students' perception of Anglo teachers' coldness toward them is magnified by cultural differences. Elsa describes her cross-cultural experience attending school in the Dominican Republic where teachers are "friends, families to the students." She contrasts that experience to the more businesslike interactional style of American teachers, who fail to "open up to us, and try to be our friends and our parents." While some students attribute this failure of their teachers to develop personal relationships with them to racist bias, Elsa has a different interpretation: "Some people say it's because we're Spanish, and I don't think it's just Spanish. I think it's all the students."

There is some research that supports Elsa's interpretation. The Latino students' unmet expectations of support from their Anglo teachers may be partly explainable in cultural terms. Studies on relationships between Puerto Rican teachers and students identify interactional styles and roles that reflect the interdependent, nurturing, supportive values that characterize the Puerto Rican extended family (Nine Curt, 1984). Montero-Siebuth and Pérez (1987) document the personalized, physical, intimate tone of interactions between a Puerto Rican bilingual teacher and her adolescent students. Colón (1989) identifies three central features of the student-teacher relationship in a Puerto Rican context: *respecto* (respect), *relajo* (relaxed kidding around), and *apoyo* (support). The data presented above suggests that the Latino students in the study feel let down by their Anglo teachers on all three dimensions. It is likely that the dominant American cultural values of autonomy, self-motivation, and independence (Stewart, 1972) translate into a teaching style that is less personal and supportive than what the students feel comfortable with. The impersonal, businesslike tone that characterizes the "professional" relationship that makes Anglo teachers feel comfortable may be interpreted by Latino students as unresponsive and uncaring. Thus, one way of looking at the breakdown in trust between Latino students and their teachers is a mismatch in expectations of the appropriate role relations between teacher and student. This interpretation is congruent with ethnographic literature that has documented the cultural discontinuity between the homes of minority students and their school environments (Delgado-Gaitan, 1987).

Yet a third explanation for the breakdown in student-teacher trust is the failure of teachers to incorporate students' cultural and linguistic backgrounds into the curriculum. Given the pressures to abandon their heritage, students experience their teachers' lack of interest in their backgrounds as delegitimizing. This perception fortifies their conviction that the teacher is not to be trusted, and it may develop into active resistance as outlined in the section above. Alicia's assertion that she and her Puerto Rican peers have an "attitude problem," a "need to speak out" as a result of being "kicked around too many times," may reflect a struggle to achieve cultural legitimacy within a curricular context that fails to validate their cultural identity. This struggle can escalate into an ongoing battle between students and teacher over cultural legitimacy. Erickson describes this conflictual cycle set into motion over the struggle for cultural hegemony and concludes:

> Teachers and students in such regressive relationships do not bond with each other. Mutual trust is sacrificed. Over time the students become increasingly alienated from school (1987, p. 348).

Conclusions and Recommendations

This study was undertaken to explore the perceptions of academically successful, Latino adolescents about their schooling experiences. The dominant image revealed by the data was one of marginalization. Students perceived their position on the social and academic periphery of the school community, mirroring the marginal economic and political status of the Latino communities in the city (Uriarte, Osterman, Hardy-Fanta, and Melendez, 1992). The Latino students in this study felt pushed out, left out, and subordinated by teachers, by non-Latino peers, and by the school as a whole. Further analysis of the data identified three ways in which the social dynamics described by the students undermine the academic achievement of Latino students. The failure of the school to incorporate Spanish language and Latino cultures, the racist school climate, and the breakdown of student-teacher trust may be seen as a denial of access to the conditions that have been found to promote academic development. The following section will discuss the implications of these three themes for research and for practice.

As mentioned in the introduction, there is a good deal of research about the need for using the native language in instructing linguistic-minority children; this study points up the need for further investigation into how the native language is used and regarded once bilingual programs are implemented. Ramirez, Yuen, and Ramey's (1991) longitudinal study of programs for Spanish-speaking children, for example, reveals that in early-exit bilingual programs, little Spanish (25 percent) is actually used in the classroom after kindergarten.

A second area that the study indicates should be explored further is the attitude of the larger school community toward bilingual education, bilingual program students, and native language. Some studies suggest that bilingual programs have become institutionalized as a remedial track within schools, with all the detrimental consequences associated with the lowest track (Ortiz, 1988; Zanger, 1987; Massachusetts Advocacy Center, 1990; Oakes, 1985). Conversely, there is a need to learn more about bilingual programs and schools that have been successful in raising the status of Spanish, such as models of integration piloted in Chelsea, Massachusetts, and studied by Brisk (1991a, 1991b).

The analysis presented in this chapter has benefited greatly from the ethnographic literature on the cultural discontinuities between home and school. There is clearly much value in continuing this line of microethnographic study, and future research efforts should focus more extensively on the three themes that emerged in this study.

There are several practical implications suggested by the finding that ignoring Latino students' language and culture has detrimental effects on their academic achievement. First, large- and small-scale efforts to restructure schools with Latino student populations must understand the central importance of this dimension of schooling. It is disturbing that both of the major education reform proposals brought before the Massachusetts legislature in 1992 failed to acknowledge the more than 100,000 linguistic-minority students in the state's schools and the implications of this linguistic and cultural diversity. Secondly, local school districts should promote effective developmental and two-way bilingual programs that create an additive context for second-language learning and promote the perception that bilingualism is beneficial for everyone. Thirdly, the present study suggests the need to disseminate instructional methods that have been found to be particularly effective for Latino students, such as cooperative learning methods (Kagan, 1986). Finally, the benefits of a meaningful multicultural curriculum, pedagogical approach, and school climate are clearly supported by this study and should be promoted. The data presented here indicates that to be most effective, multicultural education must provide all students with opportunities to both explore their own cultural heritages and to share them with peers.

If students in this study perceive their school's exclusion of Latino cultures as essentially racist, this suggests that any attempts to address issues of school climate and/or racial tensions must begin with the kinds of inclusionary issues listed above. This study also indicates that further research on intergroup relations, particularly among Latino and non-Latino students, is necessary. Such research may yield information essential in dropout prevention efforts, for example. The data from the present study suggests that the high dropout rate among Latino students at that school may be significantly related to negative relations with non-Latino peers. There is a need to investigate whether this is the case in other school settings as well. Finally, within the area of intergroup relations, there is a need to identify and promote effective prejudice-reduction techniques.

These recommendations for promoting inclusionary practices and research and for reducing racism clearly interconnect with ways to address the third theme that emerged in this study, the lack of trust between Latino students and their teachers. The pain voiced by the students in this study underscores the need for comprehensive training at both preservice and inservice levels to enable teachers to reach out more effectively to Latino students.

An impressive list of cultural competencies has been developed for new teachers seeking certification in Massachusetts (Massachusetts Department of Education, 1991). It is incumbent upon school systems with large numbers of Latino students to develop plans to train working teachers in these competencies. The little research that has been done on training teachers to be more culturally responsive suggests how difficult it is to achieve measurable results (Sleeter, 1990). There is a clear need to research and develop effective models for teacher training.

Research cited earlier suggests that effective Latino teachers serve as mentors, role models, and culture brokers for Latino students. More Latino teachers and administrators should be employed in our schools, and not just within bilingual programs. Finally, there is a need to identify the components of student-teacher relationships that promote maximum Latino student achievement, such as the relationship explored in Abi-Nader's research (1987, 1990). This information will help guide training efforts for teachers and administrators. For in the words of one of the students videotaped for this study, "They [teachers] should have patience with us. But once they get us going, we can go as far as they can push us."

Note

1. The action/research project from which this data was collected had as its objective

improving the effectiveness of monolingual program teachers working with Latino student at two high schools. The project is described in detail elsewhere (Zanger, 1989). One component of the training for teachers was to expose them to a panel discussion by linguistic-minority students. To prepare for the panel, academically successful Latino students, with the encouragement of their teachers, developed their ideas through discussion, reflection, and writing. The students understood that the purpose of the panel was to help teachers at their school better understand linguistic-minority students. A class discussion and the panel presentations were videotaped. Transcripts of the videotape were subjected to thematic analysis following procedures describe in Bogden and Taylor (1975) and Spradley (1983). Highlights of the videotape were later edited into a teacher-training tape entitled *How We Feel: Hispanic Students Speak Out* (Zanger, 1990), which is commercially available.

An earlier and significantly different version of this paper was prepared for the Third Guttenberg Conference at the State University of New York at Albany in 1990. That paper appears under the title *Not Joined In: Intergroup Relations and Access to English Literacy for Hispanic Youth*, in a volume of conference papers to be published by SUNY Press entitled *Literacy across Languages and Cultures*, edited by Bernardo Ferdman, Rose-Marie Weber, and Arnulfo Ramirez (in press).

References

Abi-Nader, J. (1987). *"A House for My Mother": An Ethnography of Motivational Strategies in a Successful College Preparatory Program for Hispanic High School Students.* Unpublished doctoral dissertation, Georgia State University.

Abi-Nader, J. (1990). A House for My Mother: Motivating Hispanic High School Students. *Anthropology and Education Quarterly, 21*, 41-58.

Banks, J. (1989). *Teacher Education and Ethnic Minorities: Conceptualizing the Problem.* Paper presented at the annual conference of the American Educational Research Association, San Francisco.

Brisk, M. E. (1991a). Toward Multilingual and Multicultural Mainstream Education. *Journal of Education, 2*, 114-139.

Brisk, M. E. (1991b). *The Many Voices of Bilingual Students in Massachusetts.* Quincy, MA: Massachusetts Department of Education.

Bourdieu, P. (1977). Cultural Reproduction and Social Reproduction. In J. Karabel and J. H. Halsey (Eds.), *Power and Ideology in Education.* New York: Oxford University Press.

Clemant, R. (1980). Ethnicity, Contact, and Communicative Competence in a Second Language. In H. Giles and W. P. Robinson, (Eds.), *Language.* Oxford, England: Pergamon Press.

Colon, N. (1989). *Understanding Why Puerto Ricans Drop Out.* Keynote address delivered at "Abriendo Caminos" conference, Holy Cross College, Worcester, MA, sponsored by Hispanic Office of Planning and Evaluation.

Crawford, J. (1992). *Hold Your Tongue: Bilingualism and the Politics of English Only.* Reading, MA: Addison-Wesley.

Cummins, J. (1986). Empowering Minority Students: A Framework for Intervention. *Harvard Educational Review, 56*, 18-36.

Cummins, J. (1989). *Empowering Minority Students*. Sacramento, CA: California Association for Bilingual Education.

Delgado-Gaitan, C. (1987). Mexican Adult Literacy: New Directions for Immigrants. In S. Goldman and H. Trueba (Eds.), *Becoming Literate in English as a Second Language*. Norwood, NJ: Ablex.

Erickson, F. (1987, December). Transformation and School Success: The Politics and Culture of Educational Achievement. *Anthropology and Education Quarterly, 4,* 335-356.

Ferdman, B. M. (1989). *Literacy and Cultural Identity*. Unpublished manuscript.

Fillmore, L. W., Ammon, P., McLaughlin, B., and Ammon, M. S. (1986). *Learning English through Bilingual Instruction*. Washington, DC: Office of Bilingual Education and Minority Affairs.

Freire, P. (1968). *Pedagogy of the Oppressed*. New York: Seabury Press.

Gardner, R., and Lambert, W. (1972). *Attitudes and Motivation in Second Language Learning*. Rowley, MA: Newbury House Publishers.

Gibson, M. A. (1987). The School Performance of Immigrant Minorities: A Comparative View. *Anthropology and Education Quarterly, 18,* 262-275.

Gilmore, P. (1985). "Gimme Room": School Resistance, Attitude, and Access to Literacy. *Journal of Education, 167,* 111-128.

Giroux, H. A. (1983). *Theory and Resistance: A Pedagogy for the Opposition*. South Hadley, MA: J. F. Bergin Publishers.

Goldman, S. R. (1987). Introduction: Contextual Issues in the Study of Second Language Literacy. In S. Goldman and H. Trueba (Eds.), *Becoming Literate in English as a Second Language*. Norwood, NJ: Ablex.

Gougis, R. A. (1986). The Effects of Prejudice and Stress on the Academic Performance of Black-Americans. In U. Neisser (Ed.), *The School Achievement of Minority Children*. Hillsdale, NJ: Lawrence Erlbaum Associates.

Heath, S. B. (1986). Sociocultural Contexts of Language Development. In *Beyond Language: Social and Cultural Factors in Schooling Language Minority Students* (pp. 143-186). Los Angeles: Office of Bilingual Education, California State Department of Education, Evaluation, Dissemination, and Assessment Center.

Hoffman, D. M. (1988). Cross-Cultural Adaptation of Learning: Iranians and Americans at School. In H. T. Trueba and C. Delgado-Gaitan (Eds.), *School and Society: Learning Content Through Culture*. New York: Praeger.

Jacobs, L. (1990). An Ethnographic Study of Four Hmong Students: Implications for Educators and Schools. In S. Goldberg, (Ed.), *Readings of Equal Education: Critical Issues for a New Administration and Congress, Vol. 10*. New York: AMS Press.

Kagan, S. (1986). Cooperative Learning and Sociocultural Factors in Schooling. In *Beyond Language: Social and Cultural Factors in Schooling Language Minority Students* (pp. 231-298). Los Angeles: Office of Bilingual Education, California State Department of Education, Evaluation, Dissemination, and Assessment Center.

Kochman, T. C. (1981). *Black and White Styles in Conflict*. Chicago: University of Chicago Press.

MacLeod, J. (1987). *Ain't No Making It: Leveled Aspirations in a Low-Income Neighborhood*. Boulder, CO: Westview Press.

Malik, A. M. (1990). A Psycholinguistic Analysis of the Reading Behavior of EFL-

Proficient Readers Using Culturally Familiar and Culturally Nonfamiliar Expository Texts. *American Educational Research Journal, 27*, 205-223.

Margolis, R. J. (1968). *The Losers: A Report on Puerto Ricans and the Public Schools.* New York: ASPIRA, Inc.

Matute-Bianchi, M. E. (1986). Ethnic Identities and Patterns of School Success and Failure among Mexican-Descent and Japanese-American Students in a California High School: An Ethnographic Analysis. *American Journal of Education, 95*, 233-255.

Moll, L. C., and Diaz, S. (1987). Change as the Goal of Educational Research. *Anthropology and Education, 4*, 300-311.

Montero-Sieburth, M., and Pérez, M. (1987). *Eschar Pa'lante,* Moving Onward: The Dilemmas and Strategies of a Bilingual Teacher. *Anthropology and Education Quarterly, 18*, 180-189.

National Coalition of Advocates for Students. (1988). *New Voices: Immigrant Students in U.S. Public Schools.* Boston, MA: Author.

Nine Curt, C. J. (1984). *Nonverbal Communication.* Fall River, MA: National Dissemination Center.

Oakes, J. (1985). *Keeping Track: How Schools Structure Inequality.* New Haven, CT: Yale University Press.

Ogbu, J., and Matute-Bianchi, M. E. (1986). In *Beyond Language: Social and Cultural Factors in Schooling Language Minority Students* (pp. 73-142). Los Angeles: Office of Bilingual Education, California State Department of Education, Evaluation, Dissemination, and Assessment Center.

Ortiz, F. I. (1988). Hispanic-American Children's Experiences in Classrooms: A Comparison between Hispanic and Non-Hispanic Children. In L. Webs (Ed.), *Class, Race, and Gender in American Education.* Albany, NY: State University of New York Press.

Rodriguez, J. D., Yuen, S. D., and Ramey, D. R. (1991). *Final Report: Longitudinal Study of Structured English Immersion Strategy, Early-Exit and Late-Exit Transitional Bilingual Education Programs for Language-Minority Children.* (Contract No.300-87-0156). Washington, DC: U.S. Department of Education.

Rodriguez, R. (1975, February 8). Searching for Roots in a Changing World. *Saturday Review,* pp. 147-149.

Roth, R. (1984). Schooling, Literacy Acquisition and Cultural Transmission. *Journal of Education, 166*, 291-308.

Schumann, J. H. (1978). The Pidginization Hypothesis. In E. Hatch (Ed.), *Second Language Acquisition,* (pp. 256-271). Rowley, MA: Newbury House Publishers.

Sleeter, C. (1989). *Multicultural Education Staff Development: How Much Can It Change Classroom Teaching?* Paper presented at the annual meeting of the American Educational Research Association, San Francisco.

Spindler, G. D. (1974). Beth Anne — A Case Study of Culturally Defined Adjustment and Teacher Perceptions. In G. D. Spindler (Ed.), *Toward an Anthropology of Education.* New York: Holt, Rinehart and Winston.

Stewart, E. C. (1972). *American Cultural Patterns: A Cross-Cultural Perspective.* Chicago: Intercultural Press.

Trueba, H. (1987). Organizing Classroom Instruction in Specific Sociocultural Contexts:

Teaching Mexican Youth to Write in English. In S. Goldman and H. Trueba (Eds.), *Becoming Literate in English as a Second Language.* Norwood, NJ: Ablex.

Trueba, H. (1988). *Raising Silent Voices: Educating the Linguistic Minorities for the 21st Century.* New York: Newbury House Publishers/Harper and Row.

Trueba, H. (1989). *Empowerment and Mainstreaming: Culture Change and the Integration of Home and School Values.* Paper presented at the annual meeting of the American Educational Research Association in San Francisco.

U.S. Commission on Civil Rights. (1973). *Teachers and Students: Differences in Teacher Interaction with Mexican-American and Anglo Students.* Washington, DC: U.S. Government Printing Office.

Uriarte, M., Osterman, P., Hardy-Fanta, C., and Melendez, E. (1992). *Latinos in Boston: Confronting Poverty, Building Community.* Boston, MA: The Boston Foundation.

Vygotsky, L. S. (1978). *Mind in Society: The Development of Higher Psychological Processes.* Edited by M. Cole, V. John-Steiner, S. Scribner, and E. Souberman. Cambridge, MA: Harvard University Press.

Walsh, C. E. (1987). Language, Meaning, and Voice: Puerto Rican Students' Struggle for a Speaking Consciousness. *Language Arts, 64,* 196-206.

Walsh, C. E. (1991). *Pedagogy and the Struggle for Voice: Issues of Language, Power, and Schooling for Puerto Ricans.* New York: Bergin and Garvey.

Weber, R. (1988). Linguistic Diversity and Reading in American Society. In *Handbook of Reading Research II* (in press).

Zanger, V. V. (1987). *The Social Context of Second Language Learning: An Examination of Barriers to Integration in Five Case Studies.* Unpublished doctoral dissertation, Boston University.

Zanger, V. V. (1989). Chats in the Teacher Lounge Are Not Enough: Preparing Monolingual Teachers for Bilingual Students. *Equity and Choice, 5,* 44-53.

Zanger, V. V. (Producer). (1990). *How We Feel: Hispanic Students Speak Out.* Falls Church, VA: Landmark Films, Inc.

Zanger, V. V. (1991). Social and Cultural Dimension of the Education of Language Minority Students. In A. N. Ambert (Ed.), *Bilingual Education and English as a Second Language: A Research Handbook 1988-1990* (pp. 3-54). New York: Garland Publishing, Inc.

Castellano B. Turner, Amaro J. Laria, Ester R. Shapiro, and Maria del Carmen Perez

Poverty, Resilience, and Academic Achievement among Latino College Students and High School Dropouts

The major purpose of this investigation[1] was the discovery of factors that are related to academic success among Latino[2] youth. We wanted to identify potential stress-protective factors involved in moderating the effects of psychosocial stress due to minority and low socioeconomic status among Latino high school students. We reasoned that these protective factors could be operating at the individual, familial, school, or social levels. They might be, at least in part, responsible for college students' resilient patterns of successful adaptation as indicated by academic achievement. By identifying these factors and increasing our understanding of the interactive processes between them, more effective interventions for preventing school dropout might be proposed.

A number of studies have found that poverty, in and of itself, generates a significant number of stressors that interfere with successful functioning and positive adaptation to any environment (Kessler and Cleary, 1980; Bullough and Bullough, 1972; Myers, Lindenthal, and Pepper, 1975). Education is universally considered a necessary step out of the cycle of poverty (Jencks, 1979); yet, poor minority children in general, and Latino children in even greater proportions, are overwhelmed by stressors and lack supports that might enable them to make use of existing opportunities for educational achievement.

Dohrenwend and Dohrenwend (1970) showed that race and class interact in producing stress. Moritsugu and Sue (1983) have demonstrated persuasively that ethnic minority status in the United States is related to a number of life stressors. Minority groups are generally more likely to be overrepresented among the very poor. They are more likely to be overrepresented among the unemployed and the underemployed and to experience chronic unemployment and chronic poverty. They are more likely to receive inferior education and health care. They are more likely to be the victims of discrimination in seeking housing, in the work place, and in a variety of social situations. Latinos in the United States have been and continue to be subjected to all of these sources of stress (Comas-Diaz, 1990; Delgado and Scott, 1979). Latino adolescents, in particular, face stresses related to poverty, ethnicity, language, and acculturation (Heacock, 1990; Texidor, 1987).

According to a study conducted by the Boston Persistent Poverty Project

(1989), 45 percent of all Latino families in Boston are living in poverty. This figure is higher than the national figure for Latinos of 39 percent. Even more dramatic and morally unacceptable is the fact that 73 percent of all Latino children in Boston under the age of six are living in poverty. Given that poverty is a source of many psychosocial stressors and limited educational attainment prefigures limited competence and unsuccessful adaptation, the picture for Latinos is, on the whole, disheartening.

Academic achievement is a crucial index of adaptation and competence in U.S. society. According to 1990 U.S. Census Bureau statistics, 79 percent of the Latino population in the United States has not completed a high school education. The median years of schooling completed by this population is nine years. In the Boston public school system, 14 percent of Latino high school students dropped out of school in 1989-90 (Horst and Donahue, 1990). This figure is the highest of all groups; it is 10 percent for blacks and 8 percent for whites. Looking at these statistics in a different way, for the 1985-89 cohort of high school students (i.e., entered ninth grade in 1985 and expected to graduate in 1989), 44 percent of the Latino cohort group dropped out at some point along the four years. Again, this figure is higher than that of any other group. These disproportionate ratios are representative of the picture nationwide. Therefore, as a group Latinos in the United States attain the lowest levels of education. Given that the Latino population in the United States is a relatively young one, these statistics tell a very depressing story about Latino youth and their prospects for the future.

The questions of this investigation arose from two distinct bodies of literature: (1) research on risk and resilience, and (2) research on academic achievement and dropping out among Latino youth.

Risk and Resilience

A focus on psychological deficits and failure has characterized the mental health and education literature. Cowen and Work (1988) have, however, described the value of a prevention orientation to psychological distress. In particular, they have shown that the discovery of the factors that make some children relatively invulnerable to significant life stress may provide avenues to the prevention of problems among those who are vulnerable. Clearly, among those Latinos in the United States who share lives of economic, educational, and social deprivation, there are some who succeed and are psychologically stable and others who are less successful and show signs of psychological distress. Much of the mental health literature focused on Latinos has attempted to understand only the relationship between the sources of stress and unsuccessful adaptation and psychopathology.

There has been some controversy in the risk and resilience literature regarding the definition of the concept of resilience. The main issue of contention is: Is resilience an individual's constitutional characteristic that is genetically determined, or does it result from the continuous interplay of biological and social processes, which in turn get internalized throughout an individual's development? Werner (1990) has pointed out that the bases of resistance to stress are both environmental and constitutional, and the degree of resistance varies over time according to life circumstances. However, resilience is still often seen as a characteristic of the individual, while protective factors are thought to include both individual and environmental characteristics that ameliorate or buffer a person's response to risk factors or stressful life events (Masten and Garmezy, 1985).

Rutter (1987) asserts that resilience cannot be seen as a fixed attribute of the individual. Resilience is concerned with individual variations in response to risk factors. However, factors outside as well as within the individual need to be considered within the context of person-environment interactions. Even in the case where social factors serve as protectors in an individual's response to risk factors, the question is: How do these external protective factors interact with individual factors to alter internal processes?

Garmezy's reviews of research on stress-resistant children (Garmezy, 1985; Masten and Garmezy, 1985) has led him to posit three broad sets of variables that operate as protective factors: (1) personality features such as autonomy, self-esteem, and a positive social orientation; (2) family factors such as cohesion, warmth, and an absence of discord; and (3) the availability of external support systems that encourage and reinforce a child's coping efforts.

In the last several years, there has been a shift in stress research from an emphasis on vulnerability to a greater focus on resilience. However, in the search for protective factors that moderate the effects of stress, different researchers have urged looking at protective mechanisms rather than just identifying single isolated factors (Werner, 1990; Rutter, 1987). Researchers have, likewise, noted that risk factors cannot be understood simply as main effects or as additive effects (Werner, 1990; Rutter, 1987). A clear understanding of risk mechanisms requires an understanding of how risk factors interact with each other as well as with protective factors. Garbarino's (1990) ecological perspective on risk and resilience seems particularly relevant in doing research with ethnic minority groups because of its emphasis on the role of social institutional and economic conditions.

Most research on resilience has focused on children rather than adolescents. The studies that have been done with adolescents have found, in general, that resilient teenagers tend to be more responsible and achievement-oriented than their age mates. The resilient teenagers attain a greater degree of social maturity, prefer more structure in their lives, and have internalized a positive set of values. Furthermore, among the resilient, both males and females share an interest in matters labeled "feminine" by society. That is, they are more appreciative, gentle, nurturing, and socially perceptive than their peers who have difficulty coping with adversity (Werner, 1985). These resilient adolescents also have a more internal locus of control and a more positive self-concept (Werner, 1990). Even though Werner's findings come mainly from her well-known Kauai study, similar results have been obtained in studies with competent black adolescents from working-class families (Lewis and Looney, 1983) and with academically successful Latino male high school students who grew up in poverty (Mason, 1967). In terms of protective factors within the family, most children identified as resilient have had the opportunity to establish a close bond with at least one person who provided them with stable care and from whom they received adequate and appropriate attention during their early years (Werner, 1990). Other elements mentioned as important within the family have been grandparents, siblings, parenting practices, and family's religious faith. Protective factors beyond the family have also been identified, such as positive relationships with peers, teachers, and other adults.

Given institutional racism and the stresses of poverty, the family becomes an enormously important protective space in providing children a positive sense of themselves, their worth, and their potential for achievement. In a review of family characteristics associated with school achievement, Weiss (1988) concluded that the following family characteristics are associated with academic success: (1) high parental aspirations; (2) warm, affectionate relationships with praise for the child's accomplishments; (3) parents who exert control over their children and are firm disciplinarians with consistent standards; (4) a large amount of time spent in a wide variety of verbal interactions; and (5) parents who spend more time talking with their children. Clark (1983) conducted an ethnographic study of ten poor, African-American, Chicago families with high-achieving high school students. Again, these families were characterized by a capacity for dialogue, warm support coupled with supervision and limits, encouragement of academic pursuits, and a sense of responsibility for their children's achievements.

As important as families are to their children's academic achievement and success, they are rarely included in school programming for improving student school experience, especially poor and minority families (Weiss, 1988). As Garbarino (1990) points out in his discussion of the ecology of early risk, poverty creates a drain and depletion for whole communities. Families within these communities, whose energy is largely consumed by survival needs and who cannot turn to equally depleted friends and neighbors for support, lack the emotional luxury of spending the psychologically necessary time in emotional engagement with their children. Fine (1991) argues, however, that poor parents typically feel a sense of helplessness in the face of rigid, bureaucratic institutions that are unresponsive to their needs and interests. She points out that when parents are given real power in their involvement with schools, such as in new school restructuring programs in Chicago, they become energetically involved in shaping a more effective collaboration between family, school, and their wider community.

Latino Students and Academic Achievement

In order to understand Latino high school students, we must understand the broader social and cultural context of Latinos in the United States. Contextual factors include the stress of migration and acculturation that many Latinos have experienced. Leaving one's homeland creates a sense of loss and uprootedness (Espin, 1987); moreover, coming into a host culture where one has to face prejudice and discrimination is even more disorienting. In addition, we must look at the historical and sociopolitical background of the migration process as well as the political relationships that are presently maintained between the dominant and the minority groups. Being a member of an ethnic-minority group basically means a lack of power in relation to the dominant group. Finally, Latinos are by no means a homogenous group; there is a great deal of diversity among different Latino groups on significant dimensions, including social class, level of identification with the country and culture of origin, and level of assimilation into the mainstream culture of the United States (Muñoz, 1982).

Some studies, in attempting to understand the behavior of Latinos, have emphasized the attitudes held by the dominant culture. Locating this issue in a historical context, Stein (1985) described the attitudes held by many educators toward Latino students during what she referred to as the "Sink or Swim Era" (1900-1960). During that long period there was a general belief in Puerto Rican "intellectual inferiority," and many newly arrived Puerto Rican children were automatically placed several grades behind the level that they had attained in Puerto Rico regardless of their English proficiency or level of achievement. In addition, school personnel generally assumed that Puerto Rican children were destined for low level jobs, and counselors frequently guided them to vocational tracks, discouraging them from entering the college preparatory track. Rodriguez (1974) clarified the destructive effects of the vocational tracking process on Latino students by describing her own experience upon entering the New York City school system after coming from Puerto Rico. The author described the confrontation with the "assimilationist ideology" that many Latinos experience coming into the United States. This ideology requires that immigrants adopt U.S. culture and completely give up their own culture. In addition, Rodriguez points out that many teachers are simultaneously unaware that they have an assimilationist ideology and unaware of any alternatives to it.

Consistent with the myth of individual responsibility promoted by the

"American dream," the "melting pot myth" encourages children of color, who are manifestly different from the dominant culture group, to make themselves into the image of the dominant group. For Latino children whose first language or family-based language is Spanish, the requirements of assimilation might create a split consciousness and a sense of loss. Recent research on cultural identity, on the other hand, suggests that healthy adaptation is associated with high positive identification with both the majority culture and the ethnic culture of origin (Phinney, 1990). Pollard (1989) concluded from a study with poor minority students that, in addition to the consequences of poverty that lead to low academic achievement, low teacher expectations as well as inefficient school practices contribute to school failures. Moreover, she points out, minority students' expectations are low because they come to believe that their efforts may not be rewarded with future occupational success. Her findings suggested that those minority students who succeeded, the resilient ones, were usually the ones who were more likely to cross cultural boundaries. Pollard concluded that schools' inflexibility forced minority students to adopt majority norms in order to succeed, at the expense of their own cultural integrity.

A study by Valverde (1987) found that the most important factors involved in Latino high school completion were positive peer group relations and grades. In contrast, dropouts were characterized by feelings of alienation, rejection, isolation, and disconnectedness. In a study conducted in five major U.S. cities by the ASPIRA Association, which promotes Latino education, Fernandez and Velez (1990) reported the following factors as important correlates of high school dropout: older age, failing grades, grade retention, truancy, father's absence from home, and lack of plans to go on to college. However, it could be argued that some of these factors are effects of a more basic problem rather than causes for students to drop out. It may very well be expected that an older student with failing grades who hardly ever goes to school and has no aspirations to go on to college will be more likely to drop out. But what accounts for the presence of such factors?

Finally, a study by Steinberg, Blinde, and Chan (1984) compared Latino students with other linguistic-minority groups. The authors found socioeconomic status to be an extremely powerful predictor of dropping out. However, controlling socioeconomic status, they also found that Latino students were more likely to drop out than non-Spanish speaking minority groups. They offered four hypotheses to explain their findings: (1) even within low socioeconomic status groups, Latino students are from lower socioeconomic backgrounds; (2) Latino communities have a stronger desire to maintain Spanish as the dominant language; (3) prejudice is stronger against Latinos than against the other groups; and (4) the circumstances of immigration tend to be more stressful for Latino groups. As we have seen, much of the emphasis on research with

Latino high school students has been on issues related to academic failure and dropping out. Studies focusing on academic success are rare.

Major Variables of the Study

This section describes how the major variables were conceptualized and operationalized in the study. In this investigation, we controlled socioeconomic status and ethnicity by limiting the study sample to Latino youth from poverty backgrounds.

Poverty was considered the major risk factor in this study. Since poverty was treated as a control factor, it was necessary to insure that the respondents each met a criterion for inclusion. Although information was obtained from respondents concerning parents' education and occupation, the major basis for inclusion was family income, adjusted for number of dependents in the family. Using the definition of the Persistent Poverty Project in Boston (1989), families of three with an income below $11,500 were included.

Psychosocial stress was assumed to be present in all respondents as a function of their shared poverty status. We did, however, include a measure of experienced stress in order to make certain that the respondents were not markedly different on this important variable.

Academic achievement was used as the major outcome variable of this investigation. We identified a group who had completed high school and were attending college and compared them to a group of youths of similar age and socioeconomic status who had dropped out of high school. In this investigation the college students were conceived of as resilient, and the dropouts were considered more vulnerable. The question was whether we could find factors that might shed light on the meaning of this difference.

Protective factors are the predictor variables of this investigation. They can also be thought of as the variables intervening between the stress of poverty and academic achievement outcome. Based on previous research and theory, we view these as both individual (internal) and social (external) factors that influence an individual's ability to adapt adequately to the environment. We placed these protective factors, somewhat arbitrarily, into four groups. First, there was the group of variables that might be viewed as most related to what the individual brings to the situation. These included level of general alienation, self-esteem, locus of control, coping style, and cognitive skills. These variables might be regarded as the relatively abiding aspects of the person, that influence the capacity to adapt to a life of stress. Second, there were family variables reflecting aspects of the family environment, including stability, cohesiveness, and support. Third is a set of external variables related specifically to the school experience, including stability, feelings, relationships, and grades. Fourth, social variables are those tapping the quality of social life outside of family and school. Social variables include relationships with community organizations, religious groups, and peers, as well as dating.

Working Model and Hypotheses

Based upon our review of previous literature, we formulated a psychosocial model to use in formulating and carrying out this study. The model consists of the following general propositions: First, in the United States poverty and ethnic-minority group status are social, structural risk factors for negative outcomes. Second, the mechanism by which poverty and minority status increases risk is by creating heightened life stress. Third, stress can be moderated by a wide range of interacting protective factors. Individuals vary in terms of available internal and external protective factors. Fourth, a combination of these protective factors can explain life outcomes, including academic achievement among Latino youth.

Based on this model, we formulated the following hypotheses, which are organized here in terms of the four proposed realms of protective factors:

Individual factors: Latino college students were expected to differ significantly from high school dropouts in terms of individual characteristics. The former were expected to be more internal, have more functional coping mechanisms available to them, have higher self-esteem, be less alienated from society, and have better school-related cognitive skills.

Family factors: Latino college students were expected to report that they have had more family stability, cohesiveness, support, and positive relationships.

School factors: Latino college students were expected to report significantly better school experiences, including their stability, feelings, relationships with school personnel, and performance. They were also expected to have been more involved in special enrichment programs than dropouts.

Social factors: Latino college students were expected to report significantly better peer relationships, to have been more involved in community organizations, and to report receiving more support from various community groups, including religious groups.

Method

The sample for the study consisted of two groups of subjects (total n = 35) who met the following criteria: (1) member of any Latino group, whether born in the United States or elsewhere; (2) came from a low socioeconomic status family (i.e., equivalent to a family of three with an income under $11,500); and (3) lived in the Boston area for at least four years[3] and attended high school in the Boston area during this time.

The first group of individuals consisted of 19 Latino college students (11 females and 8 males) attending the University of Massachusetts at Boston. The second group of individuals consisted of 16 Latino high school dropouts in the same age range as the college students (11 females and 5 males).

Instruments used in the investigation included:

Telephone-screening form: A screening form was used in a brief telephone interview to determine subjects' eligibility to participate. Items included the Hollingshead (1950) two-factor socioeconomic status index of status position, adding number of dependents in the household, years of residence in Boston, and country of family origin.

Interview schedule: Data were gathered primarily by means of individual interviews that lasted an average of 90 minutes. Questions assessed the four sets of protective factors thought important in predicting school success — individual, family, school, and social factors. Respondents were asked to refer, for the most part, to factors present during their high school years. Items covered the following general areas: personal, family, education, work, community, socioeconomic status, health, religious participation, and social/peer relations. The focus of these questions was to determine both sources of stress and support within the individual, the family (including both nuclear and extended family), the school, and the community. The interview was semistructured, including precoded as well as open-ended questions. Respondents also completed five brief self-report instruments:

1. Alienation Index Inventory (Turner, 1975),
2. Ways of Coping Scale (Folkman and Lazarus, 1985),
3. Semantic Differential Scale (Osgood, Suci, and Tannenbaum, 1957),
4. Internal-External Locus of Control Scale (Rotter, 1966), and
5. Stressful Life Events Inventory (a checklist of common stressors designed for this project).

Finally, two subtests of Wechsler Adult Intelligence Scale-Revised (WAIS-R) were administered in order to have a measure of level of school-related cognitive functioning. The two WAIS-R performance subtests were Block-Design and Digit-Symbol. These subtests measure specific cognitive skills (i.e., perceptual organization and psychomotor coordination). Verbal subtests were not used for two reasons: (1) the possibility of bias in using them with bilingual subjects; and (2) if dropouts scored lower, it would be impossible to determine the extent to which lower verbal skills were a cause or a result of dropout.

All of the instruments used were translated into Spanish. We believed that giving subjects the choice to have the interview done in their language of preference (Spanish or English) was an important consideration in ensuring that they would feel comfortable and, therefore, respond more honestly to the interview. The accuracy and comparability of the two versions was established by means of forward and backward translation. That is, all instruments were first translated from English to Spanish; next all were translated from the produced Spanish version back to English; finally, the comparability of meaning of the two English versions was evaluated by two of the investigators.

The university students were recruited using the following techniques. First, we obtained from the student advising office lists of freshman and sophomore Latino students. Second, we obtained from the Latino student organization their directory of Latino students. Third, we sought volunteers through an advertisement placed in the university newspaper. Finally, flyers were placed around the campus advertising for volunteers.

A second group of individuals was selected as a comparison sample for the first group. They were all individuals in the age range of college students who dropped out of high school. Some were friends and relatives of the college students interviewed. Others were referred to the research project by the staff of a special program for high school dropouts in Boston.

We telephoned the prospective respondents to determine their interest in participating in the study. If they were willing, we screened them for eligibility using the telephone screening form. If they met the criteria for participation, an interview appointment was set up with one of three possible interviewers on a random basis.

The interviews, which were conducted in private, took an average of 90 to 120 minutes. Then the respondents completed the scales and inventories on their own, with the interviewer available to clarify any questions. Finally, all respondents in both groups were given $10 as a token of appreciation for participating in the study.

Results

It was important to assess to what extent the groups of college students and dropouts were different on the central risk factor of poverty. The interview included a number of questions relevant to socioeconomic status, including income adjusted for number in home, mother's and father's education, mother's and father's occupation, and two ratings of family's social class standing. None of these variables showed a statistically significant difference between the two groups. Two potentially indirect indications of differences in social class were evaluated: whether the family had received public assistance and whether the family had received government food stamps. The two groups did not differ significantly on these measures. We concluded, therefore, that the relatively low social class background was shared by the two groups of respondents.

Since individuals from equivalently poor backgrounds might experience different levels of actual stress in those circumstances, we needed to establish to what extent the groups were different in reported experiences of stressful life events. The 47-item Stressful Life Events Inventory showed no statistically significant differences between the two groups on total stress reported or on subsets of stress items focused on family, school, and poverty-related stress. The two groups, then, were equivalent in initial poverty status and reported experiences of stressful life events.

The general strategy chosen to explore the differences between the groups was discriminant function analysis. The first step in this process called for an evaluation of the potential contribution of individual questions and scales to the process of discriminating the groups. Table 1 presents most of the comparison variables that yielded statistically significant *t* tests. On the variables for which *t* tests were not appropriate, Chi-square tests were computed. Table 2 presents all the dichotomous variables that yielded statistically significant Chi-square values. It is worth noting that the combination of these two tables includes all of the factors that have been presented as important in our model.

INDIVIDUAL FACTORS

The variables that achieved significance (educational aspiration during high school, digit symbol test, and self-esteem scale) are quite varied in what they reflect about respondents. As in much of our interpretation of these data, there is difficulty in each case of knowing whether to make any causal link between these variables and being in one of the two groups. The higher educational aspirations of college students, for example, may have motivated school achievement and led to high school graduation and college attendance. On the other hand, being successful in school may have increased their aspirations. The digit symbol test is one of the two subtests of the Wechsler Adult Intelligence Scale used in this study. It is worth noting that the subtest that did not show a significant difference between the groups, the block design test, is most often considered to be a measure of general intelligence. The digit symbol test, on the other hand, is thought to be much more reflective of school-related skills and experiences.

That is, this finding may reflect more the differences in length of time in school than differences in basic intelligence. The finding that college students show higher self-esteem fits both theory and previous research. Again, it is possible to interpret the difference as causing the differential school success or as resulting from school success.

Finally, as indicated in table 2, the college students were more likely to report having worked while going to high school. Again, although not predicted, the finding fits the general picture of college students as somewhat more mature and socially engaged. There is no evidence elsewhere in the data to suggest that the college students were under more economic pressure to work than the dropouts during high school.

FAMILY FACTORS

The variables achieving significance for the most part indicate that the college students felt closer to and more supported by their families than did the dropouts. Level of family alienation was the single strongest variable distinguishing the two groups, and family closeness and desired amount of time with family are consistent with level of alienation. Family transiency during high school was reported to be greater among the college students. This unexpected finding may reflect, in part, the greater likelihood that the college students came from families that migrated more recently. The significant Chi-square for helped with homework suggests that the parents of the college students were more available for help with homework.

SCHOOL FACTORS

The factors indicated in table 1 as having achieved statistical significance all support a general picture of better performance, better feelings about performance, better relationships with teachers, and more comfort in school among the college students in comparison to the dropouts. The age at which the respondent came to the United States might have been included as an individual factor or family factor. It was included here because the variable relates closely to where the person attended elementary school. As table 2 shows, the college students were significantly more likely to have spent most of their elementary school years in a country other than the United States. Finally, the college students more often reported having participated in some type of college preparation program (see table 2) — including college preparation tracks, enrichment program, and after-school programs (such as the Urban Scholars Program).

There are two aspects of these findings that are worthy of note. First, the difference in grades between the two groups was minimal during elementary school, the difference grew somewhat in middle school, and was greatest for high school performance. We interpret this trend to mean that early intervention might have prevented decline in performance and eventual dropping out. Second, the finding that the college students were more likely to have gone to elementary school in another country was unexpected. The interpretation of this finding needs to be approached with care. In exploring the data, however, we have not found any artifactual explanations. (One possible explanation is that the college students' family socioeconomic status may be low simply because these families have not been in the United States long enough to achieve their eventual higher status.) As noted earlier, having gone to elementary school in another country is closely related to coming to the United States at a later age. Although this latter correlation can be said to follow logically, it does not help to explain how going to elementary school in another country improves chances for eventual school success. We will discuss this question later.

SOCIAL FACTORS

This group of factors contains those variables that have to do with social relations outside of the family. As can be seen from an inspection of tables 1 and 2, social factors contributed few significant differences. Although there were many questions in the interview that had to do with dating and peer relationships, no differences emerged between the two groups. College students more often reported that there was someone in school that they trusted. This suggests that they were less isolated and felt more supported in their environment. The specific person seems to have been less important, since it might have been anyone in the respondent's social world — family member, friend, teacher, counselor, etc.

All variables showing individual significance were entered into a discriminant function analysis. After a series of steps that eliminated variables with overlapping contributions, the six variables listed in table 3 yielded the final discriminant function, with a canonical correlation coefficient of .88 (Wilks' Lambda = .23, Chi-square (6 df) = 45.88, $p < .001$). This suggests that the combination of these six variables accounts for a large part of the difference between the two groups.

The last column of coefficients in table 3 can be interpreted to represent the relative contribution of each of the six variables to the discriminant function. The family alienation scale and grades in high school are the largest contributors to the function and are similar in amount of contribution. On the one hand, it is not surprising that the two groups should be very different in history of school performance, and the direction of causality seems obvious. When students perform well at lower levels, opportunities open up to higher levels. The strength of the family alienation scale, however, in differentiating the groups is more noteworthy and more difficult to interpret. The model that we presented earlier gives a central role to family factors (including cohesion, support, and resources). The family alienation scale primarily reflects both a sense of family cohesion and family support. The dropouts made it clear that they felt more estranged from their families than did the college students.

The third variable defining the discriminant function was school alienation. This five-item subscale measures primarily a sense of having liked school or of believing that school contributed something meaningful to oneself. It is not surprising that such a scale would contribute substantially to discriminating between college students and dropouts. What is somewhat surprising is that family alienation was more salient in the discrimination than the school alienation scale.

Educational aspiration during high school is the next largest contributor to the discriminant function. This is the only variable in the discriminating set that addresses the respondents' future orientation. The correlation with high school grades (see table 3) suggests that aspirations are most closely related to performance. That is, if a student was getting good grades, then she or he was likely to have higher aspirations. Although the direction of influence is not determined by such a relationship, it may be of little importance, since both variables contribute to our ability to discriminate between the groups.

If a student participated in any type of college preparatory program, whether as part of the school curriculum or as an extracurricular or out of school activity, then she or he was more likely to be in the college group. The relatively large correlations between college prep experience, school alienation, educational aspiration, and grades suggest that there was a general process of orienting toward educational achievement — belonging, participating, performing, and aspiring.

Although having attended elementary school outside the United States makes the smallest contribution to the discriminant function, it is an important one. Considering how early this differential experience took place, it is remarkable that it is directly related to high school achievement at all. We have not constructed a path model in our investigation, but it is entirely reasonable that early educational success would lead to more proximate subsequent success, which would lead to eventual school success. The implications for early positive school experiences and later success will be discussed later.

Some of the variables that did not show any potential contribution to the understanding of the differences between the groups have already been mentioned (socioeconomic status, stress level) and were not used in further analyses. Neither of these findings should be surprising, since we attempted to match the subjects in terms of socioeconomic background. There were other variables that were expected to show differences between the two groups but did not. They include:

Language: A series of questions concerning use, proficiency, and preference for Spanish or English showed no significant difference. The subjects were also invited to choose Spanish or English for the interview itself; again, there was no significant difference between the two groups in this choice.

Extended family and community: There was little evidence in these data to suggest that extended family and community supports contributed to the difference between the two groups. We cannot conclude from this that these factors are generally unimportant in determining school success.

English as a second language and bilingual programs: Although some of the respondents participated in language-related special programs, there were no significant difference between the two groups in such participation.

The limitations of this investigation, which will be outlined in the next section, suggest that we must be careful in ruling out causal factors simply on the basis of these findings.

We also asked the respondents to give the reasons for their staying in school or dropping out. We could not compare the two groups, because the question was different for the groups. It is worthwhile, however, to report the most common responses given by each group. In the order of frequency, college students attributed success to: family support, self-motivation, school personnel, friends, and special programs. The dropouts attributed their dropping out to: school-related factors, social factors, school personnel, lack of family support, and life situation. Both groups seem to think that family support and relationships with school personnel were important in success or failure.

Evaluation of the Model

The findings of this exploratory investigation lend support to the proposed psychosocial model. Variables tapping all four of the realms we studied (individual, family, school, and social) contributed to the outcome of school success or failure. Although it is possible to discuss these factors as discrete contributors to outcomes, as Lang et al., (1982) have demonstrated in connection with psychological well-being, factors interact with and depend upon the other factors.

THE INDIVIDUAL AND SUCCESS

Within a developmental model of resiliency, individual attributes are continually interacting with and being shaped by the environment. At any given moment in the developmental process a person can be described as having certain traits, but those traits are not independent of the pressures and supports that exist in the environment.

A good example of this is cognitive skills and functioning. It would be surprising indeed to find that those who completed high school were not different in intellectual skills from those who dropped out. Both the inherent screening function of schools and the added opportunities to gain skills would lead us to expect better performance from those who have been successful. What a student brings to a situation at a given moment is a function of past opportunities, and what a student takes from a situation will determine future opportunities. Still, the intellectual differences that we have found between college students and high school dropouts in this study are not as large as might be expected. The two groups did not differ on a general index of cognitive ability. The skill on which the college students were significantly superior is related closely to skills practiced in school. We conclude that staying in or dropping out of school in this population of low-socioeconomic-status, Latino youth was not based upon inherent differences in cognitive abilities.

Likewise, a student's decision to stay in or drop out of school is based, in part, on perceptions of the self and on an assessment of whether she/he can survive in an academic environment. It is not surprising that we found that college students viewed themselves more positively. Success must be considered an important basis for self-esteem. On the other hand, in the model that we have proposed students' likelihood of success is also determined by their level of self-esteem. At each step, without intervention, the differences in success levels would increase the differences between them in self-esteem. Does this mean that a child must show up on the first day of school with self-esteem in order to survive and succeed? That would probably help, but that does not mean that no intervention by the schools or others could improve a child's chances. If we accept the interactive nature of self-esteem and success, it may be possible to find ways of bolstering self-esteem and highlighting success. If we view self-esteem primarily as a cause of success, then we must find ways to enhance self-esteem in the earliest school experiences. If we choose instead to construe it as a consequence of success, then schools need to find ways to provide each child and adolescent with an experience of success. The result of not doing so is to send many into the adult world not only as academic failures but as individuals with low self-esteem.

Like self-esteem, educational aspiration forms part of a feed-back loop with school success. That is, the desire to achieve academically does not emerge in a vacuum. It must be based upon a realistic assessment of probable success, which is in part based upon past success. On the other hand, educational aspirations could be based on the student's lack of appreciation of his or her potential, which would lead to unrealistically low self-expectations. It must be the school's responsibility to educate both students and their parents on what educational and vocational opportunities may be available for them. Others have found that teachers' low expectations of poor Latino and other minority students may result in tracking them into vocational training (Rodriguez, 1974; Stein, 1985). In these cases the choices have been made already for the students, and it would be no surprise that these students would have low educational aspirations.

FAMILY AND ACADEMIC SUCCESS

Coopersmith (1967) has shown that stable and secure family environments create high self-esteem. The findings of the present investigation are consistent with this conclusion and with many studies that have emphasized the important role that both the family and the social environment have in Latino culture (Comas-Diaz, 1990; Canino and Canino, 1980; Mechanic and Hansell, 1989). The psychosocial model of resilience that we are using in this study looks at protective factors within these two levels as well as within the individual. Therefore, this model is a particularly relevant one to use with the Latino population.

The set of variables that address family environment are consistent in the message they provide. High school dropouts reported feeling more alienated from their families than did the college students. It could be argued that such estrangement is a result of poor school performance. It seems to us more likely, however, that long-standing patterns of family relationships have at least some causal connection to school performance. Again, acknowledging that positive family functioning both causes success and emerges from it is consistent with the model that we have articulated. We conclude that the hypothesis that families that are cohesive and supportive produce successful students has been supported. But these findings also suggest that some families need support to carry out the important function of aiding their children toward success. One implication, then, is that we must find ways to support and empower families to serve this function.

SCHOOL EXPERIENCES AND ACADEMIC SUCCESS

The large number of school-related variables that were found to significantly differentiate the college students from the high school dropouts suggests the importance of inspecting the school experience itself in understanding success. The findings of the study provide a clear picture. The successful students were more likely to have gone to elementary school outside of the United States; they had better grades throughout the school years, but the modest early difference turned into enormous differences in high school; they had better relationships with teachers; they were more engaged rather than alienated; they had at least one person they trusted in school; and they were more comfortable in school. The variables do not, however, all have the same explanatory weight. Some of the significant differences between college students and high school dropouts are operational measures of school success. For example, the finding that college students report significantly better grades than the dropouts is hardly surprising. The path to success might be as follows:

Positive early school experiences;

Good relationships with teachers and increasing comfort;

Better school performance and opportunities for enriched school programs; and

Aspirations for higher education; high school graduation and college attendance.

How can we explain the finding that having gone to elementary school outside of the United States relates to success? One possible explanation is that in their country of origin the students were not minority group members. This implies that there was no conflict of language, no sense of being with strangers, and no problem in having parents communicate with the schools in support of their children. The greater success of these students would suggest that early school experiences may have been more positive. Another possible explanation is that teachers' expectations for Latino children are very low in many elementary schools of the United States. As these children move through the school system, they may be systematically set up for failure. A third possibility is that the elementary schools in other countries provided a stronger foundation of basic instruction than did the U.S. elementary schools. These competing explanations will be pursued in later research.

Limitations of the Study

There are some limitations of this study that may restrict the generalizability of the results. First, we used a small and nonrandom sample. The 19 students were volunteers from the population of Latino students at the University of Massachusetts at Boston, an urban commuter institution. The 16 dropouts were volunteers referred to the research project from a number of sources, including some of the students. The sample is not representative of all Latino college students or dropouts. The small sample size itself limited us in testing with confidence even two-way interaction effects. Gender, in particular, has been shown to be an important interacting variable in the study of Latinos (Gibson, 1983).

Another limitation of the study was that the information is limited to self-report and is largely retrospective. A more comprehensive future study may include interviews with parents, school personnel, siblings, peers, and community and religious leaders. School records might also be reviewed in a future study to assess the validity of the self-reports. It would, of course, be better to have longitudinal data so that we could assess influences on final outcome as they actually happen. Such a developmental approach would fit better the conceptual model we used but could not be managed in an initial exploratory project. Next, we must point out that most standard psychological instruments used in the United States, including those used in this study, were constructed for and standardized on white middle- and upper middle-class respondents. Given this, we should expect that many of these instruments present difficulties when used with minority, bilingual, and low-socioeconomic-status groups. Therefore, we must carefully interpret all results within the sociocultural context of the respondents.

Finally, Latino scholars warn of the great diversity among and within Latino cultural groups (Muñoz, 1982; Bernal and Gutierrez, 1988). In this study, because of the relatively small sample, it was not possible to control analyses for specific Latino cultural groups. Both the college student group and the high school dropout group included individuals whose families came from different parts of Latin America — the Caribbean, Central America, and South America. There was no significant difference in the national origins of the two groups.

Conclusions

Our findings support the following conclusions. First, early school experiences influence subsequent response to and success in school. In particular, Latino youth who attended grade school abroad are more likely to complete high school and enter college in the United States. Second, individual attributes such as self-esteem, aspirations, and alienation are both produced by and predict school achievement. Third, the family provides a supportive context for school achievement. Fourth, high school experiences can determine whether a student continues or drops out. Fifth, experiences of school enrichment and success are associated with the desire to stay in school. Hence, the understanding of school achievement among Latinos requires the integration of our knowledge of developmental processes, family systems, and the sociopolitical context of education in the United States.

The myth of individual responsibility for academic and economic success serves to obscure systematic social injustice toward minority groups that restricts access to educational opportunity. An emphasis on personal characteristics of minority groups such as African Americans and Latinos both protects and perpetuates an unjust social system. Current public policy attempts to avoid social accountability for racism and discrimination. Individuals who fail are considered the problem; *they* are lacking ability; *they* are not motivated; *they* have chosen a life style that is antisocial. It is easier to dismiss dropping out as personal failings rather than seek social justice through social change (Herman, 1992).

In seeking to understand the resilient individuals who succeed under the high stress circumstances of poverty and racism, we are in no way criticizing or blaming the children and families who cope less successfully with adversity. The strategy of blaming individuals for failing to succeed in the face of systematic discrimination or abuse often serves the purpose of impeding social change (Ryan, 1976). We are not interested in celebrating a few success stories as a means of justifying the destructive treatment of so many poor minority children and families, but we want to use these success stories as a means of identifying the social supports that might improve the chances for more children and families.

Notes

1. This paper is based on research supported by a grant to Castellano Turner from the Mauricio Gastón Institute for Latino Community Development and Public Policy, University of Massachusetts at Boston. The authors wish to thank those who gave assistance in the completion of this project: Hilda P. Rivera and Patricia Ballon, who helped with interviewing and coding; Elsa Orjuela of the University of Massachusetts Advising Center; Noreen Stack and Nelly Javier of the Cardinal Cushing Center in Boston; and Sandra Lopez, Wilma Marrero-Luna, and Angie Garcia, staff members of Casa Latina, the Latino student organization, University of Massachusetts at Boston. We also thank professors Joan Liem and Don Kalick, Psychology Department, University of Massachusetts at Boston, for their contributions to the early formulation of this project.

2. In this chapter, Latino refers to those with origins in Spanish-speaking Latin American countries.

3. This criterion was important because the problems of adjustment faced by recent immigrants would complicate the issues that we investigated.

References

Bernal, G., and Gutierrez, M. (1988). Cubans. In L. Comas-Díaz and E. E. Griffith (Eds.), *Clinical Guidelines in Cross-Cultural Mental Health.* New York: Wiley.

Boston Persistent Poverty Project. (1989). *In the Midst of Plenty: A Profile of Boston and Its Poor.* Boston: The Boston Foundation.

Bullough, B., and Bullough, V. (1972). *Poverty, Ethnic Identity and Health Care.* New York: Appleton-Century Crofts.

Canino, I. A., and Canino, G., (1980). Impact of Stress on the Puerto Rican Family: Treatment Considerations. *American Journal of Orthopsychiatry, 50*(3), 535-541.

Clark, R. (1983). *Family Life and School Achievement: Why Poor Black Children Succeed or Fail.* Chicago: University of Chicago Press.

Comas-Diaz, L. (1990). Hispanic/Latino Communities: Psychological Implications. *The Journal of Training and Practice in Professional Psychology, 4*(1), 14-35.

Coopersmith, S. (1967). *The Antecedents of Self-Esteem.* San Francisco: W. Freeman.

Cowen, E. L., and Work, W. C. (1988). Resilient Children, Psychological Wellness, and Primary Prevention. *American Journal of Community Psychology, 16*, 591-607.

Delgado, M., and Scott, J. F. (1979). Strategic Intervention: A Mental Health Program for the Hispanic Community. *Journal of Community Psychology, 7*(3), 187-197.

Dohrenwend, B. S., and Dohrenwend, B. P. (1970). Class and Race as Status-Related Sources of Stress. In S. Levine and N. Scotch (Eds.), *Social Stress.* Chicago: Aldine.

Espin, O. M. (1987). Psychological Impact of Migration on Latinas: Implications for Psychotherapeutic Practice. *Psychology of Women Quarterly, 11*(4), 489-503.

Fernandez, R. and Velez, W. (1990, September). Who Stays? Who Leaves? Findings from the ASPIRA Five Cities High School Dropout Study. *Latino Studies Journal,* 59-77.

Fine, M. (1991). *Framing Dropouts: Notes on the Politics of an Urban High School.* Albany: SUNY Press.

Folkman, S., and Lazarus, R. S. (1985). If It Changes It Must Be Process. *Journal of Personality and Social Psychology, 48*(1), 150-170.

Garbarino, J. (1990). The Human Ecology of Early Risk. In Meisels, S., and Shonkoff, J. (Eds.), *Handbook of Early Childhood Intervention*, p. 78-96. Cambridge: Cambridge University Press.

Garmezy, N. (1985). Stress-Resistant Children: The Search for Protective Factors. In J. E. Stevenson (Ed.), Recent Research in Developmental Psychopathology, *Journal of Child Psychology and Psychiatry,* Book Supplement No.4, 213-233. Oxford: Pergamon Press.

Gibson, G. (1983). Hispanic Women: Stress and Mental Health Issues. *Women and Therapy, 2*(2-3), 113-133.

Heacock, D. R. (1990). Suicidal Behavior in Black and Hispanic Youth. *Psychiatric Annals, 20*(3), 134-142.

Herman, J. (1992). *Trauma and Recovery.* Boston: Beacon Press.

Hollingshead, A. B., and Redlich, F. C. (1950). *Social Class and Mental Illness: A Community Study.* New York: Wiley.

Horst, L., and Donahue, M. (1990). *Annual and Cohort Drop-out Rates in Boston Public Schools: Focus on Programmatic and Demographic Characteristics.* Boston: Office of Research and Development, Boston Public Schools.

Jencks, C. (1979). *Who Gets Ahead? The Determinants of Economic Success in America.* New York: Basic Books.

Kessler, R. C., and Cleary, P. D. (1980). Social Class and Psychological Distress. *American Sociological Review, 45*, 463-478.

Lang, J. G., Muñoz, R. F., Bernal, G., and Sorensen, J. L. (1982). Quality of Life and

Psychological Well-Being in a Bicultural Latino Community. *Hispanic Journal of Behavioral Sciences, 4*(4), 433-450.

Lewis, J. M., and Looney, J. D. (1983). *The Long Struggle: Well Functioning Working Class Black Families.* New York: Brunner/Mazel.

Mason, E. P., (1967). Comparison of Personality Characteristics of Junior High School Students from American Indian, Mexican and Caucasian Ethnic Backgrounds. *Journal of Social Psychology, 73*, 115-128.

Masten, A. S., and Garmezy, N., (1985). Risk, Vulnerability, and Protective Factors in Developmental Psychopathology. In B. Lahey and A. E. Kazdin (Eds.). *Advances in Clinical Child Psychology, 8*, 1-52. New York: Plenum Press.

Mechanic, D. and Hansell, S. (1989). Divorce, Family Conflict, and Adolescents' Well-Being. *Journal of Health and Social Behavior, 30*(1), 105-116.

Moritsugu, J., and Sue, S. (1983). Minority Status as a Stressor. In R. D. Felner, L. Jason, J. Moritsugu, and S. Farber (Eds.), *Preventive Psychology.* New York: Pergamon.

Muñoz, R. F. (1982). The Spanish-Speaking Consumer and Community Mental Health Center. In E. E. Jones and S. J. Korchin (Eds.), *Minority Mental Health.* New York: Praeger.

Myers, J. K., Lendenthal, J. J., and Pepper, M. P. (1975). Social Class, Life Events, and Psychiatric Symptoms. *Journal of Health and Social Behavior, 16*, 421-427.

Osgood, C. E., Suci, G. J., and Tannenbaum, P. H. (1957). *The Measurement of Meaning.* Urbana: University of Illinois Press.

Phinney, J., (1990). Ethnic Identity in Adolescents and Adults: Review of Research. *Psychological Bulletin, 108*(3), 499-514.

Pollard, D. S., (1989). Against the Odds: A Profile of Academic Achievers from the Urban Underclass. *Journal of Negro Education, 58*(3), 297-308.

Rodriguez, C. (1974). The Structure of Failure II: A Case in Point. *The Urban Review, 7*, 215-226.

Rotter, J. B. (1966). Generalized Expectancies for Internal Versus External Locus of Control of Reinforcement. *Psychological Monographs, 80*(609).

Rutter, M. (1987). Psychosocial Resilience and Protective Mechanisms. *American Journal of Orthopsychiatry, 57*, 316-331.

Ryan, W. (1976). *Blaming the Victim.* New York: Vintage Books.

Stein, C. B., (1985). Hispanic Students in the Sink or Swim Era, 1900-1960. *Urban Education, 20*(2), 189-198.

Steinberg, L., Blinde, P. L., and Chan, K. S., (1984). Dropping Out among Language Minority Youth. *Review of Educational Research, 54*(1), 113-132.

Texidor, C. (1987). Poverty, Self-Concept, and Health: Experience of Latinas. *Women and Health, 12*(3-4), 229-242.

Turner, C. B. (1975). The Alienation Index Inventory. *Test Collection Bulletin, 9*, 4.

Valverde, S. A., (1987). A Comparative Study of Hispanic High School Dropouts and Graduates: Why Do Some Leave School Early and Some Finish?. *Education and Urban Society, 19*(3),320-329.

Weiss, R., (1988, July). *Family Support and Education Programs and the Public Schools: Opportunities and Challenges.* Paper presented for the National Association of State Boards of Education.

Werner, E. E. (1985). Stress and Protective Factors in Children's Lives. In A. R. Nicol

(Ed.), *Longitudinal Studies in Child Psychology and Psychiatry*, 335-356. Chichester, England: Wiley.

Werner, E. E., (1990). Protective Factors and Individual Resilience. In Meisels, S., and Shonkoff, J., (Eds.), *Handbook of Early Childhood Intervention*, 97-115. Cambridge: Cambridge University Press.

Table 1

Variables Yielding Statistically Significant Differences between College Students and High School Dropouts (Ordered by Size of t Value within Categories of Factors)

Variables	College Students*		High School Dropouts[†]			
	Mean	S.D.	Mean	S.D.	t	$p<$
Individual factors						
Educational aspirations	3.74	1.33	2.25	1.39	3.23	0.003
Digit symbol test	53.74	3.43	49.00	7.50	2.33	0.03
Self-esteem	10.63	2.03	9.12	1.93	2.25	0.03
Family factors						
Family alienation	17.10	2.69	12.56	1.86	6.41	0.001
How close to family	1.32	0.58	2.06	0.77	3.18	0.01
Family transiency	1.00	0.74	0.38	0.62	2.71	0.02
Feelings about family ties	2.58	0.61	2.00	0.89	2.20	0.04
School factors						
Grades in high school	2.05	0.78	3.44	0.51	6.29	0.001
Grades in middle school	1.74	0.73	2.88	0.72	4.62	0.001
School alienation	17.16	2.59	13.50	2.61	4.15	0.001
Feelings about high school grades	1.95	0.91	2.88	0.62	3.57	0.001
Comfort level in school	1.95	0.78	2.69	0.70	2.95	0.01
Age came to U.S.	7.16	5.95	2.81	5.56	2.23	0.03
Relationship with teachers	1.68	0.82	2.19	0.54	2.17	0.04
Grades in elementary school	1.63	0.90	2.25	0.86	2.08	0.05
Social factors						
Family involvement in community	2.95	0.91	3.56	0.63	2.35	0.03

[†]N = 16
*N = 19

Table 2

Variables Yielding Statistically Significant Differences between College Students and High School Dropouts (Ordered by size of Chi-square value within categories of factors)

Variables	College Students		High School Dropouts		χ^2	$p<$
	N	%	N	%		
Individual factors						
Worked during high school	15	78.9	7	43.8	4.61	0.03
Family factors						
Parents helped with homework	11	57.9	3	18.8	5.54	0.02
School factors						
Participated in college prep program	10	52.6	1	6.3	8.67	0.01
Attended elementary school outside U.S.	10	52.6	3	18.8	4.27	0.04
Social factors						
There was a trusted	17	89.5	9	56.3	5.02	0.03

Table 3

Intercorrelations and Correlations with Discriminant Function of Variables Entered into Final Discriminant Analysis

Variables	2	3	4	5	6	Discriminant function
Family alienation	.56	.54	.35	.39	.34	.57
Grades in high school		.60	.60	.36	.01	.56
School alienation			.36	.21	.03	.38
Educational aspirations				.46	.17	.30
College prep program					.01	.30
Attended elementary school outside U.S.						.20

Martha Montero-Sieburth

The Effects of Schooling Processes and Practices on Potential At-Risk Latino High School Students

Being at risk and dropping out are commonplace characterizations of underrepresented[1] student populations as a whole, yet these labels are most frequently used to describe the educational attainment of school-age Latino students, who make up one of the fastest growing populations in the United States with one of the highest dropout rates[2] and the lowest educational attainment of any ethnic group.[3] Given their high dropout rate and low educational attainment, the need to examine Latino students' experience at the high school level becomes compelling. Lack of access, limited educational experiences, low socioeconomic status, repeated student retention, and lack of high school completion have been identified by national research studies as first order explanations for becoming at risk (Pallas, Natriello, and McDill, 1989; Rumberger, 1983; Rumberger, 1987). But beyond these explanations and the numbers of students that they represent, we need to understand the factors that most affect Latino students before they become at risk in the school context.

Using qualitative methods, this study examines why some Latino students are potentially at risk, while others succeed. The study is an attempt to determine whether the students in this research displayed different behaviors and actions from those students clearly identified as being at risk, and whether any apparent differences for potential at-risk Latino students in bilingual and/or mainstream classes can be identified.[4]

To further understand how at-risk students in general and Latino at-risk students specifically are regarded within the school, the perspectives of students and their responses to the rules, regulations, and codes of the school were gathered, as well as the perspectives of schoolwide administrators, teachers, and staff. In this manner, the schooling structure in which these students and teachers function and the factors that support or constrain their day-to-day existence could all be identified and analyzed.

Use of the Term At-Risk

The term "disadvantaged students," which has now been replaced with "at risk," has evolved and shifted from its earlier 1960s definition in which the student's home and family were isolated and defined as culturally deficient or deprived vis-a-vis middle-class standards and schooling to the 1970s and 1980s definition in which those students who experience inefficient and ineffective schooling are defined as at risk. Most recently, the focus of the term has been on the exposure and quality of experiences that at-risk students have in learning in and out of schools. Thus the realm of education and of educating potential at-risk students is no longer considered the exclusive domain of the schools, but includes educational experiences provided by the family and the community (Pallas, Natriello, and McDill, 1989).

Being at risk in one or more of these domains — the school, the family, and/ or the community — can place students at an educational disadvantage (Pallas, Natriello, and McDill, 1989). Thus the influence of family, although significant in impacting academic achievement (Coleman et al., 1966), may be education-ally limited in providing children with positive learning experiences. Slavin and Madden use at-risk to define a student "who is in danger of failing to complete his or her education with an adequate level of skills" (1989, p. 4). Comer refers to "high-risk students, [as] those who underachieve in school despite adequate intellectual endowment, and as a result, will underachieve as adults" (1987, p. 13). However, while the labels of at-risk or disadvantaged do not in and of themselves characterize individual students, nor do they explain why such students are at risk, they are used interchangeably to identify populations who are educationally underrepresented and underserved.

Certain risk indicators have been identified within the at-risk literature that predict school failure: low achievement, retention in grade, behavior problems, poor attendance, poverty, single-parent families, and low socioeconomic status. However, these factors alone do not define such at-risk populations (Pallas, Natriello, and McDill, 1989; Rumberger, 1983; Rumberger, 1987). According to Pallas, Natriello, and McDill (1989), students who are labelled at-risk may be further disadvantaged by this inclusive label, more than if only one of the predicting factors is applied to them. It is important to recognize that although "large numbers of minority children...are at risk for school failure and other problems...minority status itself is not a definition of 'at riskness'" (Bempechat and Ginsburg, 1989, p. 4).

Contributions of Ethnographic Research to At-Risk Analysis

Ethnographic studies on the organizational and structural level of schools, the ways students are tracked or stratified, the way they are perceived and defined by the system, and the ways in which their experiences and perspectives are included within the schools have emerged. Page and Valli (1990) have addressed such explanations through the differentiation of curriculum and tracking for underrepresented students; Oakes (1985) has studied the effects of tracking patterns in academic placements and achievement outcomes; and LeCompte has studied the cultural context of dropping out, questioning whether "public schools are still functional, or if the schools, rather than the students have dropped out of American society" (1987, p. 233).

Fine (1983) argues that by and large the images presented of dropouts through the discourse of "risk" are only partial: "It is an image that typically strengthens those institutions and groups which have carved out, severed, denied connection to and then promised to 'save' those who will undoubtedly remain at risk" (Fine, 1990, p. 54). Fine defines the discourse of being at risk to be constructed around those issues that make controversy — that is, they offer limited perspectives on the dropout problem — or subjugate the real issues. Hence the deep seeded and more meaningful social solutions that address dropouts and require greater commitment and intervention on part of policy makers and educators are repressed.

Suarez-Orozco's study (1987) of Central American students' motivation for staying in school as a sense of "becoming somebody," Delgado-Gaitan's study (1988) of conformity among Mexican Americans, Montero-Sieburth and Peréz's discussion (1987) of survival strategies used by Latino students, Valverde's emphasis (1987) on Mexican nationalism as contributing to integration, Trueba's analysis (1989) of the meaning of success for Latinos, and Colon's explanation (1987) of circular migration to and from Puerto Rico as influencing students achievement are recent examples of the growing number of qualitative and critical ethnographic studies that seek to explore the link between Latino school failure and institutional and within-school factors.

Methodology

To conduct this study, a series of on going phases from August 1989 through June 1990 evolved. Phase I included negotiating entry to the school, selecting teachers, and identifying classrooms and students. After checking school records, a bilingual class and a mainstream class were selected on the basis of adequate numbers of Latinos. Entry to their classrooms was negotiated on a one-day per week basis with each teacher. Eight students were selected from the general pool of ninth and tenth graders[5] on the basis of their country of origin, native-born and immigrant status, and gender, and not on whether these students were known to be at risk.

Phase II involved observing the ongoing activities and classrooms of the eight selected students (referred to as the focal students) on specific days and shadowing these students for a duration of two days each to find out what these Latino students do in school.

Phase III involved participant observation of bilingual and mainstream classrooms by a team of researchers on a rotating basis. Each research assistant observed a teacher one day a week for the duration of the semester. During a two-week period, the research assistants took turns observing each other's classroom in order to draw independent inferences about what they were seeing, reducing the threats to validity. On the days the research assistants did not observe, the principal investigator rotated between the two classes. At the same time the observations were conducted, administrators, other teachers, and staff were also being interviewed about their perspectives on at-risk issues for students in general and specifically for Latino students.

Phase IV was in-depth interviews with the bilingual and mainstream teachers and focal students. The bilingual teachers were asked for their educational backgrounds, pedagogical philosophies, roles and expectations for Latino students; the mainstream teachers were asked about their backgrounds, interests, and motivational levels. Interviews with the focal students were less easy to obtain: by the third quarter, two students had dropped out of school, another had no phone, another moved so frequently he could not be located, and the remaining four, two Puerto Rican males from the mainstream class and a Puerto Rican female and Nicaraguan male from the bilingual class, were interviewed intermittently.

Phase V included preparing transcriptions of the interviews, translations from Spanish to English, data reduction of memoranda, reports, and school documentation (attendance records, final grades, and disciplinary reports from counselors), and the analysis of field notes and classroom observations. The corpus of analyzed data, themes, functions and categories of behaviors, and events were coded and categorized into matrices using cross-comparison ethnographic methods. Propositional statements were made and relationships were checked against triangulated data sets.

Research Context

Of the 1,000 students attending grades nine through twelve in the school in this study, 18 percent are white, 24 percent are Latinos, 31 percent are black, 26 percent are Asians, and less than 1 percent are native American. Close to 80 percent are bussed into a white, working-class neighborhood where over 60 percent of the residents live in public housing. The Latino students come from two densely populated, predominantly Puerto Rican and Central and South American areas. Latino enrollments in grade nine through twelve in June 1990 numbered 235 and the number of yearly dropouts per 100 Latino students was 15:8 (Boston Public Schools, 1991). One hundred and thirty-five (55 percent) of the 235 Latinos were in the bilingual program, while 100 attended the mainstream or "regular" program according to the October 1989 count. The bilingual and mainstream programs combined make up the total school personnel of about 100 teachers and staff.

The bilingual transitional program at this school has one of the lowest dropout rates for bilingual students in Boston and is also considered to be one of the exemplary programs in the state. Reportedly, over 85 percent of each bilingual senior class goes on to higher education with many students receiving academic honors. Placement of students in the bilingual transitional program occurs on the basis of language proficiency testing conducted at a Boston center and testing done at the school for English-as-a-second-language (ESL) level and academic subject level.

Within the first four years, most bilingual students have been fully mainstreamed. The mainstream or regular program, consisting of about 60 mainstream certified teachers in basic subject areas, has a majority of 20-plus-years veteran teachers from the Boston public schools and a minority of newcomer teachers with less than three years experience. To accommodate the range of student abilities within grades, basic courses in math, science, social studies, etc., in both programs are taught multiple grades.

BILINGUAL CLASSROOM

The bilingual basic math class started with 28 students in the fall, fluctuated to 39 by mid-year, and ended with 25 students during the spring term. Ms. Lopez, a native of Costa Rica in her early thirties, taught the bilingual math class. Prior to coming to this high school, she taught elementary and secondary school as well as adult education. In her two years at the school, teaching basic math, biology, and Spanish literature and directing the after-school tutorial, Ms. Lopez had met all of the Latinos in the school as well as their parents.

The focal students in Ms. Lopez class, Oscar, Leo, Edwin, and Irene, are best depicted through vignettes.[6] These students were all placed at step 2 of the Lau steps[7] because of their newness in the school system and their language assessments scores. Oscar and Leo were placed with their ninth grade cohorts because of their age. No documentation or records were on file from their countries of origin.

> *Oscar*, 16 years of age, arrived ten months ago from El Salvador and did not enrolled in school upon arrival because he knew little about the educational system and was afraid to go to the school department until his brother accompanied him. He was initially living with his brother, but

because of family tensions he sought other housing arrangements with Salvadorans. In El Salvador, he attended a rural school up to seventh grade when the war broke out. Not wanting to be drafted, he simply stayed out of school. Hearing that life was better in the United States, he first headed to Los Angeles, hoping to find work. Not having any luck there, he decided to come to Boston. His adjustment to class has been difficult. He knows how to do the mathematics required but is easily distracted by any "gossip" or any interesting social interactions within his cluster peers. Although Ms. Lopez spends much of her time calling upon Oscar and Leo to be quiet, settle down, and complete their worksheet assignments, Oscar often brags and get out of hand. He is summarily put in his place by Ms. Lopez.

Leo, age 15, came to Boston from a seaport in Nicaragua about a year ago. His paternal grandmother took care of him while his parents emigrated to the United States eight years ago. As the oldest, Leo is the pride of the family. His uncles and aunts also emigrated so that by the time he arrived in Boston, he had an extended family network. Although Leo misses his school back home where he finished seventh grade and had good grades, he is confident about what he learned in Nicaragua. The school there was small, only 70 students compared to the 1,000 here, but he feels he learned math well. Placed at Lau step 2, his goal is to learn English well within a year since he constantly uses it with his friends. Because he is smaller in size than most boys his age at the school and he doesn't feel comfortable outside of his own peer group, Leo spends most of his time with his Latino buddies from Ms. Lopez' class. He is energetic and euphoric, blurting correct answers out as he waves his arms in the air. In effect, he is the class clown; at times getting carried away, saying things quickly and causing uproars in the class. His energy level throughout the year has increased, and he has become more outspoken and assertive. At times, he has to be reprimanded, made to sit down and complete his assignment without talking constantly. Once settled, he is usually the first to finish his assignments.

Edwin, age 16, originally came with his family from a rural area in Puerto Rico. Each year, he goes back to the island for vacation. Edwin contrasts sharply with his boisterous and outgoing twin brother with whom he is often confused. He is quiet and tends to be a loner. In math class, Edwin seems lost since he never learned to apply the multiplication tables well. He struggles with each exercise but expects to pass on the basis of his work in class. He rests his head on the desk, twirls a pencil until Ms. Lopez comes around and walks him through several examples at a time, or spends time visiting with his peers and catching up with the latest gossip. When

Edwin's attention span is diverted, he moves from chair to chair until he descends upon Leo who usually ends up helping him with the assignment. At home, his mother helps him with the homework assignments. Edwin lives for the time he can go back to Puerto Rico. During the year, his family goes back at least three times. The last time they were in Puerto Rico, Edwin completed seventh grade there. He came back to Boston to finish eighth and ninth grades.

Irene, age 15, who was born in Puerto Rico, migrated with her mother, and arrived at the school in January 1990. They moved to Boston for economic and religious reasons: Irene's aunt is here, and the religious sect that her mother belongs to has an extensive network in Boston. Irene's mother is a highly religious woman who is protective about Irene. Because she could not find work, Irene's mother began to collect welfare. The financial hardships at home exert a degree of pressure for Irene to finish her schooling. While Irene misses her friends and teachers in Puerto Rico, the change in schools has proved to be positive. She had learned to work effectively with the strictness of her teachers in Puerto Rico and she carried over that work style to this high school. Her major difficulty is learning English and biology. Irene dutifully follows what she is told in class, although she spends class time reading letters from her friends or doing her make-up. Homework is left till the evening when she can get her mother to help. Whatever extra time she has, she socializes with her neighbors. Irene relies heavily on her classmates for help, yet her attempts to make friends at this school have met difficulties. When she reaches out to her Puerto Rican counterparts speaking Spanish, they answer her only in English.

MAINSTREAM CLASSROOM

The ninth/tenth grade mainstream civics class with 28 students, of which six were Latino, was taught by Mr. Laferty, a 24-year veteran social studies teacher of the Boston public schools. Of Irish-American descent, in his mid-forties, Mr. Laferty prided himself in having gone to college, supporting his studies, and working at two jobs to make ends meet. He taught, coached, and advised juniors and seniors for eight years at this school, yet this was his first year with a combined ninth/tenth grade civics class. By the end of the school year, only 17 students were on his class roster.

The focal students in the mainstream civics class were all Puerto Ricans born in the continental United States (Jose, Enrique, and Luke) except for Ariela, who was born on the island but transferred to a Boston school for her fourth grade. Jose, Enrique, and Luke were on the school's free lunch program. Since they had all been in Boston schools, their academic records were on file at the career counselor's office, although the records were somewhat incomplete. The school registrar maintained their present records, including their reading and math scores (with the exception of Enrique) on the school's computer from the time they entered the high school.

Like the bilingual students, the vignettes of the mainstream students are illustrative of how they negotiate in school:

Jose, age 15, is accustomed to the rituals of this school including being on time to class and knowing what is expected of him. He moved up the ranks to tenth grade with some difficulty, but he is determined to complete high school. This year, Jose started off on the wrong foot by having low grades; however, he felt he could make it up by doing better on the quizzes and exams. The fact that Mr. Laferty will not let him speak Spanish in class presents an obstacle. It is hard for him to make the transition from Spanish to English in class, since Spanish is spoken at home, and he likes using it with his peers. Although he knows he is expected to use English, he often reverts to Spanish. Jose banters with Mr. Laferty about silly things, but the retorts often escalate between the two, ending in verbal outbursts from Mr. Laferty who has the final word. In such instances, Jose has learned to keep his cool.

Enrique, age 16, is boisterous, excitable, and full of energy. He already has a row of zeros in Mr. Laferty's grade book. As a tenth grader, he knows he has to cooperate with the teacher if he is going to finish the year, but he feels frustrated and demoralized as remarks by Mr. Laferty and his peers mount when he speaks Spanish in class. Although English is spoken by the family at home, he knows enough Spanish to show off with his friends at school. He enjoys the privacy that Spanish gives him to joke and banter around with his friends without the teacher knowing what is being said. He does not realize this irritates Mr. Laferty. For Enrique, speaking Spanish is something he feels he controls, yet it offends his teacher deeply and gets in his way in class.

Luke, age 15 and a tenth grader, speaks English well and is able to use slang expressions that he learns from his mother. Luke's school performance is totally inconsistent. In the first quarter his grades were rows of Fs. He also has "behavioral problems" like talking in class. When he studies and stops talking in class his grades improve. According to Mr. Laferty, "If he could continue behaving, he probably would ace the class."

Ariela, age 16, came to the fourth grade in Boston after studying in Puerto

Rican private schools. Back in Puerto Rico she had been an A and B student, but soon after arriving, her grades fell. From fourth to ninth grade, she struggled academically. She is compliant and pays attention in class, is never tardy, and has only accumulated 11 absences during the year. Ariela is one of six girls in a male-dominated class of 27 students. She is quiet and rarely asked any questions. She speaks English well. During the first quarter, she started to get Fs and desperately attempted to make them up during the last three quarters by paying closer attention in class. Near the end of the fourth quarter, she met Alfredo and fell in love. It is hard to think about classwork when he is waiting outside to walk her down the hall arm in arm. Marriage was a possibility but she wanted to finish school before taking such a step. She decided to wait a year.

STUDENT OUTCOMES

From November to February, the observations and interviews revealed certain patterns for the focal students in the bilingual class. Irene and Leo were getting As and Bs, but Edwin, who struggled throughout the year in understanding the function of fractions, was consistently getting Cs, Ds, and Fs. It appeared that Edwin never academically regained the two weeks beyond the Christmas break that he and his family spent in Puerto Rico. His absences became more noticeable. By May, Irene was doing quite well in math. She had become more outgoing as well. During this time, Leo advanced to a higher level math group.

Oscar, who started out well in September, appeared to show the stress from his 35-hour-a-week job; he was frequently absent and lagged behind in his assignments. In class, he was inattentive and sleepy. Ms. Lopez placed greater demands on him, but the more she demanded, the more outspoken and disengaged he became. Despite her interventions and attempts to help, Ms. Lopez was at a loss in helping Oscar. He willingly worked with her, was only sent to the disciplinary officer once, but showed no signs of involvement in his school work after he moved out of his brother's house. Ms. Lopez did not know his whereabouts and worried about his situation. Although he continued to appear on the computer roster until after the 15 percent rule[8] had applied, by the end of April, Oscar stopped coming to school altogether. Students rumored that he was on the streets, hanging around, and had eloped. In June, after passing bilingual math, Irene and Leo were promoted on to the next grade. Edwin was to repeat math after failing. Oscar dropped out.

By the third quarter, the focal students in the mainstream class were showing signs of academic failure. Enrique accumulated ten absences during the third quarter, and even though he handed in most of his homework, his grades were poor. Jose, who was absent for five days and had completed most of his homework, did not show up to make up several tests; he either overslept or arrived late. Ariela, with only three absences, was also near failure. She was not studying as was evident from her poor grades on quizzes and tests. Even Luke, who passed every test, completed most of his homework, and was absent only three days, was "on thin ice for the semester" according to Mr. Laferty. Only better grades during the fourth marking period could save him.

In spite of their low grades, Mr. Laferty was willing to give students an advantage, especially where they were borderline, had accumulated several zeroes, yet showed consistent improvement over the four terms. In Mr. Laferty's opinion: "None of these kids have an ability problem. They all can do the work, every single one of them. It's a question of will."

By the fourth term, the status of being potentially at risk became a reality for the mainstream focal group: Enrique accumulated 41 absences; Ariela, 20; Luke, 28; and Jose, 25. Ariela barely passed onto the tenth grade with a D. Enrique left the school two months before the end of the term, leaving no information other than a discharge notice. Jose and Luke did not pass their civics class and were to repeat it or take it during summer school. By June, although most of the focal students had remained in the school throughout the year, five out of the eight students ended the academic school year failing. In the bilingual class, two students went on to the next level, and in the mainstream class only one student went on to the next level.[9] Some of these students were potentially at risk at the beginning of the year based on their general characteristics (being Latino, low grades, etc.), but even those with all of the attributes needed to succeed (English speaking, having been mainstreamed) ended up at risk. They did not pass onto the next level because the conditions in their classrooms (Spanish never spoken, stringent and absolute rules, constant retorts between teacher and students, and disregard of their culture) provided few incentives for engagement.

Discussion

A combination of in-school and out-of-school factors contribute to the at-risk conditions for Latino students. These factors appear to have less to do with being poor, having limited-English-proficiency, and being Latino and more to do with the way Latinos are perceived, the acceptance and status attributed to their language, the degree of acculturation that they have, their conformity to schooling, how they themselves perceive their role within school, and the cumulative failure that they experience in relation to the opportunities they experience for success. Against the backdrop of out-of-school factors that cannot be controlled by the school, the in-school processes and practices, which are controllable by schools and which students must understand in order to negotiate their classrooms and peer cultures, offer significant insights.

SCHOOLING PROCESSES AND PRACTICES

The schooling processes and practices most likely to influence student options for staying or leaving school are:

The fit between the student's needs and what the school offers;

Actual gains that result from staying in school, e.g., learning English, becoming skilled, getting an education;

The orientation of scheduling and actual class offerings, e.g., classes that interest the student, where his or her peers are concentrated, etc.;

School extensions into the workplace;

Availability of counselors and teachers who will talk about the student's issues;

Assistance in learning how to compete in U.S. schools;

Assistance in learning about the system and how to negotiate the rules and regulations;

Gaining skills in speaking and using English and Spanish;

Actual academic program of the school (course offerings that are challenging);

Attitudes of teachers; acceptance/rejection of students.

These processes and practices exist in schools as invitations for engagement. The student's option to stay or leave school is defined by the degree to which several of these factors work well with individual choices, acculturation, teacher-student relationships, and the ability to negotiate between their own culture and that of the mainstream.

Individual choices
From the perspective of the focal students, it appears that the decision to stay or leave school for Latino students is not arrived at on the basis of single influences such as conflicts at home or extended work hours combined with poor grades in school. Rather, the findings suggest that such decisions are arrived at by some

students over time as the cumulative effect of unemployment, family issues, and poor socioeconomic status is compounded by high absenteeism, suspensions, poor grades, and disciplinary actions. In other cases, the economic pressures, loss of a job, or need to avoid deportation snowballs and becomes a deciding factor, limiting possibilities or providing no other options but to leave school.

Moreover, becoming at risk is closely linked to the sense of power that students have in controlling their lives. This varies from student to student, but is clearly depicted by the confidence some potential at-risk Latino students show when they can garner the support of their teachers, peers, or family in dealing with an issue (as demonstrated by Leo and Irene). For those potential at-risk immigrant and nonimmigrant students who see their power to change their personal, social, and academic situations as limited (like Oscar, Edwin, Jose, Enrique, and Luke), their likelihood of persevering is also limited.

Acculturation

The degree to which potential at-risk Latino students are acculturated into mainstream culture is also worthy of consideration. For some of the immigrant Latino students, the sense of their own nationalism and their confidence in being part of a group carries them through the acculturation process to a point where they begin to gradually acquire some of the cultural and social norms of the school environment that they can accommodate into their general survival repertoire. A case in point is Leo's gradual adaptation of peer group membership to Puerto Ricans while he maintains a strong Nicaraguan nationalism. However, some of the Latinos born in the continental United States whose self-identity may have been eroded by continuous negative verbal remarks and the limits of their communication in Spanish (particularly the Puerto Ricans in the mainstream class) begin to act in deference, simply tune out, or acquire the type of resistance that is prevalent at the school, whether it be talking back, shouting down, or being aggressive.

Teacher-student relationships

The relationships students have with their teachers is conducive to their engagement or disengagement in schooling. If students like their teachers, know the teachers care about them, and like the subject matter under discussion, they show up even if the homework is not completed or is not turned in. On the other hand, if students do not like or respond positively to their teachers (like Oscar, Jose, and Luke), have difficulties with the subject matter, or feel further estranged from their peers (like Edwin), being inattentive, uninterested, or unmotivated can readily become the norm. In some instances, collusion between teacher and student occurs when the teacher will not demand attention in class as long as the student does not interfere with the teacher's process. Thus, Luke can be inattentive, bow his head on the desk, and not respond as long as he does not disrupt or cause any commotion in the class.

Significance of bilingual classrooms for students and teachers
From the perspective of these eight students and based on other previous research of bilingual students (Montero-Sieburth and Perez, 1987), it appears that bilingual classrooms afford a safe haven from much of the confusion and demands of schooling. Bilingual classes provide the only transition from home to school where these students can use not only their native language but familiar ways of relating. However, the fact that the bilingual program in this school has a greater number of resources made available to the teachers and students than the mainstream program creates problems. Several of the mainstream teachers and students perceive bilingual students as receiving preferential treatment. End-of-the-year contract negotiations and hiring period cause apprehension for bilingual students and teachers — even in an exemplary program like the one observed in this study — especially when the resources of the mainstream program are limited and mainstream teachers have no aides. While the bilingual program satisfies a transitional need for Latino students, the lack of resources in the mainstream program tends to create strife between individual teachers and the two programs, thereby placing Latino students in the bilingual program in a precarious position.

USE OF NEGOTIATION STRATEGIES

How students negotiate between their "folk" community knowledge and the knowledge required to fit in the school presents a challenge for many Latino students (Montero-Sieburth and Perez, 1987; Montero-Sieburth, 1989). The skills needed by Latino students are not only those required of other students, but they must also know how to negotiate the cultural space between their home and the school, their own culture and that of the mainstream; they must adapt to the physical space between classrooms and hallways as well as information provided by intercoms, the paperwork requirements, and verbal messages received within classrooms and from the administrative office.

Differences in motivation for schooling
Coming to school is an experience that may be traumatic for some Latinos. This is especially true for Salvadorans and Guatemalans who come from war-torn countries where they may have been in rural schools during the early grades (usually up to third grade) and have been out of school for several years avoiding the draft. This was the case for Oscar who had to relearn much of what he had forgotten from early schooling. However, because many of these students are

overage (16 to 21 years old) they are placed at the ninth grade level (since they cannot be placed in lower grades) even though they may lack the basic developmental skills.

Students like Irene and Edwin who have migrated from Puerto Rico with their families for a better life are often confronted by linguistic and academic challenges as a result of their circular migration to and from Puerto Rico, which requires constant readaptation and readjustments. Help with this readaptation and readjustment is not part of the school schedule or course offerings. Being schooled in Puerto Rico versus the United States presents students with the cultural and linguistic status differences afforded Spanish on the island as opposed to Spanish in the United States. In Puerto Rico Spanish is the acceptable communicative norm, but in the Boston schools Spanish is relegated to bilingual classrooms and is limited in use outside of classes. Knowing when and how to use it becomes confusing and alienating. For those Puerto Ricans who are already English-speaking and know the demands of U.S. schooling, being "put down" for speaking Spanish, which is still the home language and serves as a social and symbolic communicative skill among peers and family, erodes their engagement in schooling. A lack of understanding of the conditions under which Latino students learn in their home countries makes it harder for school personnel to appropriately address the students' needs when they arrive in U.S. schools.

Dissemination and use of information
The way information is disseminated and how it is implemented and internalized by school personnel creates additional challenges for Latino students. Mandates from the central office are translated into school policies via the school's administration and then disseminated either through written communications or through after-school meetings, faculty meetings, cluster program meetings, intercom communications, and a myriad of other meetings. Like their teachers, students are bombarded with information and reams of paperwork informing them about events and telling them what must be done, when, where, and how. These methods of communication contrast sharply with Latino students' accustomed word-of-mouth communication. The deciphering of school information requires that they explicitly know both written and spoken English. There is no special help for these students in learning what is expected of them and what they must do in a given situation. This is a particular problem for some of the immigrant students who navigate the system only with the help of more seasoned Latino students.

If students are tardy — a more frequent tendency for the new-coming immigrant male students and less frequent for the U.S. born Latinos — homeroom may be bypassed and important daily information may be lost. Unless peers or bilingual teachers communicate such information to them in their native language, they tend to "float" through the day, randomly picking up bits and pieces of information at lunch or on the bus home.

Another obstacle met by many Latino immigrants (Oscar and Leo are good examples) is the accuracy and quality of record data from their previous schools and how it is used in their new school situations. The absence of school records, inconsistent maintenance of records, unavailability of records, and inability to interpret records when they do exist results in the improper placement of the students.

Interpretation of school rules and policies
"A 'school' like any community, must have reasonable rules for everyone to follow. Every society has it's 'laws' and this school is no exception" (letter written by teachers on school policy). Students are presented with the rules and regulations in early September detailing the expectations of the school, the transgressions that are not acceptable, and the consequences for inappropriate behaviors and actions. The carrying out of such rules implies the existence of collective understanding of these laws — an understanding of the way that the rules function, how they are monitored and supervised at every level of the school through the principal, two assistant principals, the registrar, two disciplinary officers, guidance counselors, and teachers.

However, because these rules are presented in English and the interpretation of these rules is left to individual teachers and other school personnel, inconsistency in the carrying out of the school's procedures by Latino students are inevitable given the multitude of tasks teachers engage in. Teachers not only report student absences, tardies, and disciplinary problems, but also provide bathroom permits, notes to other teachers, notes to the office, and telephone calls to parents daily to investigate absences. All of these requirements need to be learned by Latinos as a new experience if they have not been in U.S. schools.

In other instances, the teachers interpret the rules with no understanding of the economic and social dilemmas faced by the students in their class. For example, Oscar received an F in gym because he did not bring the appropriate sneakers. He simply could not afford to buy them, so he came with his regular shoes. Enrique and Jose went from Mr. Laferty's class to gym, but because they were embarrassed about wearing shorts, they did not change into their gym clothes several times and received an F for the year.

None of the focal students in either the bilingual or mainstream class were perceived as being "serious problems" as confirmed by the disciplinary officers, despite the arbitrary nature of punishment and discipline.

The rationale for being sent to the disciplinary officer is not always clear, and the reason for some of the punishments are not readily visible to the students. In some cases, the crime does not seem to fit the punishment. For example, Oscar was sent to the disciplinary officer because he was playing with a pen in one of his ESL classes; Edwin was sent to the disciplinarian for speaking up in another bilingual teacher's class; and Luke was sent to the disciplinary officer after a warning note was issued for speaking too much in the science class. Irene was punished by having to write 150 times that she would not forget her homework in her English class.

Frequent tardiness and/or absences from school are considered critical markers leading to at-risk conditions. But avoiding these conditions requires extensive understanding of protocol and what the consequences for being late, absent, suspended, and discharged are. Being tardy or absent requires a student to bring a written explanation from their parent or guardian in compliance with the regulations of the school committee. Tardy students report to a detention of 35 minutes, either after school, at 7:00 a.m., or 11:00 a.m. After three tardies, the student may be suspended if they have not fulfilled their required detentions. Repeated tardies with more than two failures to show up for the required detention results in suspension. In-house suspension requires students to remain with a counselor all day and to make up their missed assignments accordingly. Additional detentions are given to students who fall asleep in detention, do not attend detentions, or do not attend in-house suspensions. Students who are absent more than 15 percent of any marking period fail.

Latinos are sometimes caught between different interpretations of the rules and regulations by the teachers and administrators. Some teachers waive tardiness or absences; others don't. Late students are sometimes counted absent unjustly.

The bilingual focal students observed in this study frequently learned about the consequences of their actions after the fact. They also learned the rules from the example of their peers, as a result of being chastised for a transgression, or when a teacher took it upon her/himself to explain and translate the rules for them. No transitional support mechanisms, e.g., continuous explanation in their native language or explanations that orient students to understanding and internalizing these rules, was provided. These students are thrust into the school culture as it exists with the expectation that they will quickly learn "how to be" in school. For Puerto Rican students, even without a language barrier, their disruptive use of Spanish in class and their boisterousness is interpreted as being unacceptable by the teacher, and therefore these students do not receive positive reinforcement of their language nor cultural repertoires. Disengagement is a frequent response to this dilemma.

Latino students respond to the school system in a variety of ways. While the majority will acquiesce to the rules and demands of schooling, others find ways in which "to beat the system." Cutting school is one example of behavior students use "to beat the system." Although students know that first cuts result in detention, second cuts result in in-house suspension, and any cuts thereafter lead to a parents' conference, they interpret cutting classes, leaving school, or "hookin" as acceptable behaviors as long as they are able to pass their class. Students clearly associate being present in school and passing a class as closely interrelated, but they often do not see cutting specific classes as having serious consequences. Coming back to school on day 14 to be reinstated before the 15 percent rule applies is another example of student behavior designed "to beat the system." As long as they physically appear, these students believe they are playing by the rules and are actively engaged in schooling. Another less common way "to beat the system" is to make up classes that they have failed during the year during summer school. This behavior appears to provide satisfaction because such failure in their country of origin would mean forfeiting the whole school year.

Learning about school, the norms that exist, how to negotiate their way through a school day, and how to respond and act within the structure of the school requires that Latino students learn how to survive, figure out how the system works, and how to "beat the system" when it does not work in their favor. Latino students learn more about schooling through information passed on to them socially by peers and teachers and through their own defaults than through the officially communicated rules and regulations of the school and the information they receive on a daily basis. In some instances they do not understand the function of the rules and regulations; in other instances, they ignore them; at other times, they comply out of the need to be accepted.

Concluding Remarks

Clearly, the understanding of the schooling experience of potential at-risk Latino students is complex and multilayered. While generalizations about the causes for Latino students to stay or leave school are not warranted on the basis of eight cases of potential at-risk students, five of these cases do present evidence that, despite academic opportunities, the decision to leave school or stay results over time from frustrations that are cumulative and stem from factors both inside and outside school. The external factors include work demands, family demands, illness, pregnancy, drug abuse; factors within the school include the acceptance and status of their native language, socioeconomic differences, academic expectations, degrees of acceptance and inclusion, as well as teacher attitudes. In order to "make it" within the framework of the public school system, more than academic skills and knowledge are required. Students must also learn "how to work the system...what knowledge is useful, and how to use relationships of power in very concrete ways." That is, students must learn how to deal with teachers who are insensitive and lack an understanding their backgrounds. Compelled to accommodate to their environment, potential at-risk Latino students may have their hopes and expectations diminished if they receive prescriptive responses divorced from their backgrounds and irrelevant to their own ways of accomplishing goals. The more immediate and pressing realities of available work and money appear to present concrete challenges and accomplishments that these students can attain.

Leaving school for some of the at-risk Latino students, like Oscar and Enrique, is an attractive challenge from the outside world. Those who opt to stay, like Leo, adopt a stance of "I will show them what I can do" by relying on the solidarity of values brought from home, an extended family, teachers, and peers rather than being guided by the demands of the mainstream culture. Still others, like Irene, "stick to the rules." They are quiet, come to class, comply with regulations but rebel against the demands made by the home by socially "acting out." In Irene's case, becoming pregnant allows her to take control of her life and separate to some degree from her mother's life. Still other students, like Edwin and Jose, accept repeating next year with the hope that they will succeed the second time around with a different teacher. They may be physically at school, but they are psychologically absent.

The lack of engagement for some of these students reflects the sociocultural discontinuities that Ogbu (1987), Comer (1987), Trueba (1989), and others have pointed out exist between the academic learning of schools and their homes/communities. The demands of schooling may not only be discontinuous with the home culture and exert stylistic differences between cultural ways of learning, but also the demands may indicate qualitative differences for different minority groups according to Ogbu (1982, 1989). Different underrepresented groups respond differently to the demands of academic achievement depending on the status that accompanies their adjustment to schooling (Ogbu, 1989). Puerto Rican students who move back and forth from the island face tremendous readjustment in responding to the demands and status afforded by their new context. In Puerto Rico, the use of Spanish is a premium; in the United States, it is devalued. For the Latino immigrant student from Central America, however, such adjustment may be somewhat different, based not only on the core values brought from their country of origin that sustain their opposition to the values expected in U.S. schools, but they may also have a different sense of entitlement.

More importantly, this study shows the need to understand the sociocultural discontinuities experienced by at-risk Latino students between their own culture's values and those of the mainstream school culture as well as the larger socioeconomic and political contexts in which they operate and the degree to which schooling in its delivery of rules and regulations, program policy, and directives disengages students.

While the structure of schooling affects all students, it particularly alienates Latino students from their more conventional and social conduct of life — both for the immigrant who is used to a strong relationship between school and community and also for the acculturated Latino who, knowing U.S. schooling, is viewed as foreign and a separate minority. Beyond the cultural mismatches between teachers and students and the discontinuities of home and school cultures, potential at-risk Latino students also face an environment that is committed to assimilating these students into a mass. Recognition of individual differences between Latinos — even whether they are immigrant or non-immigrant — remains unaddressed. Such lack of understanding allows for ungrounded perceptions and attitudes to prevail. The fact that Latino students are assessed on the basis of the socioeconomic status of their families to be incapable of positive learning experiences already predisposes them to be at risk. And the fact that speaking Spanish is contrasted with speaking English as a negative experience sends a strong message of unequal status. Speaking English with an accent carries the same sense of inferiority and also sets these students up to be at risk.

Much needs to be done at the school level in order to diminish the conditions identified as leading to students becoming at risk. In addition to the recommendations advocated by Lucas, Henze, and Donato (1990), there are several policies and recommendations derived from the interviews conducted with the administrators, teachers, and staff at the high school in this study:

Develop clear identification and placement procedures for potential and actual at-risk Latinos students along with an adequate and comprehensive recordkeeping systems.

Create mechanisms for transitioning immigrant and migrant students into schooling/mainstreaming through a variety of means.

Optimize human resources within schools and communities.

Engage the administration, teachers, staff, and parents in empowerment and culturally responsive educational training.

Direct the processes and practices of schooling towards the needs of Latino students, emphasizing and including their cultural contributions, language, and impact for the future.

In conclusion, this research emphasizes the need to understand the educational experiences and consequences for different Latino populations, in particular at-risk students (Jacob and Jordan, 1987), to acquire knowledge of specific differences and similarities that Latinos share in relation to language, gender, social-class status, religious beliefs, immigrant status, and country of origin, and to explore how such differences affect potential at-risk students.

Unless schooling processes and practices are analyzed and understood in terms of their actual delivery of programs and impact on students, understanding the reasons why Latino students' decide to leave school will remain "their problem," rather than the combined problem of the society, school, communities, and families. Potential at-risk Latino students will in effect become at risk if the present schooling structure remains intact, inflexible, and impermeable to immigrant and migrant Latino students' learning skills and aptitudes, their motivations, and their social forms of community networking. In recommending educational policies that will have the greatest effect, multiple rather than single approaches must be made. As schools restructure and reorganize through field-based management, curriculum reform, quality teaching, community outreach, and greater parental participation, school personnel will need to consider how effective their policies and practices are in including Latino immigrant and migrant students into the lifeblood of the schools in ways that do not place them at risk.

Notes

The research for this study was made possible through a grant awarded during 1989-90 from the Inter-University program for Latino Research and the Social Research Council. I would like to acknowledge the research assistantship and contributions of David Whitenack, doctoral candidate at Stanford University, and Dr. Carmen Ada Gonzalez, who practices psychotherapy in Boston.

This chapter focuses on only a segment of a larger study that covers not only the schooling processes but also includes classroom processes, gender differences, intragroup analysis, and sociocultural factors. The complete study will be reported in a subsequent article that will address the sociocultural contexts of schooling for potential at-risk Latino students.

The focal students and teachers of this study, as well as the administrators, teachers, and staff of this urban Boston public school, are recognized for their contribution.

1. The terms "underrepresented" or "underserved" are preferred by the author instead of "minority" because these terms more accurately reflect the present situation between mainstream and underrepresented cultural/ethnic groups.

2. Data from the *Hispanic Policy Development Project* (National Commission, 1984, Vol. I) indicates that Latino dropout rates across the country range from 32 percent to 70 percent in different urban centers. It is expected that the proportion of Latino school children will rise from 10.5 percent to 33 percent by the year 2000, with an ever-increasing number of dropouts.

3. According to Tom Blackburn Rodriguez of the *National Hispanic Reporter* (February 1992, p. 1), "More than 7 million Hispanics 16 years and older are functionally illiterate. Hispanics are making progress, yet in 1991 only 51 percent of Hispanics were estimated to have completed high school, and the percentage of Hispanics who had completed four years of college stood at 10 percent."

4. Classes conducted in more than one language are distinguished from those

conducted in English only throughout the school. The author makes this distinction sharper by referring to those classes conducted in English and Spanish as bilingual and those conducted entirely in English as mainstream.

5. According to national research studies of Latino academic achievement (Steinberg, Blinde, and Chan, 1984), the likelihood of finding potential at-risk students would be greater in the ninth and tenth grades, since this is where they are most concentrated.

6. In order to maintain confidentiality, pseudonyms are used.

7. Step 2 of the Lau steps requires students to take four or more bilingual classes combined with physical education, industrial arts, and home economics in English. Step 3 requires three bilingual classes with the same core but with Chapter I reading, math, or science, and typing in English. Step 4 requires one or two bilingual classes combined with core and with social studies, computer literacy, computer programming plus an additional English, math, science, or business course. Step 5 is fully mainstreamed except for native language and culture; all classes are in English.

8. The 15 percent rule refers to the number of days a student can be absent in a term before he or she is suspended from school. If a student is absent 15 consecutive days he/she is suspended, but many students appear on the thirteenth or fourteenth day in order to avoid suspension.

9. The following year (1990-91) Oscar returned to school, only to drop out twice during the year. He became a "serial dropout." Edwin and Luke repeated math and civics, and Enrique and Jose did not return to school. By 1991-92 Ariela, who was a senior, had gotten married and was still coming to school. Irene, now an eleventh grader, was pregnant; she came to school when she was not feeling ill.

References

Bempechat, J., and Ginsburg, H. P. (1989). *Underachievement and Educational Disadvantage: The Home and School Experiences of At-Risk Youth.* Washington, DC: Office of Planning, Budget and Evaluation Service, U.S. Department of Education and the ERIC Clearinghouse on Urban Education.

Blackburn Rodriguez, T. (1992, February). The State of Hispanic America. *National Hispanic Reporter.*

Boston Public Schools. (1991). *School Profile Tables for FY 90, High School Dropout Rates by Race.* Boston: Author.

Coleman, J. S., Campbell, E. Q., Hobson, C., McPartland, J., Mood, A., Weinfeld, F., and York, R. L. (1966). *Equality of Educational Opportunity.* Washington, DC: U.S. Government Printing Office.

Colon, N. (1987). *Cimarrones: A Study of Puerto Rican Dropouts. Harvard Graduate School of Education.* Unpublished doctoral thesis.

Comer, J. P. (1987). New Haven's School-Based Community Connection. *Educational Leadership, 44*(6), 13-16.

Delgado-Gaitan, C. (1988). The Value of Conformity: Learning to Stay in School. *Anthropology and Education Quarterly, 19*(4), 354-381.

Fernandez, R. R., and Shu, G. (1988). School Dropouts: New Approaches to an Enduring Problem. *Education and Urban Society, 20*(4), 363-386.

Fine, M. (1986). Why Urban Adolescents Drop into and Out of Public High School. *Teachers College Record, 87*, 393-409.

Fine, M. (1990). Making Controversy: Who's At Risk? *Journal of Urban and Cultural Studies, 1*(1), 55-68.

Jacobs, E., and Jordan, C. (1987). Theme Issue: Explaining the School Performance of Minority Students. *Anthropology and Education Quarterly, 18*(4).

LeCompte, M. (1987). The Cultural Context of Dropping Out: Why Remedial Programs Fail to Solve the Problems. *Educational and Urban Society, 19*(3), 232-249.

Lucas, T., Henze, R., and Donato, R. (1990). Promoting the Success of Latino Language-Minority Students: An Exploratory Study of Six High Schools. *Harvard Educational Review, 60*(3), 315-340.

Montero-Sieburth, M. (1989). *Bilingual Teachers Ideologies in the Integration of Hispanics and Southeast Asian Immigrant Students: An Initiative between Practitioners and Researchers.* National Association for Bilingual Education Conference, 1988-1989, Washington, DC.

Montero-Sieburth, M., and Perez, M. (1987). Echar Pa'lante. Moving Onward: The Dilemmas and Strategies of a Bilingual Teacher. *Anthropology and Education Quarterly, 18*(3), 180-189.

National Commission on Secondary Schooling for Hispanics. (1984). *Make Something Happen: Hispanics and Urban School Reform*, Vol. I and II. Washington, DC: Hispanic Policy Development Project.

Oakes, J. (1985). *Keeping Track: How School Structure Inequality.* New Haven: Yale University Press.

Ogbu, J. U. (1982). Cultural Discontinuities and Schooling. *Anthropology and Education Quarterly, 13*(4), 290-307.

Ogbu, J. U. (1987). Variability in Minority Performance: A Problem in Search of an Explanation. *Anthropology and Education Quarterly, 18*(4), 312-334.

Ogbu, J. U. (1989). The Variability of Ethnic Groups in School Achievement. Presentation for the Institute on Multicultural Education, Harvard Graduate School of Education, Summer, July 24-28.

Page, R., and Valli, L. (1990). *Curriculum Differentiation. Interpretive Studies in U.S. Secondary Schools.* Albany, NY: State University of New York.

Pallas, A. M., Natriello, G., and McDill, E. L. (1989). The Changing Nature of the Disadvantaged Population: Current Dimensions and Future Trends. *Educational Leadership, 18*(5), 16-22.

Rumberger, R. W. (1983). Dropping Out of High School: The Influence of Race, Sex and Family Background. *American Educational Research Journal, 20*(2), 199-220.

Rumberger, R. W. (1987). High School Dropouts: A Review of Issues and Evidence. *Review of Educational Research, 57*(2), 101-122.

Slavin, R. E., and Madden, N. (1989). What Works for Students at Risk: A Research Synthesis. *Educational Leadership, 46*(5), 4-13.

Steinberg, L., Blinde, P. L., and Chan, K. S. (1984). Dropping Out Among Language Minority Youth. *Review of Educational Research, 54*(1), 113-132.

Suarez-Orozco, M. (1987). "Becoming Somebody": Central American Immigrants in U. S. Inner-City Schools. *Anthropology and Education Quarterly, 18*(4), 287-299.

Trueba, H. T. (1989). Rethinking Dropouts: Culture and Literacy for Minority Student

Empowerment. In Trueba, H., G. Spindler, and L. Spindler (Eds.), *What Do Anthropologists Have to Say About Dropouts?* Pp. 27-42. Philadelphia, PA: Falmer Press.

Valverde, S. (1987). A Comparative Study of Hispanic High School Dropouts and Graduates: Why do Some Leave School Early and Some Finish? *Education and Urban Society, 19*(3), 320-329.

Part IV
Future Directions

Sonia Nieto
Creating Possibilities: Educating Latino Students in Massachusetts

Research on the presence, progress, and experiences of Latino students in Massachusetts public schools has been accumulating steadily over the past decade. Much of it points to disturbing trends that must be aggressively addressed in the years ahead if the Commonwealth is to fulfill its stated goal of equal educational opportunity for all students. In particular, data related to retention, high school graduation rates, and the impact of bilingual education on academic achievement have serious implications for the future success or failure of our growing Latino population. No longer a case of not knowing, we are now faced with increasing evidence that, in general, the schools of the Commonwealth are not providing Latino youth with the access, preparation, and skills that they need to become active and productive participants of a democratic society.

The chapters in this book have added substantially to the body of information and analysis about the education of Latino students in Massachusetts. Whether the research they report concerns vocational or bilingual education, parental involvement, or the complexity of factors that either help or hinder Latino students' school success, the message is quite clear: Without access to quality education, many Latinos are faced with severely limited options and, consequently, poor life choices. Both this volume and previous research provide us with evidence that a new direction needs to be taken.

The purpose of this chapter is to suggest that responsibility for the education of Latino students in Massachusetts needs to go beyond blaming students and the conditions under which they live and instead address school policies and practices that create either roadblocks or possibilities. Although further research may help educators and policymakers understand the causes and implications of the present state of affairs, there has been enough research over the past three decades to make it clear that the need to move beyond research to practice has never been more urgent. The author of a 1968 report commissioned by ASPIRA, an educational advocacy organization for Puerto Rican students, was among the first to sound this message: "The many Puerto Rican parents who complain that their children 'are not being taught to read or do their arithmetic' are usually right. No new study is required to confirm their anxieties...." The author goes on to review research done in the 1960s highlighting the high dropout rates and low reading and math scores of Puerto Rican students and the meager efforts of most school systems in confronting these issues. He adds, "The title of this report — 'The Losers' — refers to us all. The children are losing all hopes of learning or succeeding; the schools are losing all hopes of teaching; and the nation is losing another opportunity, perhaps its last, to put flesh on the American dream" (Margolis, 1968, p. 1). Reading these words, some 25 years after they were written, is a disheartening reminder of lost opportunities and of the little progress that has been made.

In the remainder of this chapter, I will suggest that rather than continuing to blame conditions outside of the school as the sole or primary reasons for Latino students' failure, we need to create possibilities for their academic success by focusing on school policies and practices that will improve educational outcomes. I will end with a series of scenarios that demonstrate how schools for Latinos can differ dramatically in their policies and practices by using a model of varying levels of multicultural education.

Reconceptualizing Our Responsibility to Educate Latino Students

It has been standard practice for educators and policymakers to look outside the schools for the causes of Latino students' failure. Even well-intentioned critics have been guilty of pointing the finger at uninformed parents, low socioeconomic status, unstable family structure, and linguistic and cultural differences as the root causes of student failure. Less sensitive critics have blamed uncaring parents, the "culture of poverty," drugs, and violence for students' lack of success. Although it is now largely unacceptable to use the term "culturally deprived" popular in the 1960s, the less harsh but equally damaging term "at risk" has taken its place. Children are labeled at risk if they are poor, speak a language other than English, or live in a single-parent household. Sometimes just being a member of a particular ethnic or social group places children in the at-risk category (Rumberger, 1987; National Council of La Raza, 1990).

Ironically, in her research on social class and its effect on educational equality, Persell (1989) found that students are more different from one another when they *leave* school than when they *enter*, due in part to the kinds of schools they attend, the curriculum to which they are exposed, and the length of time in which they stay in school. Thus, poverty in and of itself cannot be blamed for student academic failure, although we cannot discount the effect that living in urban or rural areas characterized by poverty, racism, and violence can have on the education of many students, Latinos included. Stressful situations to which many children are exposed include not only poverty, but adult unemployment, poor medical attention, inadequate and even dangerous housing, dysfunctional families, physical abuse, and the other attendant problems faced primarily by those who are unfortunate enough to be poor in our society. The decade of the eighties was an especially cruel one for children of all backgrounds, making them the poorest segment of our society: 20.6 percent of all children currently live in poverty, an increase of 2.7 million poor children since 1979 (National Education Association, 1992). In addition, of the more than 21 million children under the age of six in 1987, an alarming 23 percent were living in poverty (National Center for Children in Poverty, 1990). Among Latinos, the situation is much worse: Nearly two of every five Latino children live in poverty, compared with one in five in the general population (Human and Civil Rights Committee, 1991).

As desperate as this situation is, however, it fails to explain why some children, in spite of their experiences with the disadvantages of poverty, are nonetheless successful in school. In some cases, even families who are struggling for survival are able to counteract the negative messages of schools; in other cases, the schools have taken the lead by changing the way they do things (Greeley, 1982; Clark, 1983; Edmonds, 1986; Taylor and Dorsey-Gaines, 1988; Nieto, 1992a). Research suggests, for example, that academic success for Latino students who are considered by schools to be "at risk" is often the result of modifying the environment in which they learn and the messages they receive, whether from family or school, rather than continuing to focus on the problems with which they may live. Such modifications include having high expectations, dispensing with academic tracking, and respecting and affirming students' language and culture.

Our public schools have a public trust to educate all children in an equitable manner, not only those students who happen to come from wealthy, two-parent families and speak English. Even if one were to accept the theory that Latino children fail in school primarily because of their family structure, poverty, or the low educational achievement of their parents (an assertion that is difficult to prove in any case), the fact is that teachers and schools can do nothing to make poor children middle class or to find fathers for them. Research by Steinberg and others, for example, has found that although socioeconomic status is a powerful predictor of dropping out, when it is held constant, Latinos still drop out of school at a higher rate than the general population. They suggest that there is some evidence that prejudice against Latinos on the part of school personnel is widespread and impedes their educational progress (Steinberg, Blinde, and Chan, 1984).

Parents, teachers, and other concerned advocates of Latino children are increasingly asking that schools, rather than persisting in looking for problems in the students' families, cultures, and communities, examine their own policies and practices in order to help Latino students have a better chance at succeeding. In this chapter, tracking, curriculum, and pedagogy will be briefly reviewed as examples of these policies and practices (for a more detailed description, see

Nieto, 1992a). Expectations of student achievement, often accompanied by institutional racism, will be discussed as a separate issue that undergirds several policies and practices in schools.

TRACKING

Tracking is the placement of students of roughly matched ability within classes, subject areas, or specific programs. A common practice that is found in most public schools from first grade through high school, the tracking of students is often made with the best of intentions. Through it, teachers and schools expect that students will be able to progress at a rate that is commensurate with their ability. Unfortunately, the results of tracking have not borne this expectation out.

Tracking decisions made early in a student's academic career often develop a life of their own. Rather than being flexible decisions that can change as students progress, first- and second-grade children who are tracked are likely to remain in the same track for the duration of their schooling, and children of color and poor children are generally the ones in the lowest tracks (Goodlad, 1984). Furthermore, Oakes (1985), based on research in 25 junior and senior high schools around the country, reported almost exclusively negative results of tracking. Even more disturbing, she found that tracking has a particularly adverse effect on those students most alienated from the educational setting, including those from linguistically and culturally diverse families. Closer to home, the Massachusetts Advocacy Center (1990) reported that in the Boston public schools, African-American, Latino, and Asian students from some backgrounds are most likely to be classified by their presumed "deficits," while European, American, and Asian students from other backgrounds are classified by their presumed "talents." This means that Latino students are overrepresented in special education and underrepresented in programs for gifted and talented students.

Academic tracking is the primary way that many schools provide what they consider an equitable education for all their students. Although the goal is commendable, the means to reach it is questionable. Nevertheless, simply "de-tracking" a school may not be the solution either because it may have little effect on student achievement if no provisions are made for the very real differences in learning styles, skills, and interests that children do indeed have. Tracking in and of itself is usually not the culprit for students' poor achievement, but the messages that students learn through the process of tracking may create and reinforce the poor expectations they have of themselves while perpetuating teachers' and schools' initial low evaluation of students' abilities. The conclusion that they are neither worthy nor intelligent does not need to be stated explicitly; rather, it is voiced silently every day in classrooms where little is expected of, and even less is delivered by, students. The implications of this practice for Latino students in Massachusetts could not be clearer: Tracking decisions may at best jeopardize and at worst prevent their academic success.

CURRICULUM

Curriculum is a powerful force in schools. It serves as one of the key methods of social control, and students learn that what may be regarded as important at home is often negated in the school. This is certainly the case with linguistic and cultural disconnections. Yet, the curriculum to which most Latino students in Massachusetts schools are exposed has little to do with their culture, experiences, or needs. For instance, it is all too often the case that Latino children find themselves in Spanish classes at the middle- and high-school levels where their Spanish is rejected for being "incorrect," this in spite of the fact that they may be the only truly fluent speakers of the language in the classroom, teacher included. In one of the classes where they could shine, Latino children are often made to feel inferior. It is not unusual for many of these students to drop out of Spanish classes altogether or to fail them. Among Puerto Rican school children in one city in Massachusetts, Walsh (1991) found that there was a reluctance to admit being fluent in Spanish because of the negative connotations of bilingualism in the school and community in which they lived. Research by Commins (1989) also found that even those children who were Spanish-dominant were reluctant to speak their native language in school because it was widely perceived as the language of "dumb" kids.

Latinos, culturally and linguistically members of a subordinate group, are absent from most school curricula. When they are included, it may be in insensitive, inaccurate, or stereotypical ways. The depiction of Latinos in even current textbooks is little improvement over decades ago (Sleeter and Grant, 1991). A similar situation has been found in most children's literature which, though certainly more multicultural than was true in the past, still marginalizes the experiences of Latinos in general (Nieto, 1992b). A number of curricula focusing specifically on Puerto Rican and other Latino communities has recently been developed in Massachusetts and elsewhere, but most of these are still largely unknown and therefore not used by the majority of schools Latinos attend.[1]

Another way in which curriculum is often at odds with the educational needs of Latino students is that it is "watered down," that is, simplified in order to be more appropriate for them. Although teachers may dilute the curriculum in a sincere attempt to address what they feel are educational deficits of their students, it is a strategy that often backfires because children perceive that teachers expect less of them than of other students. Invariably, a watered-down curriculum is also an undemanding and boring one. In contrast to this approach, Moll (1988) found that teachers of successful Latino students, although modifying the curriculum, still taught at the highest level possible. In effect, they adapted the curriculum with the assumption that their students were capable of doing challenging and intellectually rigorous work.

There is also a mismatch in much of the curriculum because it is in direct conflict with the experiences students have in their schools and communities. For example, while they may study the Declaration of Independence and the Constitutional Convention in their history classes, many students see absolutely no connection with these events and their everyday lives. Although this is a problem with many students, not only Latinos, it is particularly severe in schools with high proportions of poor, African-American, and Latino children (National Coalition, 1985). On the other hand, if teachers take the opportunity to encourage students to become informed and active citizens of their classrooms, schools, and communities, the serious contradiction between teaching civic responsibility in the abstract and being citizens of autocratic school systems in practice would be dramatically lessened.

The absence of Latinos in the curricula of Massachusetts public schools is not a new situation. In this volume, the research reported by Frau-Ramos and me points out how, even in a school system with a student body that is two-thirds Puerto Rican, no course on the history and culture of Puerto Ricans is taught in English. It is no surprise that Latinos pick up the message that what is "important" history has nothing to do with them. Schools need to find ways to increase the visibility of their students in the curriculum, and using the community as a resource is one way in which students' lives could become more connected with what they learn at school. Until that happens, curricula will continue to be one of the key ways in which Latino children are marginalized in schools.

PEDAGOGY

Teaching practices, including instructional methods and the very way in which teachers and schools view the nature of learning, also influence student success or failure. Latino children are perhaps even more affected by pedagogy than are others for a number of reasons, including having less experienced teachers, being subject to more rigid methods focused on basic skills than students in more affluent neighborhoods, and being in environments where their learning styles are more at odds with the teaching styles of their teachers. For instance, a recent report by the California Commission on Teacher Credentialing found that a disproportionate number of poor students and those from culturally and linguistically diverse backgrounds are taught by the least-qualified teachers because of high teacher turnover, misassigned teachers, and classrooms where teachers hold only temporary certification (García and García, 1992). Given similarities in the changing demographics of students in Massachusetts, it is not unlikely that schools in the Commonwealth face a similar situation.

Pedagogy can also be a problem when it is subverted to the content to be covered. At the middle- and high-school levels, subject matter often dominates pedagogy, and the content to be covered becomes more important than student learning because standardized tests act as gatekeepers to promotion and school success. Frequently, tremendous pressure is put on teachers to finish the course of study at all costs, and they are often forced to rush through the curriculum without focusing in any depth on the important concepts or principles of the subject matter. This situation was confirmed in a study on language-minority students in which three classroom features that led to the deterioration of their academic performance were identified: "the relentless pace of instruction;" the fragmentation of settings and activities; and inattention to the children's cultural adjustment (Trueba, 1987). Moreover, between 1972 and 1980, when many test-oriented measures were instituted in the nation's schools, pedagogical methods that focus on higher-order skills such as student-centered discussions, the writing of essays, research projects, and laboratory work all decreased (Darling-Hammond, 1991).

As we have seen through several of the research studies reported in this volume, in classrooms dominated by Latino and other educationally disenfranchised students, the pedagogy is often rigid and dry because the focus is on basic skills rather than on critical thinking. Although there need not be a bifurcation between basic skills and critical thinking, unfortunately there usually is. Thus, students in basic levels are rarely exposed to intellectually stimulating and creative pedagogy, while those in high-level classes tend to have more access to this kind of pedagogy, although it is also true that the pedagogy to which most students in most classrooms are exposed is neither innovative nor exciting (Goodlad, 1984).

Much recent research indicates that relying on rote learning or instruction in basic skills feeds into the deficit syndrome. In the words of Means and Knapp:

> Children from impoverished and affluent backgrounds alike come to school with important skills and knowledge .... Instead of taking a deficit view of the educationally disadvantaged learner, cognitive researchers developing alternative models of instruction focus on the knowledge, skills, and abilities that the children possess (1991).

A stagnant and uninspired pedagogy, particularly for students whose culture and language have historically been maligned, may result in further alienating them from the academic process. According to Cummins (1989, p. 4), teachers are in a position to either empower or disable their students by their interactions with them and their families. He concludes that "the kind of education that minority students experience is very much a consequence of the ways in which teachers and other educators have defined their own roles both within the school and in relation to minority communities." This line of thinking echoes the work of Paulo Freire (1970), who maintains that education is either "liberating" or "domesticating," that is, that it can result in students becoming either critical learners or passive followers.

There are a number of concerns related to providing critically empowering pedagogy for Latino students. First, the process of education needs to be addressed so that it is not simply a matter of substituting Latino "heroes and holidays" for European American "heroes and holidays." Whether students can name a few Latino superstars like Roberto Clemente and Cesar Chavez, for instance, is not as important as being aware of their own history, including the struggles and goals of the Latino community in their own city or town and their responsibilities as learners and citizens. A pedagogy that stresses depth and critique must go beyond simply multiculturalizing the curriculum at the level of glorification and superficiality or "Dick and Jane in brownface."

There is an equally important implication for bilingual classrooms. Research investigating the effect of bilingual education on academic success has been overwhelmingly positive (see Frau-Ramos and Nieto, this volume). In the words of the Massachusetts Advocacy Center (1990), bilingual education has been found to act as a "buffer" in preventing dropping out of high school. In spite of the very real benefits it can have, bilingual education has not achieved as much success as it can for a number of reasons including lack of support at the state and local levels. In terms of pedagogy, bilingual education is in a unique position to challenge stale pedagogy that relies on textbooks, tests, and ability grouping. All sorts of pedagogical arrangements, from peer tutoring to cooperative learning, are possible in bilingual programs, which are not as highly regulated or have as many required texts or tests as nonbilingual programs. By using the linguistic and cultural strengths of students in the pedagogy and curriculum, bilingual programs can offer alternative means of achieving academic success. Yet, too often, bilingual programs follow traditional programs in lockstep fashion, simply substituting one language for another. Massachusetts, the home of the first mandated law in bilingual education, has the opportunity to go beyond legal obligations to assist school systems in developing pedagogically sound, empowering bilingual programs that use students' native languages and cultures in innovative ways.

Expectations of Student Achievement

Underlying the policies and practices found in schools are attitudes and perspectives that can dramatically promote or limit the access that Latino students have to an equal and high quality education. One of the most significant of these is expectations of student achievement. The term "teachers' expectations" refers to teachers' views about their students' abilities and is generally used to define research that has focused on low expectations of students based on their socioeconomic status, race/ethnicity, or language. It is a misleading term, however, because it assumes that teachers have the sole influence on the learning of their students. Instead, the term "expectations of student achievement" is more accurate in describing attitudes and beliefs about students that are held not only by teachers, but by schools, communities, and indeed the society at large.

Placing teachers at the center of student achievement is both an unrealistic and incomplete explanation of students' success or failure because it effectively takes schools and society off the hook for their own responsibility and complicity in students' failure. Expectations of student achievement need to be understood within the broader framework of societal expectations that are acted on by teachers, schools, and others. Although their role is indeed crucial, if we refer only to teachers we place the blame on them for policies and practices that are often out of their control. By referring to expectations of student achievement, the complex interaction of teachers, schools, and communities in producing failure can be understood. The role of institutional racism in constructing low expectations of students from particular backgrounds cannot be underestimated, for it is generally those students from marginalized and oppressed racial and ethnic groups who are the target of the lowest expectations. Thus, institutional racism and low expectations of student achievement often feed upon one another, setting up a dynamic for failure.

The research on expectations of student achievement that began in the 1960s and 1970s was a major breakthrough because, prior to it, students' failure in school was ascribed completely to individual or family circumstances (Rosenthal and Jacobson, 1968; Rist, 1971). The possible influence that the attitudes and practices of teachers, schools, and society could have on such failure could now be considered as well. The most compelling implications of this breakthrough were for the education of those students most seriously disadvantaged by schooling, including Latinos.

Although Latinos have not been at the center of many of the studies related to expectations of achievement, a growing body of research confirms that attitudes others have about their ability can indeed influence their experiences in school. In this volume, the chapters by Wheelock, Darder and Upshur, Montero-Sieburth, and Frau-Ramos and Nieto all allude to the damaging messages about Latinos that are perpetuated in schools and affect how students feel about themselves, their future, and even their intelligence.

Other studies corroborate the effect that expectations of Latino students have on the quality of the education they receive. Ortiz (1988) compared the educational experiences of Latino and non-Latino children in order to determine the quality of the educational experience they receive in a variety of contexts. After observing almost a hundred classrooms over a six-year period, she concluded that the differential delivery of educational services to Latino students occurs equally in situations in which they are the majority and the minority and is both programmatic and interpersonal. Not only is their educational experience affected by inadequate and inequitably distributed material resources, but it is also affected by personal resources under the control of the teachers — resources that are also denied.

In schools and classrooms where they are in the majority, Latino students receive an inferior education through particular structures including remedial programs, tracking, and teachers' negative reactions to cultural awareness workshops. In classrooms with few Latino students, Ortiz found that teachers believed that Latino students were not as capable as their peers. The results of these perceptions were that teachers allocated fewer resources to Latinos, had less eye contact, interaction, and physical contact with them, and only reluctantly allowed them to engage in activities involving abstractions. In addition, while non-Latino students received more teacher time, Latino students received more drill lessons and were praised for mediocre or poor performance. In both cases, the expectations teachers had of Latino student achievement seem to have been factors in the quality of the education they received.

On the positive side, research has also considered the impact that teachers and schools can have on the success of their Latino students. For example, a case study of an inner-city school in California found that dramatic differences in the children's knowledge and use of written language were visible only a few months after the school began a process of pedagogical transformation (Flores, Cousin, and Díaz, 1991). The transformation, according to the researchers, had to do with the schools' rejection of the "at-risk" label and all it implies and the acceptance of positive assumptions about the ability and intelligence of the children they taught, including a large number of Latinos. Changes in student achievement were visible after teachers began questioning the myths associated with the "at-risk" label, reorganizing for the teaching of language and literacy, and focusing on the children's strengths.

Research by Moll (1988) on effective schooling for Latino students began with the selection of several classroom teachers judged by peers and administrators as outstanding teachers of Latino children. In all cases, their students were achieving at or above grade level on standardized measures of academic achievement. In observations of two of these teachers, Moll found that the expectations they had of their students led them to teach at the highest level possible. Specifically, he found:

In contrast to the assumption that working-class children cannot handle an academically rigorous curriculum, or in the case of limited-English-proficiency students, that their lack of English fluency justifies an emphasis on low-level skills, the guiding assumption in the classrooms analyzed seemed to be the opposite: that the students were as smart as allowed by the curriculum. The teachers assumed that the children were competent and capable and that it was the teachers responsibly to provide the students with a challenging, innovative, and intellectually rigorous curriculum. Rote-like teaching of low-order skills simply did not take place (p. 467).

A large-scale study of six schools that are highly effective in teaching Latino, language-minority students adds substantially to the research in this area. The schools in this study were characterized by eight features, some of which are directly related to high expectations of student achievement and antiracist behaviors. For one, the schools valued students' language and cultures and demonstrated this by treating the ability to speak Spanish as a benefit. Moreover, teachers learned Spanish and showed support for students' backgrounds in numerous ways. A second feature of the schools was that they held high expectations for Latino, language-minority students and showed this by helping them prepare for college, using challenging curricula and varied strategies and materials, and recognizing student success publicly (Lucas, Henze, and Donato, 1990).

Congruent with this study is an overview of recent research by García (1991) that addresses effective instruction for students who enter schools from homes and communities in which English is not the primary language of communication. In interviews with classroom teachers, he found that they were highly committed to the educational success of their students and perceived themselves as instructional innovators who used new learning theories and instructional philosophies. These teachers continued to be involved in their own professional development, had a strong commitment to home-school communication, and felt empowered to create or change the curriculum. According to García, "These instructors 'adopted' their students: They had high academic expectations for all of them .... They rejected any suggestion that their students were intellectually or academically disadvantaged" (p. 5). Principals in these schools tended to be well informed and articulate about the curriculum and instruction in their schools and supportive of teachers' autonomy. In addition, parents expressed satisfaction with and appreciation for their children's educational experiences.

Research such as this demonstrates that Latino student failure need not be a given. Changing teacher, school, and community expectations is one step in the process toward turning Latino school failure around. There is also an urgent need to review school policies and practices that are undergirded by low expectations and racism and that result in Latino students in Massachusetts and elsewhere experiencing inordinately high rates of academic failure. Changing some school policies and practices can help by providing alternative messages to students that they are capable of high achievement or, in the words of the students, that they are "smart" rather than "dumb."

Reconceptualizing Cultural and Linguistic Differences

Reconceptualizing cultural and linguistic differences means moving away from a deficit view of diverse cultures and languages and toward an affirmation of them. Yet, because most of us have been educated in schools with a monocultural philosophy, that is, a philosophy in which diversity is neither valued nor rewarded, this reconceptualization will take time, energy, and a creative leap. In the remainder of this chapter, a number of scenarios for affirming Latino students within a multicultural approach will be described based on a model of multicultural education (Nieto, 1992a). The model begins with *tolerance* and moves through *acceptance*, *respect*, and finally to the highest level, *affirmation*, *solidarity*, and *critique*, and the scenarios describe what educational environments for Latinos moving through the grades from kindergarten through high school in Massachusetts might look like.[2]

Models, no matter how well-meaning, are problematic and can be misleading because they provide an unrealistic way of looking at change, as if it were linear and simplistic rather than complex and interconnected. Curricular and pedagogical change are highly complex processes that are dependent on the mix of students, teachers, administrators, and community in a particular school and, in the final analysis, are imbedded in the sociopolitical context of the society and world in which we live. In spite of these limitations, I am proposing this model because it helps us to understand that multicultural education is not a simple or unitary concept, but a series of frameworks through which we can understand varying levels of support for student differences. It is in this spirit that the scenarios are offered as responses of various schools to their Latino students.

TOLERANCE

Many schools believe that they have a comprehensive multicultural program if, in their mission statement, they make reference to tolerance. Yet, tolerance is the very lowest level of multicultural education. To tolerate differences means that they are endured, but not necessarily embraced, so that what is tolerated today may be rejected tomorrow. Nevertheless, tolerance represents a step up from the monocultural and monolingual education that is practiced in most schools.

In terms of school policies and practices, tolerance may mean that cultural and linguistic differences are at least understood as inevitable in a pluralistic society. For Latinos, this might mean that structured English-as-a-second-language instruction is offered for those who do not speak English. Nevertheless, teachers, even if they spoke Spanish, would probably avoid using it with their students so that they not develop a "crutch" on the language. A number of special programs focusing on Latino heritage month might be featured, and the curriculum might include reference to a few Latinos, mostly from Puerto Rico or Mexico and not from Massachusetts or other places in the United States.

In the high school, no course on Puerto Rican, Caribbean, or South American history and culture would be available. In the textbook used for the U.S. history course, there might a reference to the Jones Act, which made Puerto Ricans U.S. citizens, and to "Operation Bootstrap," a U.S. program for the economic development of the island; Mexicans might be mentioned in reference to the Alamo. The beginnings of support for more in-depth community service might mean that the high school would offer a cross-generational tutoring program for younger Latino students in an after-school program at one of the schools.

Parents are grudgingly accepted in schools, but rarely openly welcomed. The only exception to this is a series of parenting classes in which the registration of Latino parents is actively sought.

ACCEPTANCE

Acceptance is the next level of multicultural education. Here, differences are more readily accepted and their importance is neither minimized nor denied. For Latinos, this means that the schools acknowledge linguistic and cultural differences in visible and supportive ways. Thus, a transitional, bilingual-education program is available for all students who need it until they learn sufficient English to be "mainstreamed" to a "regular" program. That usually happens in three years, but many Latino students are referred for special education after they leave the bilingual program because they have a hard time understanding the work in the mainstream classes.[3]

The curriculum in the bilingual class includes some information about the Taínos, the flag and the shield of Puerto Rico, and some songs and dances. A number of multicultural fairs, schoolwide community dinners, and special assembly programs are held for "Puerto Rican Discovery Day" in November and "Cinco de Mayo." Parents are asked to cook typical meals for these events.

Teachers are required to go to a number of professional development activities that emphasize different learning and teaching styles, language development, and other kinds of diversity. The school's communication with parents in newsletters and notes is bilingual, and parents are invited to the school to be volunteers. At the high school, community involvement is acknowledged as an increasingly important part of the curriculum, and there are a number of community service projects including peer education about drugs in a local community agency where students receive academic credit for their work.

RESPECT

The third level of multicultural education, respect, is characterized by admiring and holding diversity in high esteem and therefore using it as the basis for much of the curriculum. Schools at this level offer developmental, bilingual-education programs, that is, programs where Latino and other language-minority students are able to use their native language throughout their schooling, not simply as a bridge to English. Being bilingual is not viewed as a liability, but as an asset.

The curriculum at this level is more explicitly multicultural because education is defined as knowledge that is necessary for living in a complex and pluralistic society. As such, the curriculum includes topics not generally discussed in schools such as racism, sexism, and other forms of discrimination. In addition, there are courses both in English and in Spanish on Puerto Rican, Caribbean, and South American history and literature, and these courses are available to all students.

Ability grouping has been discarded at both the elementary and secondary levels. Instead, schools have developed a variety of strategies for involving students of varying abilities in learning. These include individualized instruction, cooperative work, peer tutoring, and cross-age and cross-school classes.

Latino students feel at home in their schools, as do other students. The cultures and languages of all students are apparent in the bulletin boards and classroom materials, many of which have been designed by the teachers. Parents are welcomed into the school to give their opinion on what their children need to learn. A respect for parents, students, and teachers is apparent through the interactions they have.

AFFIRMATION, SOLIDARITY, AND CRITIQUE

The fourth and highest level of multicultural education, affirmation, solidarity, and critique, is more complex than the others. The languages, cultures, interests, and lifestyles of all students are used as the primary basis for the curriculum, and students, teachers, and parents develop relationships based on affirmation and solidarity with one another. In addition, because multicultural education is concerned with equity and social justice for all people and because basic values of different cultural groups are sometimes diametrically opposed, conflict is inevitable. As stated by Kalantzis and Cope (1990), passively accepting the status quo of any culture is inconsistent with multicultural education: "Multicultural education, to be effective, needs to be more active. It needs to consider not just the pleasure of diversity but more fundamental issues that arise as different groups negotiate community and the basic issues of material life in the same space — a process that equally might generate conflict and pain."

At this level, culture itself is understood as dynamic and problematic.

Multicultural education includes critique and does not remain at the exotic or romantic stage. Thus, students learn to transcend their own cultural experience so that they do not simply glorify heroes or incidents from the past. This education helps them to reflect on and critique the content to which they are exposed in school. What this might mean at the classroom level is that children learn not only about some romanticized version of indigenous civilization as it existed when Columbus arrived in the Caribbean in 1492 and 1493, but that they discuss the impact of the arrival of Europeans on indigenous cultures in general and the meaning of slavery and exploitation within that experience, as well as the similarities and differences among the experience of Africans, Mexicans, American Indians, Chinese, Irish, Italians, Jews, and others in U.S. history. Schools at this level of multicultural education use the language and culture of students in a consistent, critical, comprehensive, and inclusive way. This means developing multicultural settings in which all students feel reflected and visible, for example, through two-way bilingual programs in which all the languages of students in the school are used and maintained meaningfully in the academic setting. The curriculum is characterized by inclusiveness and a wide variety of courses and perspectives are available so that all students have the opportunity to study, for example, Caribbean history, the civil rights movement, and the U.S. immigrant experience from a multitude of perspectives.

The teachers and administrators in the schools at this level are highly diverse themselves because the school system has vigorously recruited staff representative of the inclusiveness that it espouses. The school takes advantage of this diversity by having teachers share unique talents, whether these are speaking another language or poetry writing skills. Teachers, working together, develop innovative and varied instructional strategies so that all students are successful learners. They also serve as expert advisors to one another through peer review and evaluation and professional development activities. Parents and other community members are actively supported as the first and most important teachers of their children, and their experiences, viewpoints, and suggestions are incorporated into classroom and school programs and activities. They too are exposed to experiences and viewpoints different from their own, which in turn helps them to expand their horizons.

Most important of all, there are high expectations for all students. Teachers refer to Latino students as "gifted" because they speak Spanish, and they seek their help in learning the language. There are constant reminders, through instructional materials, bulletin boards, letters sent to parents, and in daily interactions with students, that they are capable of reaching the highest levels of learning. Remedial math is scrapped and everybody is given the opportunity to study algebra and geometry, while provisions are made for students to complete these courses in various lengths of time depending on their individual needs. Rigid programming is replaced with flexible classes of one-, two-, or three-hour segments, even at the high school level. In addition, the schools at this level become community centers that are used by a variety of groups and organizations for everything from family literacy classes to cultural events. In short, the schools at this level truly become "a community of learners" for all involved, including students, teachers, staff, and parents.

Conclusion

The scenarios sketched above help to reconceptualize what successful learning and inclusion for Latino students at varying levels of multicultural education might look like. Although there is probably no school in which these levels are apparent in as pure a way as described, all schools are characterized by varying levels of support for diversity in different aspects of their operations. It is clear from even a cursory reading that some levels of multicultural education are more supportive of differences than others, although each level has its own advantages and is a step toward more inclusion.

The level of affirmation, solidarity, and critique provides the best opportunity to affirm Latinos in the most direct and supportive ways because it is based on a more critical understanding of culture and its impact on learning. In the final analysis, a school based on this model supports not only Latino students, but all students, for example, by providing two-way bilingual programs that result in all students becoming fluent in two languages, clearly a benefit in our increasingly diverse world. Thus, the result of developing excellent, high-quality, and affirming education for Latino students is that all students in the Commonwealth benefit.

Although research can help guide us in developing appropriate and affirming learning environments for Latino children, enough research has been done to demonstrate that we need to change our institutional policies and practices. The challenge for all citizens and the educational system in Massachusetts is to decide that Latino students are capable and worthy of the best education and then to develop approaches and curricula that are based on this assumption. In the process, a shift in thinking must take place towards possibilities for academic success and away from blaming and academic failure.

Notes

1. Some of these resources are: *Caribbean Connections: Classroom Resources for Secondary Schools*, 1990, by D. Menkart and C. A. Sunshine, Eds. (Washington, DC: Ecumenical Program on Central America and the Caribbean and the Network of Educators' Committees on Central America); *Building Bridges of Learning and Under-*

standing: A Collection of Classroom Activities on Puerto Rican Culture, 1990, by Marla Perez-Selles and Nancy Carmen Barra-Zuman (Andover, MA: The Regional Laboratory for Educational Improvement of the Northeast and Islands and the New England Center for Equity Assistance); *Literature and Society of the Puerto Rican People: A Syllabus for Secondary Schools*, no date, by Roberto Márquez and Sonia Nieto (NY: Ford Foundation).

2. The inspiration for developing these scenarios was suggested to me by a wonderful paper by Peggy McIntosh, "Interactive Phases of Curricular Re-Vision: A Feminist Perspective" (1983). In it, she uses a number of young women who move through her five phases of curricular revision to demonstrate how differing curricular ideologies impact on their lives.

3. This scenario is not unusual. In fact, according to Cummins, there is a direct link between "mainstreaming" students from bilingual programs prematurely and their placement in special education classes (Cummins, 1984).

References

Clark, R. (1983). *Family Life and School Achievement: Why Poor Black Children Succeed or Fail.* Chicago, IL: University of Chicago Press.

Commins, N. L. (1989, January). Language and Affect: Bilingual Students at Home and at School. *Language Arts, 66*(1), 29-43.

Cummins, J. (1984). *Bilingualism and Special Education: Issues in Assessment and Pedagogy.* Clevedon, England: Multilingual Matters.

Cummins, J. (1989). *Empowering Minority Students.* Sacramento, CA.: California Association for Bilingual Education.

Darling-Hammond, L. (1991, November). The Implications of Testing Policy for Quality and Equality. *Phi Delta Kappan*, 220-225.

Edmonds, R. (1986). Characteristics of Effective Schools. In U. Neisser (Ed.), *The School Achievement of Minority Children: New Perspectives.* Hillsdale, NJ: Erlbaum.

Flores, B., Cousin, P. T., and Díaz, E. (1991, September). Transforming Deficit Myths About Learning, Language, and Culture. *Language Arts, 68*(5), 369-379.

Freire, P. (1970). *Pedagogy of the Oppressed.* New York: Seabury Press.

García, E. (1991). *Education of Linguistically and Culturally Diverse Students: Effective Instructional Practices. Educational Practice Report 1.* Santa Cruz, CA.: National Center for Research on Cultural Diversity and Second Language Learning.

García, E. E., and García, E. H. (1992, April). Not the Best or Worst of Times, but Times of Challenge. *The Council Chronicle (National Council of Teachers of English)*, p. 16.

Goodlad, J. (1984). *A Place Called School.* New York: McGraw-Hill.

Greeley, A. M. (1982). *Catholic High Schools and Minority Students.* New Brunswick, NJ: Transaction Books.

Human and Civil Rights Committee. (1991, December). *Ethnic Report: Focus on Hispanics.* Washington, DC: National Education Association.

Kalantzis, M., and Cope, B. (1990). *The Experience of Multicultural Education in*

Australia: Six Case Studies. Sydney, Australia: Centre for Multicultural Studies, Wollongong University.

Lucas, T., Henze, R., and Donato, R. (August, 1990). Promoting the Success of Latino Language-Minority Students. *Harvard Educational Review, 60*(3), 315-340.

Margolis, R. J. (1968, May). *The Losers: A Report on Puerto Ricans and the Public Schools.* New York: ASPIRA, Inc.

Massachusetts Advocacy Center. (1990). *Locked in/Locked Out: Tracking and Placement Practices in Boston Public Schools.* Boston, MA: Author.

McIntosh, P. (1983). *Interactive Phases of Curricular Re-Vision: A Feminist Perspective.* Wellesley, MA: Wellesley College Center for Research on Women.

Means, B. and Knapp, M. S. (1991, December). Cognitive Approaches to Teaching Advanced Skills to Educationally Disadvantaged Students. *Phi Delta Kappan,* 282-289.

Moll, L. C. (1988, September). Some Key Issues in Teaching Latino Students. *Language Arts, 65*(5), 465-472.

National Center for Children in Poverty. (1990). *Five Million Children: A Statistical Profile of Our Poorest Young Citizens.* New York: Author.

National Coalition of Advocates for Students. (1985). *Barriers to Excellence: Our Children at Risk.* Boston, MA: Author.

National Council of La Raza. (1990). *Hispanic Education: A Statistical Portrait 1990.* Washington, DC: Author.

NEA Today. (1992, April). *Families With Children: Fewer, Smaller, Poorer.* Washington, DC: National Education Association.

Nieto, S. (1992a). *Affirming Diversity: The Sociopolitical Context of Multicultural Education.* White Plains, NY: Longman.

Nieto, S. (1992b). We Have Stories to Tell: A Case Study of Puerto Rican Children's Literature. In V. A. Harris (Ed.), *Teaching Multicultural Literature in Grades K–8.* Norwood, MA: Christopher-Gordon Publishers.

Oakes, J. (1985). *Keeping Track: How Schools Structure Inequality.* New Haven, CT: Yale University Press.

Ortiz, F. I. (1988). Hispanic-American Children's Experiences in Classrooms: A Comparison Between Hispanic and Non-Hispanic Children. In L. Weis (Ed.), *Class, Race and Gender in American Education.* Albany NY: State University of New York Press.

Persell, C. H. (1989). Social Class and Educational Equality. In J. A. Banks and C. A. M. Banks (Eds.), *Multicultural Education: Issues and Perspectives.* Boston, MA: Allyn & Bacon.

Rist, R. C. (1971). Student Social Class and Teacher Expectations: The Self-Fulfilling Prophecy in Ghetto Education. *Challenging the Myths: The Schools, the Blacks, and the Poor,* Reprint Series #5. Cambridge, MA: Harvard Educational Review.

Rosenthal, R., and Jacobson, L. (1968). *Pygmalion in the Classroom.* New York: Holt, Rinehart & Winston.

Rumberger, R. W. (1987). High School Dropouts: A Review of Issues and Evidence. *Review of Educational Research, 57*(1), 101-121.

Sleeter, C. E., and Grant, C. A. (1991). Race, Class, Gender and Disability in Current

Textbooks. In M. W. Apple and L. K. Christian-Smith (Eds.), *The Politics of the Textbook*. New York: Routledge and Chapman Hall.

Steinberg, L., Blinde, P. L., and Chan, K. S. (1984, Spring). Dropping Out Among Language Minority Youth. *Review of Educational Research, 54*(1), 113-132.

Taylor, D., and Dorsey-Gaines, C. (1988). *Growing Up Literate: Learning from Inner-City Families*. Portsmouth, NH: Heinemann.

Trueba, H. (1987, April). *Cultural Differences or Learning Handicaps? Towards an Understanding of Adjustment Processes in Schooling Language Minority Youth*, Volume III. Proceedings of the University of California Linguistic Minority Research Project Conference, 45-79, University of California, Los Angeles.

Walsh, C. E. (1991). *Pedagogy and the Struggle for Voice: Issues of Language, Power, and Schooling for Puerto Ricans*. New York: Bergin and Garvey.